S0-AIU-771

MODERN EDUCATIONAL CONTROVERSIES

Edited by

David Tavel
University of Toledo

Theodore Lownik Library
Illinois Benedictine College
Lisle, Illinois 60532

UNIVERSITY
PRESS OF
AMERICA

LANHAM • NEW YORK • LONDON

370
.973
M689

Copyright © 1984 by

University Press of America,™ Inc.

4720 Boston Way
Lanham, MD 20706

3 Henrietta Street
London WC2E 8LU England

All rights reserved

Printed in the United States of America

Library of Congress Cataloging in Publication Data
Main entry under title:

Modern educational controversies.

   Bibliography: p.
   1. Education—United States—Addresses, essays,
lectures. 2. Minorities—Education—United States—
Addresses, essays, lectures. 3. Education and state—
United States—Addresses, essays, lectures. 4. Education-
al sociology—United States—Addresses, essays, lectures.
I. Tavel, David.
LA217.M63   1984   370'.973   84-15395
ISBN 0-8191-4273-5 (alk. paper)
ISBN 0-8191-4274-3 (pbk. : alk. paper)

All University Press of America books are produced on acid-free
paper which exceeds the minimum standards set by the National
Historical Publications and Records Commission.

Modern Educational Controversies is an outgrowth of two
decades of an introductory foundations course organized in
terms of contemporary educational issues. Some of the topics
have persisted through that time, even in a supposedly rapidly
changing world. Others are being emphasized because of events
now occurring. Still others are not included here primarily
because interest in them is currently in decline.

Designed for a single academic term, this book consists
of discussions of thirteen controversial issues selected in
part to provide students with some understanding of the historical, legal, philosophical, political, and sociological
foundations of our present system of public education. It has
been edited with a view to serving as an introductory text at
the undergraduate level or for students taking their first
foundations course at the graduate level. It is also appropriate for experienced teachers, who should be sensitive to
current debate over public schooling. One might add that for
the same reason it would be useful to interested lay persons.

The pro-con format was adopted to generate student interest and involvement. Because bibliographies on contemporary concerns quickly get out of date, and because the
search for additional information and interpretations should
be part of the learning process, the material in these pages,
except for brief introductions, is limited to the authors'
statements and notes. I have attempted to provide some consistency in format throughout the various articles, but re-
calling the Emersonian observation that foolish consistency is
the hobgoblin of little minds, I have shown deference to those
contributors who favored particular stylistic elements. Thus,
for example, in some articles the reader will find the term
"black" used as a racial designation, but when reference is to
cultural characteristics the word is capitalized, as with
English, French, or Canadian. Writers' individual styles will
become evident in the following pages.

I am especially grateful to the authors whose contribu-
tions have made this volume possible. My sincerest apprecia-
tion is extended to David Barr and William Collie of Wright
State University, Frederick Buchanan of the University of
Utah, Malcolm Campbell of Bowling Green State University, June
Canty-Lemke and Leo Leonard of the University of Portland,
Joseph Conn of Americans United for Separation of Church and
State, Herbert Douglas of Glassboro State College, Philip
Kearney of the University of Michigan, Dal Lawrence of the

Toledo Federation of Teachers, Edward Remington of Concerned Educators Against Forced Unionism, James Riccitelli of the Center for Biblical Studies in Toledo, Virginia Schaefer of the Toledo Public Schools, James Stull of Eastern Kentucky University, and John Thomas of the Roman Catholic Diocese of Toledo. My deepest thanks also go to colleagues at the University of Toledo: Samir Abu-Absi, David Balzer, Langston Bannister, Leon Carter, John Cryan, James Gress, Thomas Lopez, Edward Nussel, Philip Rusche, Robert Wilhoyte, Peggy Williams, and especially Sam Snyder who contributed two articles, proofread others, and assisted with the introductions. Finally my thanks to Eva Hattner-Hulisz who typed every word of this manuscript.

David Tavel

Toledo, Ohio
June, 1984

TABLE OF CONTENTS

INTRODUCTION

The purpose of this book is to introduce the reader to controversial issues in education in the hope that present and future teachers will increasingly realize the nature and breadth of concerns which influence what takes place in the school, and thus hopefully will become involved with them. Too often there is a tendency to think of the educational enterprise as the teaching and learning occurring within a school's walls, and to wonder why anyone other than a school parent or a disgruntled taxpayer would show any interest. We are inclined to think of the scope of educational decision-making in a very limited way, and fail to recognize the mutual interaction of events and issues inside the school and those in the larger society.

The really critical educational questions are answered by those who dominate society's power structure. Educational decisions are political decisions. Politics often gets in the way of sound educational decisions, and instead of solving educational problems we merely change the scene of the action and the names of the players. Bussing for purposes of desegregation may be an excellent case in point. Educators had little impact on decisions to transport youngsters between neighborhoods, and in regard to most educational issues they have had little impact throughout our history. Were it not for the fact that when a teacher closes his classroom door he can, within reason, do whatever his professional judgment dictates, we would soon realize how minimal a role the teacher plays in policy making.

For three notable reasons many citizens are reluctant to have educators involved in determining policies. Historically our public schools have been the creation of the local community, and with a conviction that proves surprising to persons from other countries, local citizens expect the school to reflect their values, needs, and interests, and do not hesitate to pressure educators to do just that. A second factor is the strain of anti-intellectualism manifested in the suspicion of "book learning," the disdain shown educators, and the unwillingness to keep children back in grade, unless of course they are athletes who could benefit from an extra year's physical growth. Additionally, teachers have seldom demonstrated any expertise which would give them the recognition (or begrudging acceptance) shown physicians and lawyers. Most teachers have a bachelor's degree, which is likely to mean no more schooling than what many voters possess.

The first step to intelligent involvement in policy making is developing an understanding of the issues. Thirteen such issues are examined in this book. With American society undergoing rapid change, it is inevitable that the schools, too, will change. Even a cursory examination of the questions here debated should reveal their actual and potential impact on teachers. Policy changes regarding any one of them could mean significant changes in what teachers do and how they do it. The questions posed here are, therefore, not solely theoretical. Some of the proposals could, if implemented, drastically alter the educational enterprise. Teachers thus need to know what currently is in dispute, what are the proposed alternatives, and what are the implications for their chosen profession.

The positions presented in this book by the several contributors are not necessarily definitive; more could be and frequently is being written on all of them. The format employed here, with one article taking the "pro" side and one the "con," is intended to encourage further investigation. Not just educational publications, but commercial ones -- magazines and newspapers -- are useful sources of viewpoints and data. The reader should seek to determine what assumptions underlie the positions expressed, be they by professors or politicians. Sometimes a superficial statement sounds impressive, but an examination of the unstated ideas which form the basis for the viewpoint leads to a different judgment. Educators especially should seek to keep abreast of research findings. In a society whose bottom line usually is "does it really work," the results of painstaking investigation should carry more weight than collections of slogans, myths, and wishful thinking.

PART ONE -- COMPULSORY ATTENDANCE

Should the nation's youth be required to attend school, or have compulsory attendance laws outlived their usefulness?

In 1852 the General Court or Massachusetts enacted the country's first compulsory school attendance law. Before the end of the nineteenth century over half the states and territories passed similar statutes, although historians differ as to the effectiveness of such legislation. During the first half of the current century compulsory attendance became reality throughout most of the nation. The past few decades, however, have seen challenges to these laws. The Supreme Court's 1972 decision in <u>Wisconsin vs. Yoder</u> only fueled the arguments.

The first article treats schooling as primarily political in nature and contends that, of all the purposes assigned to the American public school, the most important is the development of a sense of community and responsibility for the general welfare. Compulsory attendance laws, to the extent that they assure the exposure of all youngsters to experience which contribute to a realization of this purpose, are highly desirable, if not necessary.

The second article asks whether compulsory schooling is the best way to achieve our educational goals, and whether compulsion is consistent with the ideals of a democratic society. In practice these laws may infringe upon religious and cultural freedom. Finally, it is but an assumption that without them people would not seek an appropriate education for themselves and their progeny.

DAVID TAVEL, editor of this book, is Professor of Educational Theory and also Director of the Division of Educational Foundations at the University of Toledo. Previously he taught at Boston University, Colorado State College, and in three Massachusetts public school systems. He holds a doctorate from Boston University.

FREDERICK S. BUCHANAN is Associate Professor in the Department of Educational Studies at the University of Utah. He also serves as chairman of the Division of Cultural Foundations of Education at Utah. He formerly taught in the Bountiful, Utah High School and at the University of Toledo. His doctorate is from Ohio State University.

1

A CASE FOR COMPULSORY SCHOOL ATTENDANCE

David Tavel

Compulsory schooling, in one form or another, has been a feature of the American scene almost continuously ever since the Massachusetts Puritans began to fear that their offspring might not believe and behave as their parents desired. These English Calvinist settlers held to the view that parents were responsible for the upbringing of their children -- a good idea somewhat falling into disuse nowadays. Either because they were only partly successful in this endeavor, or because their neighbors were only partly successful -- it is easier for historians to determine actions rather than motives -- they deemed it necessary to enact laws to promote their beliefs. Thus legislation in 1642, 1647, 1654 and later aimed to insure that the young were properly educated. The first of these made town officials responsible for seeing that youngsters learned how to read, that they knew the basic laws of the colony, and that they received religious instruction. The second, the famous "Old Deluder Satan Act," required the establishment of schools and the hiring of teachers. The third called for the supervision of teachers. Each law was succeeded by a later one, and that succession was clear evidence of the failure of the predecessor to achieve the objectives which inspired its passage.

The one requirement not enacted into law by the leaders in the Massachusetts Bay Colony was that youngsters would have to attend school. This would have been too extreme a departure from their English traditions. After all, it was not until late in the nineteenth century -- long after the establishment of the American common school -- that England itself began to take serious steps to get all children into school. The education laws beginning with that of 1642 can be regarded as our first compulsory education statutes. Although they only partly achieved their aims, they are of major significance in America's educational history because they established the precedent of the civil government assuming responsibility for education by requiring communities and parents to make provision for the schooling of the young.

There was, of course, no United States in the middle of the seventeenth century. Indeed, few of the colonies in North America had anything in common with one another. Europe's religious wars of the 1500's and 1600's were part of the first hand experience of many colonists, and laws of Puritan Massachusetts discriminating against Baptists, Quakers

3

and Roman Catholics were typical of what was found on both sides of the Atlantic. Fragmentation and dispersion, rather than centralization, was the order of the day. Even where a government might attempt to prescribe for an entire colony, it was always possible for the discontented and displeased merely to pack up and head over the hill and out of the effective reach of the authorities.

Effective centralized government did not exist. When thirteen of England's thirty-odd American colonies finally gained their independence, their various governments emerged with only limited ability to control the populace, and with few funds to do much of anything. Thus the schools of the young nation remained in the hands of the towns and villages. Indeed, the American experience in this respect is somewhat unique. Throughout most of the world school systems have been imposed on the people by the national government. By way of contrast, the schools of the United States have arisen from the efforts of the local community. Our early schools, furthermore, tended to come into existence in areas where limited population meant an equally limited financial pool from which to draw resources for buildings, staffing, and equipment. We, therefore, find ourselves in the mid-1800's before state compulsory attendance laws make their appearance.

Several developments during the first half of the nineteenth century set the stage for laws requiring school attendance. Where they were most prominent the first compulsory attendance statutes were enacted. The first two of these developments were urbanization and industrialization. By bringing large numbers of people together in one community, they made universal taxation a feasible way of financing schooling for the city's youth. The rise of the city and the changing of the family from a primarily productive unit to a primarily consuming one brought stresses and strains -- poverty, slums, and crime. Schools -- schools under the control of the community -- became increasingly viewed as one means of combatting these problems. Furthermore, the first wave of immigration brought to the cities people whose numbers and clearly different values were often viewed with alarm. They had to be Americanized, and what better way than by requiring their children to attend school.

Finally, the battle for the common school was being won. Schools founded by individuals or private societies, and supported by philanthropy and rates charged parents for each enrolled child, had dominated the American educational scene. Largely due to the efforts of men such as Horace Mann and Henry Barnard the public was becoming increasingly receptive

4

to a new type of school. This was to be a school not for children whose parents were of a particular religious persuasion or a particular social class, but for all children. It would be supported not by the uncertain donations of the rich or by enrollment fees which placed the poor at a disadvantage, but by universal taxation. It would, therefore, be responsive not to the demands of the few, but to the desires of the many. It would teach not what the upper classes accepted as appropriate preparation for further schooling including college, but rather commonly agreed upon subjects taught in the common language. In sum, this was not to be an exclusive school serving a select clientele, but rather a common school serving society as a whole.

The common, or public, school followed logically from the ideas of the American Revolution, ideas which inspired republican government. If the authority exercised by government were to be derived from the will of the people, the people had to be educated. Jefferson is author of the often cited observation that a people which "expects to be ignorant and free, in a state of civilization, expects what never was and never will be." A republican society requires an intelligent electorate, and the best guarantee of such an electorate is a system of universal schooling. To assure that everyone attends, schooling has to be free, which is to say financed by a system of universal taxation.

The mere creation of schools does not, however, guarantee attendance. Varied motives explained the support given to the concept of compulsory attendance. In slightly modified form some are appropriate still today. Already mentioned is the need to prepare youngsters for a role in the political system. The American republic was to many an experiment, for self-government was far from the most common political system in the western world. Self-government necessitated civic or political education, and since all people would in some way be involved in the governing process, all needed that civic education.

The fast multiplying industries were giving rise to other reasons. Factories made use of child labor, usually for long hours and under harsh conditions. Children working in these factories were unlikely to get any schooling. The humanitarian sentiment to get them away from conditions on the job combined with concern that the youngsters would remain ignorant gained some support for compulsory schooling. Then there were the immigrants who, in their ignorance of American ways, also had to be protected against possible exploitation. And as the factories attracted people from rural areas and the lower class, the more affluent city dwellers became concerned with what they viewed as the undesirable habits and relative ignorance of the newcomers. In time some factory owners saw merit in compulsory schooling, for this was one useful means of teaching skills and attitudes that would enable people to function better on the job. Workers needed to be able to follow written directions and read orders. It was most desirable that they be punctual, sufficiently clean so that they would not be disease carriers, accustomed to taking orders, and imbued with republican sentiments that minimized susceptibility to foreign ideologies.

The very same civic, economic, and social motives which had led to the creation of the common school gave rise to compulsory attendance laws. The first such laws applied to working children. Then in 1852 Massachusetts passed a law which applied to all children. After the Civil War other states enacted legislation so that by the end of the century thirty states had compulsory attendance laws. In 1918 Mississippi became the last of the original 48 states to pass a compulsory schooling statute.

Early efforts to enforce these laws often met with the same problems found today in "third world" countries. There might be an inadequate number of classrooms, or schools, or even of teachers, although the normal schools were doing their best to turn out sufficient numbers of trained persons. State enforcement agencies, if they existed at all, lacked the resources and experience to implement the new statutes. It was a story often repeated on the American scene. Unrealized ideals inspire legislation, but effective implementation is hindered by the very same conditions which give rise to the legislation.

These laws did not wither on the vine, however, because they were consistent with the goals of community building and the development of national unity. The conditions which gave rise to the common school not only still existed at the end of the century, but appeared more acute in light of the greatest period of immigration in the nation's history. Half a million people a year were entering the United States, and in the last decades of the 1800's they were coming from central, eastern, and southern Europe, areas but little removed from the middle ages. They crossed not only an ocean, but centuries. The combination of sheer numbers and acute cultural differences posed a threat to a growing sense of national unity. If ever there was a time for programs of Americanization, the turn of the century was such a time. If some feared the new arrivals as endangering the American way, others recognized the oppor-

tunity to promote assimilation through humanitarian and demo-
cratically oriented efforts. The schools could aid in such
efforts by exposing immigrant children to the same teaching as
given to American pupils, and thus provide the first training
in citizenship.

Increasingly through the early years of the twentieth
century cities did a better job implementing compulsory attendance legislation. Truant officers were hired, child labor
laws were more carefully enforced, and school censuses were
regularly taken. One factor which made enforcement increasingly effective was the decline of large and unwieldy school
boards which were being replaced by boards of far fewer members. These smaller boards, furthermore, were becoming increasingly dependent upon superintendents who were management
oriented.

There is no way of knowing what percentage of the children were in school because the law required it. Attendance
figures and writings from the post-Civil War decades lead to
the inescapable conclusion that most parents sent their children to school because they wanted them there. Parental
motives may have varied, but as the industrial system changed
family functions it became easier to consider postponing the
economic benefits of putting one's children to work. What
income children did not generate while in school would be
more than made up as a result of an education which would make
better jobs available to them in the long run.

Not only were parents seeing children in a different
light, but social reformers were re-assessing the relative
roles of community and parents in the upbringing of the young.
Where parents appeared incapable of providing moral instruction or vocational training, or even adequate child care,
intervention by government was called for. The welfare of
society was at stake. Thus the school and other social
agencies through the current century have taken a more prominent role in the life of children. So encompassing has this
role become that many parents are turning over the socialization of their offspring to the school, and education -- what
the family once provided -- has become synonymous with schooling.

A century ago elementary schooling was all the "book
l'arnin'" youngsters expected. Life in the United States
changed drastically in the next fifty years, however, and one
impact this had on schooling was to draw students to the high
school. By 1930 nearly one-half of the 14 to 17 year olds
were in high school. Today, half a century later, over 50

7

percent of the population enrolls for some college work. Given such increasing dependence on our schools, it is easy to understand how compulsory attendance laws became all but universally accepted.

The compulsory attendance laws passed by the states did not dictate which school a youngster had to attend, nor did they specify the course of study to be pursued. These laws set the minimal length of the school year, the ages at which children had to attend school, and the various enforcement mechanisms. They were not federal statutes, but state enacted. After the 1954 Supreme Court decision in <u>Brown v. Board of Education</u> three southern states repealed their compulsory attendance laws in an effort to avoid integrating their schools. Today Mississippi is the only state without such a statute.

In 1972 the Supreme Court in <u>Wisconsin v. Yoder</u> exempted Amish children from attendance beyond the eighth grade. For several decades Amish parents in a number of states had run afoul of the law in attempting to keep their children from schooling which, they believed, would undermine the beliefs and values they wanted their young to hold. Since the end of World War Two minority views have increasingly sought a hearing in the courts, and their successes have been highly publicized. Thus encouraged, three Amish parents defied Wisconsin's compulsory attendance law which required them to send their children to a public or private school until age sixteen. In ruling for the parents, the Court stressed their unique life style, and noted that the Amish had a record of being law-abiding and economically productive. It rendered its decision on the basis of the Amish experience, and provided no explicit encouragement to other groups to seek the same exemption.

Critics of the American public school, however, did see the ruling as encouraging them, if not to oppose compulsory schooling laws, at least to divert tax moneys to sectarian and other non-public schools. In delivering the Court's <u>Yoder</u> decision, Chief Justice Burger spoke of schooling as an alternative to children displacing adult workers and to "forced idleness." If this was the reason for having schools surely one school was as good as another. Some critics thus sought the establishment of voucher plans, and more recently, tuition tax credit schemes. Others called for abolishing the public school. Even within the educational profession there were voices raised in support of amending attendance laws to excuse pupils of high school age.

The prominent report of the National Commission on the Reform of Secondary Education appeared in 1973 with the title <u>The Reform of Secondary Education</u>. One of its recommendations called for dropping the formal school-leaving age to fourteen. If implemented, argued the Commission, we would be recognizing the liberation of youth which had been legally established as a result of court rulings in the previous decade. We would be recognizing the right of teen-agers <u>not</u> to undertake formal schooling beyond age fourteen. Noting school violence and the high degree of truancy in many cities, the Commission viewed compulsory attendance statutes as both ineffective and contributory to conditions which blocked effective instruction in schools. It recommended abandoning compulsory attendance, but retaining compulsory education, arguing that students still needed to acquire certain skills. The traditional high school was not the only place where such skills could be developed. The Commission admitted, however, that these alternative modes of education did not exist, and that reducing the age requirement to fourteen would be equivalent to abandoning many teenagers. (It is interesting to note that 1983 -- ten years later -- saw a spate of highly publicized reports on education, none of which called for reducing compulsory schooling.)

The courts appear equally unwilling to endorse immediate changes, and have proceeded to discourage those who saw the Amish ruling as equivalent to declaring open season on the concept of compulsory attendance. In 1981, in dismissing an appeal by a Nebraska church, the U. S. Supreme Court upheld a decision by the Nebraska Supreme Court which had ruled that the state's compulsory education law did not violate any First or Ninth Amendment rights of church-operated schools. That same year the Supreme Court of Iowa agreed with a district court's verdict of guilty against parents who refused to send their children to a public school or to an equivalent non-public school which employed certified teachers. Also in 1981 the North Dakota Supreme Court ruled that the state's compelling interest in providing an education to all through a compulsory attendance law outweighed the detriment to plantiffs who objected to compulsory attendance on religious grounds.

While the legal status of compulsory attendance laws thus remains fluid, consideration of the desirability of such laws needs to be made. An appropriate starting point is the recognition that our world has become increasingly complex, the technology of the industrial revolution is being succeeded by that of an electronic revolution, and our storehouse of knowledge is increasing at a rapidly increasing rate. These conditions are placing far greater educational demands on each of us, requiring additional technical and professional competence. Literacy has to be redefined. It can no longer consist merely of the ability to pronounce the printed word. Indeed, even technical skills by themselves are inadequate for the active participant in a democratic society.

We need an articulate public whose members are able to communicate with one another as part of the decision-making process. Such communication is painfully absent from current American life as witness the language used by government officials who appear to be deliberately seeking to confuse and confound us. The communications media themselves do not really communicate, seeming to be far more interested in the noise they make than in what, if anything, they say. An articulate electorate is a necessity in a democracy, but where is such articulation to be learned and mastered if not in the school? The previously noted decline of family influence has resulted in a decreasing ability of the home to insure that adequate and appropriate communications skills are developed, not to mention other aspects of education.

A few years studying our national history accomplishes little. We live in an increasingly interdependent world. The more advanced a nation, the more dependent it is on other nations. Our young people need more -- not less -- time in school to develop a global outlook. The same need exists when we consider other aspects of modern life and their school counterpart the course of study. One could contend that the primary purpose of school is to equip the individual with those tools which will enable him to educate himself. Such self-education requires more maturity than a fourteen year old -- even today's sophisticated fourteen year old -- is likely to possess. The extra two to four years of compulsory schooling may constitute more than a mere quantitative difference.

Several criticisms of compulsory schooling for high school age youngsters merit some recognition. They note the number of pupils who have high absence rates, the boredom of many youngsters, the lack of accomplishment in school, outbreaks of violence among pupils, and the alleged inappropriateness of some courses and activities. Without question some school programs do need to be overhauled, and it would be difficult to argue against excusing (or expelling) incorrigibles and other trouble-makers from our schools. Repeal of compulsory schooling would, however, invite wholesale departures, many of which would be regretted as the drop-outs found no place for themselves in the economic world. Those currently at the lower end of the achievement ladder would, by leaving school, soon find themselves at an even greater disadvantage in competition with young people succeeding in school.

Compulsory schooling need not mean twelve years within the walls of the traditional school. It could well mean required work-study programs for some students. With a population increasingly oriented toward attending college there is distinct merit in having some work experience during the high school years. Such experience might help combat the widening social gap between "hand" and "head" labor. Were we to lessen the number of years of required schooling, one likely result would be the cramming into fewer years the same amount of work currently attempted in twelve. We would probably succeed only in making school work more intense and schooling more pressure-packed, all to the detriment of the goal of helping young people experience a sense of satisfaction in accomplishing something worthwhile.

Schools would play less of a custodial role if educational activities could be increasingly individualized. Schools could individualize instruction if educators put less faith in teaching so-called essentials and developing minimal competencies. It would also help if colleges and state departments of education stopped requiring certain subjects which are, in effect, regarded as either eternal verities or the sine qua non of a high school diploma and college admission. In addition, some creativity and imagination on the part of educational leaders could go a long way toward alleviating undesirable conditions in some of our schools. Throwing the baby out with the bath by abolishing compulsory schooling partly or totally is not necessarily part of the solution, or an answer to the critics.

Some critics of compulsory education have their sights set not only on the attendance laws, but on public schooling itself. Some of these see the American school as an instrument of oppression run by a ruling class intent on maintaining its hold on the country. Others view the school as purveyor of false doctrine and even immorality. In all likelihood teachers would be surprised to hear themselves described as instruments of the ruling class deliberately holding down the lower classes, or as secular humanists determined to rid the schools of morality, decency, and just about everything else that's good.

We could lump with these critics those who charge that schools overeducate people who then become unhappy with their jobs or even above work. It is true that an educated person

11

would become unhappy with narrow routine tasks. Such work is dehumanizing, offering little opportunity for a sense of personal accomplishment or for individual growth. The problem, however, lies not with people having too much schooling, but with the values which dominate American commerce and industry.

What good alternatives are there to keeping youngsters in some type of educational program? Where are school leavers to go, and what are they to do? We already have a high youth unemployment rate. The probability is overwhelming that the drop-outs will find inferior or no positions in the job market. In either instance they are likely to become burdens to themselves, their families, and society at large. The morality of letting young people leave school unprepared for what we know they will find is highly questionable.

The boys and girls most likely to suffer from a reduction in the years of compulsory schooling are, as already pointed out, those currently educationally disadvantaged. Dropping out will result in their slipping further behind the more advantaged individuals who remained in school. Widespread recognition that there must be expanded career opportunities might lead to a form of distributive education for all students. Such arrangements would put students in contact with potential employers, but the young people who dropped out would miss this, and be at an even greater disadvantage. Where better than in school can young people get practice in making career decisions, in coping with problems of finding a job and paying the bills?

What is beyond the power of the school may be the major concern. Society has not yet provided places for the drop-out to go. The answer then to the question of alternatives is a simple one. There are no acceptable alternatives to compulsory schooling at this time.

The case for compulsory attendance laws has noted the need for more schooling in an increasingly complex world, has remarked on criticisms of the current operation of some of our schools, has revealed the ulterior motives behind the actions of some critics of the public school, and has pointed out the absence of viable alternatives. It remains for us to consider a final but far from insignificant reason for maintaining existing statutes. The development of compulsory education, traced in the first part of this article, has throughout our history coincided with the desire to achieve certain social goals. These goals may have varied in importance depending on times and circumstances, but one element was common to all of them. They were public goals, relating to the promotion of the general welfare.

Training for a job, good emotional adjustment, mastery of "basics" -- these are personal or private goals. Their importance in schooling is not to be disparaged. In a day, however, when we are encouraged to take care of "number one"; when public confidence in government sinks even lower; when the officials in government respond primarily to the demands of single issue groups; and when individual loyalties are increasingly provincial, ethnic, and religious, there is an overwhelming need to concentrate on public goals and public purposes. In the last analysis, such public purposes constitute the bedrock upon which the justification for compulsory attendance laws rests.

In the United States today a major thrust of education must be to strengthen the always tenuous sense of community. It is the American commitment to pluralism which has precluded our taking that sense of community for granted. Thus, for example, we have relied on the pledge to the flag and the singing of the national anthem to give overt expression to the value of community. Psychologists might view such activity as compensation for the discrepancy between the ideal and reality. America as one community is indeed a very fragile entity today. If America as a single society is worth preserving, young people will require some experience in living and working with others who are products of different backgrounds and holders of some different values. The public school is the institution most likely to provide an environment within which this contact can regularly take place.

From the first Puritan communal educational efforts we have held schools responsible for promoting the general welfare. It is precisely because the general welfare was involved that it was possible to enact compulsory attendance laws in the late nineteenth and early twentieth centuries. Since no institution other than the public school existed to provide experience in developing and sharing common values, it was the school that was called upon to provide all children with common experiences. The ideal was a school which would enroll children of the rich and children of the poor, children of the working classes and children of the managerial class, children from traditional American homes and children of immigrants. In school they would learn that the entire world does not think the way they as individuals do, that beliefs which they hold without question are held by some people only very tentatively and by others not at all. They would learn not only toleration of different views, but also how to work

13

with people who hold them. The response to those who point out how far we still are from fully realizing the ideal is that our democratic ideals are for us what the North Star is for the mariner. They serve as a guide, as a constant reminder of the direction we have decided upon.

Eliminating compulsory attendance, or reducing it to the elementary and junior high years, would make it harder for the school to meets its obligation to build a sense of community and responsibility for the general welfare. More young people than is currently the case would by dropping out miss those years of school during which they, because of emerging maturity, would be best able to learn how to put these social ideals into practice. They would be having up to four years less experience in developing and mastering the skills and knowledge required to make citizenship effective in a democratic society.

THE CASE AGAINST COMPULSORY SCHOOL ATTENDANCE

Frederick S. Buchanan

In one of its most significant decisions affecting schools, the United States Supreme Court in the 1943 case of West Virginia State Board of Education vs. Barnette gave an eloquent expression to the rejection of "official orthodoxy" in American society. In holding that the children of Jehovah's Witnesses could not be compelled to salute the American flag during school exercises Chief Justice Jackson asserted that:

> If there is any fixed star in our constitutional constellation, it is that no official, high or petty, can prescribe what shall be orthodox in politics, nationalism, religion, or other matter of opinion or force citizens to confess by word or act their faith therein.[1]

Another religious group, the Old Order Amish, was the means of having the Court in 1972 examine whether the Wisconsin law requiring compulsory attendance at school beyond the eighth grade applied to the Amish. The Court held for the Amish on the grounds that the state had no compelling interest in forcing them to attend schools beyond the eighth grade and that to force such would be a contravention of the Free Exercise Clause of the First Amendment.[2] In other words, Amish parental claims to religious freedom had priority over the state's interest in compulsory schooling beyond the eighth grade. It should be recognized, however, that the Court at the same time upheld the idea that the state may impose "reasonable regulations" respecting the control and duration of education, including apparently, the compelling of attendance for even the Amish during the first eight grades.

In spite of this affirmation of the tradition of compulsory schooling, the Yoder decision is still a significant departure from the norm in that it raised questions concerning the idea of universal compulsory schooling in a nation where the concept has taken on an aura of sanctified "conventional wisdom." The Amish intransigence in refusing to allow their children the "benefits" of formal schooling beyond the eighth grade added a new dimension to the perennial debate over the respective roles of state and parents in the education of children. It is the purpose of this essay to argue that using the state's power to compel children to attend schools is not a "reasonable regulation" and may be detrimental to not only

15

the children of a small group such as the Amish, but to the education of children in general.

In nothing has America acted on faith more than in its belief in an assumption that compulsory schooling is a necessary adjunct to "life, liberty, and the pursuit of happiness." Over the years compulsory school attendance has been gradually accepted as necessary on the basis not of studied research, or of closely reasoned analysis, but on the assumption that it is necessary for the general welfare of the nation. Like the purveyors of miraculous elixirs on the American frontier, the promoters of compulsory schooling have touted their nostrum as a cure for:

The aches, the quakes, the palsy and the gout.
All ills within and all ills without.

Whatever ills, imagined or real, have stricken the body politic, the notion of compulsory school attendance has promised relief -- from the threat of urban crime in the 19th century, through the threat of adolescent sexuality at the turn of the century, to the ideological and technical threat of Soviet Russia in the 20th century, the remedy of schooling has been applied, with vigor. John Dewey's characterization of many "progressive" practices in education as stale mustard plasters which continue to be used, in spite of a loss of efficacy, fits the concept of compulsory schooling as a conventional panacea for society's problems.[3]

The idea of compelling people to attend school is not just an educator's dream -- it is derived in part from deeper, social roots not the least of which are the assumptions of the "Enlightenment" notion of universal progress in the late 18th century. For Enlightenment philosophers the key to a "better, rational society" was education and "given a rational education, there was no limit set to the progress of humanity to become 'happy and powerful.'"[4] Few people are likely to object to such a stance, but it must be remembered that this "Enlightenment" position was an expression of a hope, of a faith in human potential, not a statement of empirical fact.

Another earlier and less idealistic source of compulsory schooling is derived from the needs of those who wield power in society to make sure that their power is preserved. In 16th century Germany, for example, Martin Luther advocated schooling to "compel adherence to Lutheranism, and to aid in the suppression of dissent from the established church."[5] Calvin in Geneva advocated compulsory schools for similar reasons and the tradition continued in Massachusetts with the

16

attempt there to impose compulsory schooling through the "Old Deluder Satan Act" of 1647. It is worthwhile noting that the only New England colony which did not establish a compulsory system was Rhode Island which had been founded by dissidents from orthodox Calvinism.[6] Adolphe E. Meyer in surveying colonial educational developments contrasts the two approaches toward compulsory schooling in New England:

> There remains Rhode Island, a mere grain of earth as colonies go, but inhabited by a free-spirited and highly nonconformist folk. In 1647, for example, while Massachusetts was making history by seeking to slip a bridle on that old deluder Satan, Rhode Island for its part gained immortality when, the first among English-speaking people, it inscribed a bill for freedom of worship into its ordinance. Not given to the theocratic revelation, Rhode Island kept state and church in separate corners. In consequence, in an age when religion was education's main reason for being, Rhode Islanders were content to leave the matter to their various congregations and localities, and the colony never adopted a general statute for compulsory instruction.[7]

The seeming relationship between compulsion in matters of religion and compulsion in matters of education is not lost on contemporary opponents of compulsory schooling, who see today's secular state taking on some of the characteristics of the officially sanctioned religions of the past and using the public schools to enforce educational orthodoxy. Neither the Enlightenment faith in human potential nor the efforts of religious orthodoxy to maintain the status quo justify compulsory schooling as a means of promoting education. If anything, they are examples of why compulsory schooling may be unnecessary and counterproductive.

Later generations did not concern themselves with such niceties, however, and eventually between 1852 and 1918 compulsory attendance at school to promote "progress" became the cri de guerre of all educational systems in the United States. What could not be achieved by persuasion was therefore brought about by compulsion -- legislated compulsory schooling was now the key to a "better, rational society." While some of the ideals of America's founders have been used to support the notion that the state has an obligation to promote a "better, rational society" through fostering widespread social and economic equality, those ideals did not include enforced attendance at schools as the means of attaining the "just society." It was the school reformers of the 19th century who

17

made that necessary "leap of faith" and widely and religiously heralded compulsory public schooling as the answer to problems of inequality, un-Americanism, and public and private immorality. For these schoolmen and their successors, the American public school, mandated and supported by the state, was increasingly identified as the panacea for social and individual ills; it would be, they believed, "an equalizing power -- a leveling engine." 8

Thomas Jefferson is often cited as one of the architects of the American public school system because of his proposals for tax-supported schools in Virginia. However, as Lawrence Cremin notes, although Jefferson was "a great believer in schooling ... it never occurred to him that schooling would be the chief educational influence on the young."9 Nor, it must be added, did he ever propose that the schooling that he outlined should be compelled by the state. A man who had spent so much energy championing the separation of church and state and opposing "all forms of tyranny over the human mind" would not be likely to want one set of compulsions (however, virtuous or praiseworthy) replaced with another set in the guise of saving humanity from ignorance.

Of course, Jefferson and his compatriots of the "Enlightenment" era had a general faith and hope that mankind with appropriate education could and would solve many of the perplexing problems confronting them, but to assume that is quite different from assuming that one can force such desirable ends by compulsory school attendance. They leaned toward persuasion rather than compulsion in matters of politics, religion and education.

It is readily admitted, of course, that society does have an interest in encouraging its citizens to be well-informed, rational and intelligent, and even in promoting equality of opportunity for as many citizens as possible. The question at issue is: is compulsory schooling the best way of achieving these aims? After all, there are numerous desirable conditions which make for a "good society" and the "good life." Take health, for instance. Who can argue that health and freedom from disease are not desirable ends. But in spite of this, no one suggests that every person must by law be required to submit to a physical or mental examination at regular intervals so that society can maintain its health. In the absence of a "clear and present danger" that a person may spread a contagious and potentially dangerous disease, the state does not enforce its will on the public at large. Likewise in the absence of a "clear and present danger," compulsory schooling is not necessarily the best and only way to

promote the social good. Persuasion and argument in an atmosphere free of coercion and restraint seem most conducive to
the aims of education as a means of promoting inquiry and
progress among a free people. In Einstein's words: "It is a
very grave mistake to think that the enjoyment of seeing or
searching can be promoted by means of coercion and a sense of
duty." [10]

   The issue of universal, compulsory schooling in fact
involves the very matter of freedom and the conditions which
nourish and promote it. Noted constitutional lawyer Leo
Pfeffer asserts that the Amish rejection of compulsory schooling beyond the eighth grade raised religious freedom to a
first place position among our traditional constitutional
freedoms -- a position which, according to Pfeffer, it has[11]
always held in the hearts and thought of the American people.
The Yoder case, in Pfeffer's view, simply makes what was implicit, explicit. In the process, this notion of freedom must
now be seen as a chief contender with another American article
of faith -- the deeply held belief that compulsory public
schooling is necessary for national and individual "salvation" in the secular realm. From the tenor of the Supreme
Court decision it would appear that compulsory schooling,
rather than take its place as a supporter of religious freedom and of a religious orientation, is now a potential an-
tagonist of that very freedom. The Amish clash with public
schooling is but an instance of the conflict which Kenneth[12]
Boulding identifies in his "The Emerging Superculture."
According to Boulding the major problems confronted by modern
man center around the tension created by the clash of the
superculture and the traditional culture. With the compulsory
public schools acting as an agent of the superculture by
transmitting the superculture's secular value orientations,
it should be easy to understand why the Amish object to its
sophisticated content and why compulsory public schooling has
become a focal point of tension between the values of the
technological society and those of the folk society, and by
extension to those of the community and the family.

   The most crucial issue dealt with by the Wisconsin decision is the Amish claim that enforced attendance at public
schools which do not reflect the small society's religious
values constitutes an infringement on the religious liberty
to be Amish. Quite apart from the constitutional issue, it is
evident that the Amish fear is well justified -- today in
Europe there are no Amish as the acculturation processes of
the superculture have absorbed those who chose to stay in
their homeland. The fact that this is a "natural" process of
social evolution does not mean, however, that the state's

19

power should be used to speed up the process of the disintegration of small societies. If a group such as the Amish relies for its continuance on certain cultural boundaries as means of maintaining its integrity and independence, it must resist, as a matter of survival, the attempts of external forces to dissolve those boundaries. The public school's function as an active agent of national unity and acculturation, in which cultural and religious differences are minimized or even obliterated, warrants the Amish perception of public schooling as a threat to their way of life. Religious groups like the Amish are particularly vulnerable to the influence of the secular society's agents of acculturation (the schools) because of the rejection of the world's <u>modus operandi</u> and their refusal to utilize "worldy" means to achieve their ends. (They have historically refused to be aggressive litigants because of their rejection of the world and agreed to involvement in the Wisconsin case only when the state initiated the original action and the appeal to the Supreme Court.)

The impact of the schools upon such an unwordly group as the Amish is more likely to have a greater disruptive influence, culturally speaking, than upon groups like the Mormons, for example, who have not withdrawn from the world but who seek to change it through an aggressive proselytical program. For instance, unlike the Amish, who until recently had little to do with organizing an Amish school system, the Mormons not only exert a powerful influence on public school policies in Utah, but they have a highly organized seminary system based on the released-time principle as an antidote to the secular orientation of the school curriculum. Public schools are less likely to have a secularly-oriented socializing impact if school patrons are able to exert an influence over the educational content and process as well as over teachers and administrators. However, this can only be done if the religious group has enough concentrated power to influence the schools to be more sensitive to their particular frame of reference. The tension between the superculture and the traditional culture is somewhat reduced when the traditional culture is able to adapt itself to the processes of the superculture and use them to protect its independence and existence. This the Amish refused to do, and the Supreme Court reinforced their refusal by agreeing that the issue involved, for the Amish at least, the principle of freedom of religion.

Does this decision, then, only apply to small withdrawn sects who appear helpless in their confrontation with the larger society? Is the potential threat to the personal beliefs of committed individuals lessened any because their particular group is, unlike the Amish, more integrated into the larger society, socially and economically? Does the fact that one does not belong to a separated group imply that the threat to individual religious freedom is lessened when compulsory schooling promotes points of view at variance with the person's religious orientation?

However much the secular society values, in theory at least, critical thinking and the rigorous examination of belief systems, for some citizens these dispositions are perceived as threats to religious freedom and are perceived as involving the school in the task of undermining parental control over children. One can imagine, for instance, the Jehovah's Witness' response to the generally accepted stress on voting and civic duty as a prerequisite of good citizenship. In effect the child of Jehovah's Witness parents may be made to feel inadequate and unworthy as a consequence of the compulsory social studies curriculum. What of the children of Evangelical Christian parents who have been taught at home and church to regard the Biblical creation account in a very literal sense and are confronted with the evolutionary conception of creation? Likewise, the beliefs of the children of Christian Scientists may be threatened by the inclusion of units on health care and disease in the public school curriculum. Indeed, in some instances such children have been excused from taking required courses on the grounds that their religious values are being unnecessarily threatened by state mandated courses in "proper" health care.

It can be argued, of course, that such an "unprogressive" stance against civics education, scientific evolution and health education simply reflects the parents' "blind faith" in a particular religious tradition and if these idiosyncracies are legitimized it will give warrant for every conceivable kind of excess in the name of religion: for example, plural marriage among Mormon fundamentalists, the refusal to bear arms in time of war, or the practice of drinking poison and handling snakes among some American religious groups. It must be admitted that in an open, pluralistic society committed to freedom of belief and expression, the possibilities of individual or group excesses are always present, but unless there is evidence which indicates that an individual or the society as a whole is being substantially injured such a society must tolerate those who hold and even practice unreasonable or bizarre ways of life. The alternative is to give the state a mandate to prescribe what are or are not appropriate beliefs and behaviors. For many parents compulsory schooling verges uncomfortably close to such a mandate.

When parents feel compelled on religious grounds to instruct their children to answer test questions on evolution, history or health the way the teacher wants, but to make mental reservations about the truth of such claims, might this not promote a condition detrimental to the child's integrity? Consider also the emphasis in the public school curriculum upon celebrations such as Halloween, rooted as it is in pagan beliefs, or upon the secularized versions of Christian events such as Easter, Christmas and St. Patrick's Day. Are public schools infringing upon the personal beliefs and values of Jews, Christians or even non-believers when they construct their curriculums around such events and teachers come to school dressed as witches, Easter bunnies, leprechauns, or even Santa Claus?

If compulsory attendance at the sophisticated public schools is viewed as potentially destructive of the Amish faith, way of life, and religious freedom, is inclusion of content which is perceived as being potentially destructive of the faith or integrity of Jehovah's Witnesses, Christian Scientists, Mormons, Jews, Evangelical Christians and numerous other religious groups any less a threat to religious freedom? Could such groups use Yoder's rationale to force changes in the curriculum or to stay away from compulsory schooling? In 1976 the actions of community activists in Kanawha County, West Virginia in protesting the kinds of materials used in public schools seemed to be based on the fear that the schools would promote values antithetical to the religious values of the parents and community. Although widely misinterpreted as a call for a backward, traditional approach to education, the then U. S. Commissioner of Education T. H. Bell's plea for more sensitivity on the part of educators and publishers to the value systems and standards of school patrons is similar in emphasis to the Yoder decision and actually closely parallels the policy of making textbooks used by minority children more relevant to their needs. Do fundamentalist parents of sincere religious convictions (no matter how irrational or unscientific) have the right to textbooks which are relevant to their values or at least do not directly assault those values by inclusion of offensive materials? Is the inclusion of such controversial materials and their use in compulsory schooling a threat to freedom of religion?[13]

These questions are not easily answered, if indeed they ever can be, because they involve us in making choices between the personal freedom to believe, if we wish, in an unreflective manner and the expectation that our participation in society demands that we be reflectively critical of the claims of politicians, economists, religionists and even of educationists. However, the fact that there are no obviously "correct" answers to such questions should give us cause to pause and make us wonder at the ease with which compulsory schooling has been, and still is, accepted as the best approach to raising the level of social intelligence. Perhaps we need to examine alternative approaches which might preserve both the values of pluralism and the values of critical inquiry without sacrificing either.

But quite apart from the argument against compulsory schooling as a threat to religious and cultural freedom, it may also be viewed as a threat to the very thing the schools are supposed to nurture -- intellectual freedom. Given the "closed society" nature of the Old Order Amish, it is apparent that intellectual freedom to pursue science, art, or literature, was not what the Yoder case was about. However, if compulsory schooling can be interpreted as an infringement of Amish religious beliefs and freedom might it not also be perceived by some as an infringement on personal intellectual freedom, of which religious freedom is but one aspect? Indeed the Supreme Court decision in Welsh vs. The United States (1970) seems to give some credence to this interpretation when it expanded the meaning of religious beliefs and accepted Elliott Welsh's devoutly held personal, non-theistic moral beliefs as grounds for his claiming exclusion from military service as a conscientious objector.[14]

Apparently what is or is not a religious belief is open to debate and it is conceivable that if non-theistic moral beliefs have equal standing with religious beliefs the distinction between intellectual freedom and religious freedom is also clouded. Thus some people who do not agree with the generally accepted definition of what constitutes "truth" and "knowledge" could challenge the conventional wisdom of scientific methodology, which permeates much of the compulsory school curriculum, as an infringement on their intellectual-religious beliefs. Intentionally or not, the compulsory nature of schooling gives the curriculum and values promulgated in schools a compulsory tone. Indeed one of the reasons why academic freedom in public schools is a much more limited concept than academic freedom in higher education is the fact that attendance is compulsory. This acts as a constraint on teachers and necessarily limits their academic freedom. Similarly compulsory critical thinking or scientific inquiry is perceived as an infringement on those who do not share the assumptions on which these approaches to education are based.

23

The removal of the compulsory aspect to public schooling would allow schools greater freedom to pursue intellectual inquiry without the constraints of having to be sensitive to the needs of the captive audience in attendance because of the law. True, some schools might then become the domain of "uncritical" segments of society, but in the long term, competition in the marketplace of ideas would challenge the quality of education in such institutions as it should in public schools.

The actions of religiously-oriented parents in establishing private schools where their belief systems will be respected, and the attempts to pass laws which promote a "balanced" view of the teaching about creation cannot be dismissed simply as expressions of a "crack-pot" fringe. They are, rather, expressions of a commitment to personal freedom of the mind which our constitutional system is bound to uphold -- no matter how unorthodox they may appear to be to the majority. The tendency for institutions to exert pressure toward conformity (whether for ideological or efficiency reasons) certainly suggests that compulsory schooling could very well inhibit student freedom to think and freedom to act intellectually as well as religiously.

The question then becomes -- does compelling children to attend school infringe upon their personal freedom? Those who argue that ignorance is a much greater threat to personal freedom than compulsory schooling have a point. Certainly in the modern world we cannot ignore the need for trained intelligence, for reading, for writing and for critical, reflective thinking. But the issue under consideration is not that of "no-schooling" versus "schooling." We are not arguing for ignorance and illiteracy, although proponents of the compulsory school system seem to imply that without compulsion we would revert to a barbaric state. That conclusion is neither obvious nor accurate when one examines the historic record.

To equate compulsory schooling with particular aspects of a good education is to claim more for it than is justified -- it also assumes that given freedom, people will not choose education over ignorance. That people can be made capable of making rational choices is the very essence of the "Enlightenment" faith in education, but it should be through persuasion rather than compulsion. Making schooling a matter of persuasion and choice is in fact an expression of faith in human beings that if they are given choices they will choose what is "best" for them. Two historical studies of schooling seem to bear this out: according to E. G. West, even prior to the onset of compulsory schooling in Great Britain and the United

States, most parents actually chose to enroll their children in non-compulsory schools. West's studies convinced Milton Friedman of the University of Chicago that compulsory school attendance could only be justified if unschooled children became a threat to the community. In Friedman's words:

> The work done by West and others has persuaded
> me however, that the overwhelming majority of
> children would be schooled even in the absence
> of compulsory schooling.[15]

The research of Albert Fishlow reveals that

> levels of literacy and school attendance were
> very high in the United States before the common
> school revival of the 1840's and 1850's --
> second, perhaps only to Germany; he estimates that
> white adult literacy was about 90 percent in
> 1840 -- a dozen years before the first compul-
> sory education law. Before Americans generally
> accepted the idea that schooling should be
> publicly controlled and financed they clearly
> believed in the education of the public.[16]

Perhaps at a time when communication was limited and society insecure (as in the early national period of the U.S.) a case could be made for compulsory schooling as a means of getting things going -- a sort of starter or "leaven in the lump" necessity. However, given the sophistication of today's educational technology and the possibility that home computers linked to educational terminals may make future classroom instruction unnecessary and extremely inefficient, it is not inconceivable that part of the early 19th century rationale for compulsory schooling -- efficient transmission of information and technical know-how -- is now, at the gateway to the 21st century, redundant.

In the foreword to his stimulating book <u>Freedom to Learn</u> Carl Rogers asks:

> Can the traditional system as a whole, the most
> traditional, conservative, rigid, bureaucratic
> institution of our time ... come to grips with
> the real problems of modern life? Or will it
> continue to be shackled by the tremendous social
> pressures for conformity and retrogression,
> added to its own traditionalism?[17]

The remainder of Rogers' book attempts to support his contention that individuals ought to have the freedom and responsibility to learn. For Rogers, it is an article of faith that if given choices, people (including students) will choose what is best. Rogers also quotes Albert Einstein's criticism of school instruction as tending to "strangle the holy curiosity of inquiry" and that such inquiry "stands mainly in the need of freedom." Perhaps if schools were not compulsory, custodial institutions they would promote more intellectual freedom than they do. Of course, accepting the perspective that freedom is better than compulsion requires a certain degree of confidence in humanity, but it is no less a leap of faith than that which supports compulsory schooling as the system necessary for educating people in a mass society.

If one accepts the notion that compulsory schooling is antagonistic toward religious and intellectual freedom, it might still be argued that it has a necessary social function to perform, which transcends the academic aims of schooling. In this sense compulsory attendance at school is viewed as a necessary aspect of social control without which society and its economic institution could not survive. Schools then exist in large measure to keep masses of unemployed children off the streets and to keep them from competing with adults in the marketplace. They actually function as holding tanks, and compulsory attendance at such school is a means, not of raising the intellectual standard of society or of providing democracy with informed citizens, but of solving a social and economic problem -- what to do with unwanted youths! Given the affect which increasing automation has on still further reducing the number of youths who can be employed, some "social engineers" have in the past suggested that the best solution to this economic problem is to raise the compulsory school leaving age and mandate that more and more youths (and eventually young adults) be added to the rolls of compulsory schools.[18] There is, of course, a certain logic in such a proposal, but only if one assumes that the schools are indeed the best means of remedying what is essentially a socio-economic problem. It appears, however, to be but another instance of laying more non-educational responsibilities on the schools and raising the expectation that they will be the panacea for social ills.

The rationale for compulsory attendance has also included socialization and assumes that without an official mode (if not content) of education, the masses would become ungovernable. Such a stance is saying in effect that without government controls people can't be trusted. The historical evidence previously cited points to the conclusion that the

United States was _not_ in a condition of anarchy prior to the enactment of compulsory school legislation, nor was it in danger of being overrun by ignorant masses when most parents _chose_ to send their children to non-compulsory schools. While some minimum form of regulation of human affairs is no doubt necessary to promote the "general welfare," to protect individual citizens in their exercise of basic rights, and to protect individuals from the state and the state from some individuals, the exact meaning of "reasonable regulation" is hard to gauge and is the main reason, of course, for judicial reviews as in the _Yoder_ case. Traditionally, Americans have tended toward the notion that "that government governs best which governs least" and while the setting of minimum standards for basic literacy would appear to be "reasonable," the degree of coercion implicit in compulsory schooling legislation is hardly an example of minimum regulation, touching as it does almost every person in the nation. A free and open democratic society has less need for compulsory schooling than do authoritarian regimes which feel compelled to control as much as possible the lives of their citizens; too much freedom, they believe, promotes disorder and disequilibrium and ultimately threatens the existence of the state.

Of course, some people might use their freedom to _not_ become educated just as some choose not to attend church, not to take books out of the public library, or not to learn how to swim. Unfortunate, perhaps, as this might be, who would hold that compulsory church attendance, compulsory membership and activity in the public library, or compulsory swimming should be enforced by legislative fiat? Indeed the whole concept of compulsory attendance at school smacks somewhat of the practice of forcing people to attend church with which some New England colonies dabbled. The rationale that they wouldn't know God's will for them unless compelled to attend finally gave way to the notion that salvation cannot be compelled -- nor, it should be added, can education, even if one is compelled to attend school!

Obviously the U. S. Supreme Court had the social control issue in mind when in deciding for the Amish in _Yoder_ it said that the Amish failure to attend school beyond the eighth grade was not "a substantial threat to public safety, peace, order or welfare." Presumably the Court in stressing that the decision was meant for the Amish only and did not have universal applicability, was in fact saying that to extend freedom to other than the Amish would actually threaten "safety, peace, order or welfare." That may indeed be the case, but it is not beyond dispute and perhaps more importantly, it says very little for our concept of democracy to maintain that it

27

is upheld not by freedom of choice, but by state mandated compulsion. Is our political, social and economic fabric so fragile that it is dependent upon compulsory schooling for its survival?

In the absence of compelling historical or contemporary evidence that our society would indeed deteriorate dramatically if the compulsory nature of schooling was rescinded, it would appear that in spite of the Court's own disclaimer to the contrary, the Yoder decision, in theory at least, opens the door and gives justification for freedom of schooling and freedom from compulsory attendance at school. In the Court's words: "However strong the State's interest in universal compulsory education, it is by no means absolute to the exclusion or subordination of all other interest." Taken literally this statement has far-reaching implications for compulsory school attendance.

Given the resilience of the American constitutional system and its ability to reverse and modify its opinions to follow the "election returns" or the shifting sands of social, economic and political reality, it is entirely possible that some future Court may add "schooling" to Chief Justice Jackson's clarion call for liberty and say:

> ...that no official, high or petty, can prescribe what shall be orthodox in politics, nationalism, religion, schooling, or other matters of opinion or force citizens to confess by word or act their faith therein.

It needs to be continually borne in mind that the notion that compulsory school attendance is necessary for social and individual well-being is in large measure a "matter of opinion" which has become, by virtue of its alignment with social, economic and political interests, the "orthodox" way to increase individual and social intelligence. To continue to uphold compulsory attendance at schools is to demonstrate blind faith in the system's efficacy; it is to have faith in a mustard plaster gone stale.

Notes

[1] West Virginia State Board of Education vs. Barnette, 319 U.S. 624 (1943).

[2] Wisconsin vs. Yoder, 406 U.S. 205 (1971).

[3] Cited in Lawrence A. Cremin, The Transformation of the School (New York: Knopf, 1961), p. 349.

[4] Sidney Pollard, The Idea of Progress: History and Society, (New York: Basic Books, 1968).

[5] Murray N. Rothbard, "Historical Origins" in The Twelve Year Sentence: Radical Views of Compulsory Schooling, ed., William F. Rickenbacker, (LaSalle, Ill.: Open Court, 1974), p. 12.

[6] Ibid., p. 14.

[7] Adolphe E. Meyer, An Educational History of the American People, 2nd edition (New York: McGraw-Hill, 1967), p. 48.

[8] Horace Eaton as cited in Henry J. Perkinson, The Imperfect Panacea: American Faith in Education 1865-1965 (New York: Random House, 1968), p. 12.

[9] Cited in Lawrence A. Cremin, The Genius of American Education (Pittsburgh: University of Pittsburgh Press, 1965), p. 5.

[10] Cited in George Leonard, Education and Ecstasy (New York: Delacorte Press, 1968), p. 233.

[11] Albert N. Keim, ed., Compulsory Education and the Amish: The Right Not to be Modern (Boston: Beacon Press, 1975).

[12] Boulding's essay is in A. Kurt Baier and Nicholas Rescher, eds., Values and the Future (New York: Free Press, 1969).

[13] The materials dealing with the issue of compulsory schooling and religious freedom are taken, with some minor changes, from my review essay "How Compelling is Compulsory Education?" The Review of Education, II (July/August 1976).

[14] Welsh vs. United States, 398 U.S. 333 (1970).

[15] E. G. West, "Economic Analysis: Positive and Normative" in Rickenbacker, The Twelve Year Sentence, pp. 163-191. (Note: This book contains an excellent 29 page bibliography of

legal and other citations relating to compulsory schooling.)
The Friedman comment is found in Dennis J. Chase, "Compul-
sory Attendance: Sense or Nonsense?", Nation's Schools,
XCIII (April, 1974), 43.

[16]Cited in David B. Tyack, One Best System: A History of American Urban Education (Cambridge, Massachusetts: Harvard
University Press, 1974), p. 66.

[17]Carl Rogers, Freedom to Learn (Columbus, Ohio: C.E. Merrill,
1969), p. vii.

[18]Paul Goodman, Compulsory Mis-Education (New York: Vintage
Books, 1965).

PART TWO -- RELIGION IN THE PUBLIC SCHOOLS

Is there a place for religion studies in our schools?

The century of secularization of American education has been succeeded by efforts since the early 1960s to put religion alongside the "three R's," science and social studies. The movement to include such study was in part spurred by Supreme Court rulings outlawing devotional exercises in public schools, and in part by reaction to an apparent decline in the influence of religion in society at large.

If teaching religion is now forbidden by law, is it nevertheless desirable to teach about religion? The first of these two articles contends that within guidelines which can be drawn from the rulings in the Engel and Schempp cases, teaching about religion is both possible and desirable. Several projects concerned with teaching the Bible as literature and with comparative study of the world's religions have resulted in the development of instructional materials and in programs in some schools. Although such programs are not widespread, the authors believe religion studies will continue to find their way into the curriculum, albeit slowly.

The second article takes the position that the complexities related to implementing studies about religion are likely to involve the schools in problems which may have an adverse impact on the total educational program. The sensitive nature of the subject of religion, problems in defining religion, constitutional restrictions, and practical instructional difficulties should be sufficient to deter a school system from undertaking such a program. The study of "religion" may actually prove dysfunctional as schools attempt to develop an objective understanding of the religious institution in a social environment where students, parents, and clergy regard religion as a matter of faith which is not in need of and should not be subject to any intellectual examination.

DAVID BARR is Professor of Religion, Religion Department Chairman, and Co-director of the Public Education Religion Studies Center at Wright State University in Dayton, Ohio. He is co-author of Religion Goes to School (Harper, 1968) and co-editor of The Bible in American Education (Scholars and Fortress, 1983). WILLIAM COLLIE is Professor of Education, Director of the University Division, and Co-director of the Public Education Religion Studies Center at Wright State. He is co-editor of Teaching About Religion in Public Schools (Argus, 1977). The article by Barr and Collie is an updated version of one appearing under the same title in the March, 1981 issue of Church and State. It is reprinted in revised form with the permission of Americans United for Separation of Church and State.

JAMES STULL is Professor of Education in the Department of Administration, Counseling and Educational Studies, College of Education, Eastern Kentucky University. His teaching and administrative experience have extended from Ohio to Florida to Guam. He holds the doctorate from the University of Toledo, and is editor of the journal Eastern Kentucky University Educational Review.

RELIGION IN THE SCHOOLS: THE CONTINUING CONTROVERSY

David Barr and William Collie

A vigorous campaign by the President of the United States to amend the Constitution and overturn a ruling of the Supreme Court in the winter of 1984 fell only eleven votes short of success. The strength of the campaign, the intensity of the rhetoric, and the degree of public support were surprising, for the ruling the President was trying to overturn was over twenty years old. But the issue was an emotional one, with a strong natural constitutency: prayer in public schools.

Most observers assumed that the death of Senator Everett Dirksen in 1969 marked the end of the so-called Prayer Amendment Movement. Dirksen had led the fight to overrule the 1962 and 1963 Supreme Court decisions which found it unconstitutional for the public schools to conduct religious exercises. There had been a great public outcry, but all of Senator Dirksen's eloquence could not move the proposed amendment out of committee. Senator Birch Bayh, chairman of the subcommittee on constitutional amendments, stood firmly opposed to the amendment. The case seemed closed.

But times change. Senator Bayh was not reelected to the 79th Congress. The Democrats lost their majority status, and Senator Strom Thurmond, a proponent of prayer in the schools, became chairman of the Senate Judiciary Committee. The 1980 Republican Platform supported the reestablishment of socalled "voluntary" prayer in the schools. Public support for an amendment has been continually stirred by the religious right. Today no one would predict that the Prayer Amendment is dead.

Yet much of the current rhetoric seems unaware of the real nature of the Court's decisions and of the significant developments that have taken place sine then. We cannot pretend that the last two decades have not happened; we must understand our past to gain any perspective on our future. This article summarizes these developments, surveys what is currently happening, and makes a few tentative predictions about the immediate future of religion in the schools.

Twenty-two years after the Supreme Court ruled that the religious freedoms guaranteed in the First Amendment applied equally to the states as to the federal government ((Cantwell v. Connecticut, 1940, 310 US 296), it drew the logical conclusion of that ruling: that the public schools as organs of the states could not sponsor religious practices without violating the proscription against establishing religion (Engel v. Vitale, 1962; 370 US 421). The public outcry that followed this decision caused the Court to consider the issue more broadly when it was confronted with two similar cases involving school sponsored prayer and Bible reading for opening exercises less than a year later. While the constitutional issue was clearcut in this 8-1 decision, the Court produced five separate opinions in the case (Abington v. Schempp, 1963, 374 US 203). In three of these opinions the justices tried to emphasis the legitimate, if limited, ways in which the public schools could deal with religion. Writing for the majority, Justice Clark asserted:

> It might well be said that one's education is not complete without a study of comparative religion or of the history of religion and its relation to the advancement of civilization. It certainly may be said that the Bible is worthy of study for its literary and historic qualities. Nothing we have said here indicates that such study of the Bible or of religion, when presented objectively as part of a secular program of education may not be effected consistently with the first amendment.

In a lengthy concurring opinion, Justice Brennan added: "The holding of the Court today plainly does not foreclose teaching about the Holy Scriptures or about the differences between religious sects in classes in literature or history."

Justice Goldberg added his own concurrence, joined by Justice Harlan, asserting:

> Government must inevitably take cognizance of the existence of religion and, indeed, under certain circumstances the First Amendment may require that it do so. And it seems clear to me from the opinions in the present and past cases that the court would recognize the propriety ... of the teaching about religion, as distinguished from the teaching of religion, in the public schools.

While these dicta did not assuage the public outcry, and in fact were ignored by the popular media, they did clarify the proper role of religion in public education and contributed to a series of diverse efforts aimed at implementing the suggestions of the Court.

It would be impossible to recount all the many local and regional projects and conferences that followed in the wake of the Court's decision. One can get a feel for the diversity of the developments up to 1967 from the fourth chapter of Religion Goes To School: A Practical Handbook for Teachers, by James V. Panoch and David L. Barr (Harper and Row, 1968). Four states initiated significant projects and one national interfaith publication was stimulated. Although initiated before the Court ruling, this interfaith project was redefined in the light of that ruling and subsequently published as The Bible Reader (Walter Abbot and others, eds., Bruce Publishing Co., 1969). Selections from the Bible that have been important in the development of Christianity and Judaism were chosen and commented on by Catholic, Protestant and Jewish scholars.

In Nebraska, the Curriculum Development Center at the University of Nebraska was encouraged to develop units on religious literature as part of the general English curriculum being created. These outstanding units were eventually published as The God-and-Man Narratives and Themes (University of Nebraska Press, 1968 and 1971).

In 1965 the legislature of Pennsylvania, where the Schempp case originated, enacted a law permitting "the literature of the Bible and other religious writings" to be taught "as regular courses in the literature branch of education." This mandate was taken up by the Department of Religious Studies at Pennsylvania State University and, after a great deal of controversy and revision, resulted in the publication of The Religious Literature of the West (by John Witney and Susan Howe, Augsburg Publishing House, 1968, 1971).

In Florida the State Board of Education established a committee on Religion in Public Education which eventually prepared a set of guidelines and fed into the work at Florida State University to produce social studies curriculum materials. An initial series on religious issues in American, Western, and World Cultures for use in secondary social studies classes was developed with the assistance of grants from the Danforth Foundation and published as the Issues in Religion series (Addison-Wesley, 1972, 1973). A subsequent series on religion in the elementary social studies was developed at the same institution under grants from the National Endowment for the Humanities and partially published by Argus Communications (Learning About Religions/Social Studies, Levels 1-3, 1976).

Indiana initially appointed a new state committee of English teachers to revise its 50 year old curriculum on the Bible as literature, but the curriculum was so dated and the revision so inadequate that the results were never published. However, the need in Indiana was soon filled by a longterm project at Indiana University. A series of summer workshops, funded largely by the Lilly Endowment, were conducted under the direction of James Ackerman, professor of Old Testament at Indiana, and Thayer Warshaw, an innovative English teacher from Newton, Massachusetts. The fruitful collaboration of these two men, Bible scholar and teacher, Christian and Jew, led to a most exciting teacher training project and the publication of a shelf of resource materials (a listing of which can be found in the Foreword to <u>Handbook for Teaching the Bible in Literature Classes</u>, by Thayer Warshaw, Abingdon, 1978).

What was still lacking was a curriculum on world religions. That need was met by a project that grew out of a controversy over school-sponsored religious practices in the St. Louis Park School District in suburban Minneapolis. In this instance, controversy led to constructive action and a curriculum project was initiated with a grant under Title III/ IV Part C of the Elementary-Secondary Education Act. This project eventually developed an extensive and exciting multi-media curriculum later published by Argus Communications (1978 and following). Units on Religious Expression, Hindu, Buddhist, Jewish, Christian, and Islamic Traditions are available; others are projected in the <u>Religions in Human Culture</u> series.

From one perspective, it is encouraging to note that in less than two decades since the Court decisions we have seen the development of responsible and objective curricula on each of the aspects of religion to which the Court called attention: the Bible as literature and as history, world religions, and the impact of religion on other aspects of culture. It must be noted, however, that no new projects are being undertaken, that these already published materials have been slow to be adopted, and that several of these projects are incompletely published and may never be finished. The reason for this delay in publication is the practical concern of sales. While the study of religion has found some acceptance in every area of the curriculum, it has not been widely implemented. While the attention it has received is promising, the degree of implementation has been too limited to sustain large-scale publishing ventures. The range of current practice is described in Nicholas Piediscalzi and William Collie, eds. <u>Teaching About Religion in Public Schools</u> (Argus, 1977).

In brief, a great deal of innovation in the study of religion has occurred in every area of the curriculum. A wide
range of study is currently going on, though the rapid growth
phase seems over. Implementation of study about religion has
occurred in school districts throughout the nation though the
pattern is spotty. The gains of these two decades of development, however, are clear, and we seem in no immediate danger
of slipping back into the neglect of religion that characterized public school curricula prior to 1963.

However, if we turn from a direct examination of the
curricula to a consideration of the organizational support
which has emerged for public education religion studies, we
have less reason for optimism. A large number of organizations have responded to the issue of religion in public
schools as one part of their concern, including notable contributions from the Education Division of the National Council
of Churches and from the Religious Education Association. REA
has devoted several issues of its journal to this concern over
the years. There also have been a large number of groups
formed in distress -- what we might call prayer amendment
movements. Only a few groups, however, have taken public education religious studies as their primary concern while attempting to work within the framework of the Court decisions.

All indications are that the era of rapid development and
expansion is over. Certainly the support organizations no
longer seem able to attract significant funding. We are in a
period when gains in one place are off-set by losses in
another. Religion studies are only managing to hold their own
in the curriculum. We must now consider why this is so and
what it portends for the future.

Why has study about religion faced such a slow acceptance
within public education at the elementary and secondary levels
in the years since the Schempp case? Certainly part of the
answer lies in the very complexity of American public schooling. Despite constant pressures to bring about educational
reform from myriad forces, the curriculum of American schools
has proven to be remarkably resistant to change. By and
large present-day public school curriculum at elementary and
secondary levels is disturbingly similar to that experienced
by this generation of schoolgoers' parents and grandparents.
With schools across the U.S. organized into thousands of independent school districts overlaid by state and national
agencies with varying degrees of control, curricular reform is
a difficult task. It certainly cannot be imposed from the top
down for there is no centralized control over the schooling
process.

Curricular rigidity, however, has prevented virtually every special interest group from attempting to see that the schooling process addresses its particular concerns. Hence public education religion studies find themselves seeking a share of the school day along with environmental education, career education, consumer education, global education, and sex education, at the very time when many citizens are responding to the call for a return to a basic education which would restrict curricular offerings. The competition for a portion of the curriculum is keen, however valid the rationale for the study being proposed. Despite the frequently heard despair with public schooling, it seems there is no lack of suitors waiting at the door, wooing the schools for their curricular attention. And the competitors have usually held the edge, because they have been able to pay their own way. Economic education has received ongoing financial support from the business community. Career education has had support from the business community and from other advocates of vocational education.

The objective study of religion has found few ardent supporters, however, and even fewer willing to provide financial support. Limited funding for a number of teacher education programs has come from the National Endowment for the Humanities and such private organizations as the Lilly Endowment. Large grants from either private or public sources have not been available to sustain long-term development of public education religion studies. Another disadvantage religion studies have in relation to competition for school time is the potential danger of controversy created when such studies are implemented in the curriculum. Since the public is not familiar with a "creature" called religion studies, it may be misunderstood as inappropriate religious instruction. With the schools already bombarded by myriad problems, public school administrators are often loathe to support any curricular innovation which might stir further public consternation.

Impact for any new curricular emphasis appears limited in the near future given the other pressing needs facing public schooling. Reeling from the financial blows of inflation, limited revenues due to a stagnant economy, and shrinking student population, the schools do not appear headed for a decade of curricular reforms in the 1980s. Faced with basic issues of institutional survival, public education's priorities in the near future are not likely to be focused on curricular expansion. Indeed, fiscal pressures plus public support for the "basics" will probably lead to a trimming of curricular experimentation such as mini-courses and elective areas of study, particularly at the secondary level. In addition, we surmise that the call for a "return to basics" often places its emphasis on return, a return to an idealized and secure past.

On the one hand this becomes a call to return to past religious practices. Since social conflict seemed to soar just at the time prayer and Bible reading were ruled inappropriate for public schooling, a restoration of such practices might once again return the nation to some sense of cultural unity and direction. From this wishful desire for a condition which in fact never existed, stems some of the impetus for the movement to amend the Constitution, if necessary, to reinstate prayer in public schools. For such persons, academic study about religion, however valuable, is an insufficient corrective for the lack of Godly direction now pervading public schooling. No amount of study about religion can replace the direct reliance on God as an integral part of the educational process.

On the other hand, a return to basics may also be a longing for a more simple past. Religion studies open us up to our differences, a feature shared with other forms of multicultural education. The rationale for such multicultural education is that mutual respect and tolerance depend on mutual understanding. Only by examining our differences, including our religious differences, can we find ways to work together as a society.

This approach argues that cultural uniformity is not a prerequisite to societal stability, but rather acceptance of, support for, and celebration of the freedom to be different can itself be the common bond which holds our nation, and indeed our world, together. From this viewpoint cutural diversity is not only an accurate interpretation of present reality, but it is also a true strength of it. What is needed then is education to learn how to live together in reasonable public harmony rather than attempts to deny or to eliminate our cultural differences. Opponents of this approach argue that such objective study about religion, examining religion from the viewpoint of "what is" rather than asking "what ought to be," fails to provide adequate guidance for students. They see such objective study as one further example of the shift by the public schools from their traditional role as purveyor of the cultural heritage and tutor of the basic skills of reading, writing, and computation to the role of promoter of social change.

Advocates of multicultural education argue that it is not a reform movement aimed at reshaping society but an attempt to more adequately prepare students to deal with the world in which they already live. For example, an objective study of Islam is not aimed at spreading the Muslim revolution but it may help us live more safely in a world in which that revolution is a reality.

Whenever the call for a "return to basics" includes a plea to return to a more unified and religious past, it must be unmasked for the fraud it is. For if the schools' past religious practices provided only a patina of national cultural oneness and unity which in reality did not exist, then the critics' own position is not conservative; it is reactionary. It calls for a return to an idealized past. It forces an impossible role on the public schools, asking them to portray a cultural and social oneness which did not exist in the past and is most certainly not existent today.

We see, then, that several factors within public education itself have contributed to the slow acceptance of study about religion: the enormity of the public educational enterprise without any central policy body, competition from a variety of special interest groups -- some of them with much more tangible support, controversy over religion, a concern for "basic" education with less curricular diversity, and a certain sort of cultural nostalgia which would minimize rather than highlight our differences. This leads us to a final consideration of the broader social context and its impact on public education religion studies.

Nicholas Piediscalzi has argued that the common conception of religion held by many Americans likewise limits their understanding of what study abour religion can contribute to a person's general education. For many, religion is equated with adherence to the beliefs of a given religious community. In the popular conception some people are religious, namely those who belong to a certain community of faith, while others are non-religious or even irreligious. From this perspective there does not seem to be much value in studying the religion of those others. In addition, religion is generally viewed as a set of beliefs, so that religion study appears to be an exercise in theology. Most people have had little exposure to religion studies as an endeavor to interpret human action, and to explore the role of myths, rituals, symbols and communal life as expressions of the meaning of being human even as others study literature or history.

Paradoxically, even though many equate being religious with holding the beliefs of a given tradition, they also view religion as a private matter -- something that is experiential and personal and hence not open to study. But such a focus ignores the cultural and historical dimensions of religious experience and religious communities. Construing religion narrowly as belief may blind people to the fact that they simultaneously may hold two commitments not entirely in harmony with each other. For example, a personal commitment to a religious community's faith in nonviolence and self-sacrifice may conflict with the person's public commitment as a citizen to a general civil religion which identifies God with country in a way that readily justifies military action. Such overlooking of the complexity, centrality, and cultural relevance of religion has hampered the push to make religion studies an integral aspect of public schooling.

This endeavor has been further complicated by past public school involvement with religious practice. For a long period in our nation's history, the public schools served as the de facto organs of the Protestant establishment. They served to nurture students in Protestant doctrine and ethics. Bible reading (usually the King James Version), recitation of the Lord's Prayer in opening exercises, and focus on the Ten Commandments as the model for social stability were the keystones of these efforts. Much of the present controversy over public education religion studies is due to the residue of fears and anguish engendered particularly among Jews, Catholics, Christian sectarians and non-Christians by this (often unwitting) attempt to shape their children in the white, Anglo-Saxon Protestant mold. While Court rulings have made it clear that any academic study of religion must be objective and pluralistic in its approach, for these persons the educational benefits promised by religion studies advocates is not worth the risk of opening the schools once again to the potential of abuse of children's civil and religious rights.

Another factor on the current social scene that affects public education religion studies is the resurgence of Evangelical Christianity. One might expect such a resurgence to support religion study, but only rarely has this been the case. Although many Evangelicals endorse the objective teaching about religion in public education, it has never become a central part of the Evangelical agenda. In some ways it goes against that agenda, since the goals of the two movements differ widely. Groups like Moral Majority or Christian Voice are endeavoring to make a "Christian America"; that is, they wish the organs of our common life -- government, business, education -- to adopt and reflect the values of conservative Christianity. Thus they are more likely to support the call for a prayer amendment and to try to preserve Christmas celebrations than they are to call for a serious and objective study of religions. They simply do not accept the pluralism inherent in such a study.

If you add to this the pervasive suspicion and even rejection of public education often found in the Evangelical Movement (most obvious in its endeavor to build an alternative system of Christian schools), it becomes clear why the current revival of Evangelicalism has not produced a boon for public education religion studies. While many, perhaps most, Evangelicals continue to be involved with the public schools, the impetus of the movement has been to withdraw and build a better, more godly system. Whether the issues have been evolution, the inquiry-method, or sex education, Evangelicals have felt threatened by the major movements of public education. Add to that the serious problems many schools face with discipline and resources combined with the seduction of the idea of providing a wholesome, Christian environment for their children and there is little wonder that the thrust of Evangelicalism has turned toward private education. This too seems to be a long-term trend.

There is thus a real paradox in the contrast between the present resurgence of interest in religion, when religious paperbacks are marketed in the millions in our supermarkets, and the current low level of support for teaching about religion in public schools. The increase in evangelical religious activity contributes to the decline in public education religion studies both because its own goals have more in common with the proscribed religious practices and because such goals increase the anxiety of those who have suffered under earlier attempts to enforce religious conformity within the schools. In addition, "religion studies" as a discipline is so poorly understood among the general populace that it can be considered an unnecesary frill to basic education. Two decades of development have done much to allay the fears of minorities and to demonstrate the viability of such study, but the excitement of that development has not been communicated to the average citizen and does not coincide with the agenda of a resurgent evangelicalism. We do not expect any of these factors to change significantly in the near future.

The ironies of our present situation should not be lost. The most significant advances in public education religion studies over two decades spring from a court decision many conservatives would like to overturn. Excellent curricular materials are available, but not widely used. The only on-

42

going national organization concerned exclusively with support of public education religion studies has to date been largely ineffective. Public schools are so concerned with a basic education that they are losing their flexibility to deal with the most basic of all human actions. While the primary stimulus for the growth of public education religion studies was a decision of a federal court, almost no federal money has supported such study. The more seriously people take religion personally, the less inclined they seem to be to support public study of it.

Given such ironies, forecasting the future of public education religion studies seems perilous. Nevertheless, certain trends seem established. Lacking legislative mandate, judicial order, outspoken public demand, or governmental or private funding to foster its growth, public education's response to the opportunity to help students examine religion in an academic setting has been, and probably will continue to be, lukewarm at best. The development of public education religion studies will continue to take place slowly, largely in piecemeal efforts as individual classroom teachers recognize the need to deal with the religious dimension in their teaching as they attempt to help their students understand the complexities of our social world.

Taken together, the factors on the present scene suggest that most of the pressures in the immediate future will be toward reinstituting religious practices in the schools. With the significant conservative shift in leadership in the Senate, it would not be surprising to see a continued push for a prayer amendment or some other legislative tactic designed to allow school-sponsored prayer. An alternative scenario could be developed if we recall that the next President will probably replace several of the current justices of the Supreme Court with judges of his own choosing. A conservative domination of the court could result in new rulings in this area. The current low level of responsible and objective study of religion in public schools will contribute to this pressure, since it is obvious that the school should do something with religion.

Of course, not all the gains of the past two decades have been lost; many excellent programs exist and will continue. Emphasizing these proper responses to religion will be one way to redirect some of the pressures toward illegal and ill-advised religious practices. However, as we survey the developments of the past two decades and examine the pressures of the contemporary social scene, we are not optimistic that the immediate future will see any significant upsurge of support for religion studies in public education.

RELIGION IN THE PUBLIC SCHOOLS? NO!

James Stull

Religion's place in the public schools is one of the continuing issues in American education. It is highly controversial because of the range of religious pluralism in the United States and the widely differing views of the numerous religious groups. It is probable that arriving at a universally accepted, hence enforceable, solution may prove more difficult than resolving the problems of racial segregation. There has been for many years a consensus that racial segregation violates the rights of citizens in a democratic society. On the other hand, there is noticeably less consensus concerning the many issues involving religious freedom and the separation of church and state. This absence of agreement is prominently reflected in decisions of the United States Supreme Court, which on several occasions in church-state related cases has split five to four and at least once (the famous flag salute dispute) reversed itself.

The issue of whether religion should be taught in the schools is not peculiar to the United States. An examination of school systems in various parts of the world reveals a wide variety of solutions to the problem. For example, in some countries it is compulsory to teach the faith of the majority: Roman Catholicism in Spain, Protestantism in Norway, Islam in Pakistan. In others the teaching of religion is prohibited. This policy prevails in the Soviet Union where religious education is forbidden on ideological grounds. In other countries which are characterized by religious pluralism, established policy permits released time for instruction by visiting clergy, as in Australia and New Zealand, while the British and Canadians permit comparative study of traditional religions.

Advocacy of a more religious orientation to education has had its spokesmen throughout American history. Recent increases in crime and violence, a relaxation in the traditional attitudes regarding sex and marriage, the growth of materialistic concepts encouraged by technological developments, the seeming absence of civic and social responsibility, and the high incidence of drug usage have stimulated a renewed interest in religion. The view held by some is that these conditions have come about as a result of a decline or disintegration of values, which in turn has been encouraged by the secular nature of American education. Naturally, one of the "solutions" to these social problems lies in a more religious approach to education in the public schools.

The argument for placing a stronger emphasis on religiously oriented courses, i.e. religion, in the public schools appears at first glance to be plausible. Many of the assumptions supporting such a move seem simple, reasonable and logical. However, when these presumptions are examined more thoroughly, many prove to lack substance. Secondly, many individuals are unaware of the vast array of complex questions which arise when consideration is given to the teaching of religious related courses. The purpose of this essay is to examine some of the major assumptions supporting a more religious orientation in American education and to point out several of the concerns which would emanate from policies based on such assumptions.

The Law and Religious Instruction

Many advocates of religious instruction in the public schools speak from a very limited legal knowledge of the situation. Comprehending the issue of religious instruction in American education is not possible without an understanding of what is and is not currently permissible under the laws as they are presently interpreted. The legal history of the church-state issue and its related educational implications is both long and controversial.

The first significant step in this legal history of church-state relations occurred in 1789 with the adoption of the First Amendment to the Constitution, which reads in part: "Congress shall make no law respecting an establishment of religion or prohibiting the free exercise thereof." On the surface this statement appears clear and uncontroversial, but in actual practice it has stimulated much debate. Most agree that it prohibits the establishment of a national or state church; the debate focuses on the issue of whether the amendment does or does not prohibit equal government assistance to all religions.

A second major advance in providing for the separation of church and state took place when the Fourteenth Amendment was adopted in 1868. This is a long amendment and will not be quoted in totality. However, the key part which impinges on the discussion here says that "no state shall make or enforce any law which shall abridge the privileges or immunities of the citizens of the United States." While the First Amendment dealt with the federal government and established, in the view

46

of many, a "wall" between church and state, the Fourteenth Amendment concerned the individual states and in essence placed the same limitations on them as the First Amendment did on the federal government. Although the meaning of statements included in the First and Fourteenth Amendments may appear clear, practical implementation has proven controversial. Schools in many communities continued with religious practices until, and even after, objections resulted in a number of court cases.

In one of the more celebrated cases (McCollum v. Board of Education, 1948), the United States Supreme Court declared religious instruction on public school property to be in violation of the First Amendment. Students in Champaign, Illinois were released from regular classes for one hour per week to attend religion classes in their school. The Court found this practice unconstitutional. Just four years later in a very similar case (Zorach v. Clauson, 1952) the Court upheld a released time program in New York. The significant difference, the majority of justices claimed, was that in the New York situation the students were receiving the religious instructions in churches or other sites away from the public schools.

Although the first of these released time decisions generated protests from some church people, this was nothing compared to the outrage which followed later rulings banning organized prayer and devotional Bible reading from the public schools. The first case in point involved the one-sentence prayer "Almighty God, we acknowledge our dependence upon thee and we beg they blessings upon us, our parents, our teachers and our country," adopted for school use by the Board of Regents of New York state. Unimpressed by the state's claim of nonsectarianism, the Court found the prayer to be in violation of the principle that the state should be neutral in religious matters (Engel v. Vitale, 1962). The very next year, ruling on cases brought to it from Pennsylvania and Maryland, the Court found statutes requiring the reading of a chapter from the Bible and the recitation of the Lord's Prayer to constitute an establishment of religion. Bible reading and prayer were religious exercises, and the fact they were required by state law acted as an advancement of religion. They were, therefore, in violation of the neutrality concept, hence unconstitutional.

In summary, the opportunities for religious-oriented instruction in the public schools are limited by law. Any experience which would tend to encourage or discourage a student's faith in religion are currently illegal. Any type of religious instruction per se must be provided off school property. The courts have ruled such activities as Bible reading and class prayer as unconstitutional because they promote religion. Courses which teach about religions are examples of experiences that fall within what the courts consider acceptable.

The question then is: Should the public schools become involved with teaching courses that include religious concepts? The position of this author is "No." The complexities related to the practical implementation of such a policy are enormous. Religion is a very sensitive subject; teaching it in the public schools could raise a storm of protests related to content and methodology, thereby rendering attempts counter-productive. The possibilities of emotionalism prevailing, politicians being swayed, and laws altered could be enhanced, all of which might lead to proselytism on the part of aggressive or dominant religious sects.

The Problem of Defining Religion

A very real problem in trying to implement a policy which encourages teaching about religion is that of defining terms. Agreement on the meanings of church, denomination, sect, and cult is far more likely than agreement on a definition of religion. Not only is the latter term a far more value-laden concept, but because the working definition sets the parameters for study, agreement such as between theologians and sociologists, or between anthropologists and psychologists may be exceedingly difficult. Even further apart may be representatives of different lay groups trying to establish a school board policy on teaching about religion.

Anthropologists and philosophers might define religion in comparatively broad terms. The definitions could include statements such as one's comprehension of the cosmos, an individual's view regarding the totality of existence, or a person's view of life. If this type of definition is accepted, teaching about religion could become almost philosophical in nature. How many advocates of a more religious approach to American education would be satisfied with having doctrines and rituals of their church organized and taught as a specific cultural phenomenon rather than as something divinely inspired?

Religious history in the Western world reveals a tendency to view religion in a very ethnocentric fashion which when defined tends to exclude all other forms. The traditional Western view of religion is that of a system of concepts and

48

beliefs about the one God and the universe. Such a definition excludes the various forms of polytheism which abound in other areas of the world. Most Western religions are not only monotheistic, but require that adherents accept on the basis of faith a large body of sacred literature which provides a complex system of behavior patterns designed to serve God. Even if this more traditional view of religion is accepted, there are approximately 250 different religious groups existing in the United States today. Given the religiously pluralistic nature of American society, the inflexibility of religious beliefs, and the legal guarantee of religious freedom, how does one decide which religions and definitions of religion will be dealt with in courses that teach about religions, but cannot possibly teach about all of them?

When the typical American thinks about religion, the Jewish faith, Roman Catholicism and Protestantism immediately come to mind. Are these more prominent religions the only ones which should be treated in courses that teach about religion? Why not teach about the faiths of the Mormons, the Christian Scientists and Jehovah's Witnesses, for example? Should we let American students learn to appreciate only those religions indigenous to this country? What about the great Oriental religions such as Buddhism, Islam, and Hinduism, which include more adherents than most American groups? Should schools deal with viewpoints based on ethical principles, such as those espoused by the American Humanist Association and the Ethical Culture Society? How are the beliefs of the followers of Reverend Moon and eastern gurus to be treated? Will the schools discuss agnostic and atheistic viewpoints, and are these religious?

If agreement could be reached on a functional definition of religion and if criteria could be established for deciding which religions should be included in courses about religion, how does a teacher prevent Christianity, which in one form or another is the belief of most American students, from being used as the standard against which other religions will be judged? If a teacher does permit Christianity to become the basis for judging other religions, does this not become the promotion of a religion and thus violate at least the spirit of the religion clauses of the First Amendment?

The educational problems related to teaching about religion would still not be solved even if agreement could be reached on a functional definition and even if decisions were made on which religious systems were to be included in these types of courses. The question must then be asked: Should the school take on this added responsibility? Many people believe that educational experiences related to religion should be the responsibility of the home and church. In addition, the school is already being heavily criticized for not adequately performing currently assigned duties. Adding more courses to an already crowded curriculum would only compound existing problems. The introduction of new courses related to religion would require school systems to increase faculty. The current financial condition of many school districts makes this an impossibility.

Difficulties in Teaching about Religion

Teaching courses dealing with religious concepts raises a multitude of vexing questions. Historically such teaching has been mere indoctrination. Criticisms of this approach generate emotional responses which make rational approaches to answers exceedingly difficult. Knowledge based on experience is deficient, and many of the suggested techniques have not been sufficiently examined or tested.

One of the first questions which must be asked after one assumes religious courses should be offered in the schools is: At what level should these experiences begin? Would it be wise to initiate these activities in the early elementary grades and follow each year with more complex concepts much as mathematics and language arts are currently taught? Many educators question the practice of exposing young children to the pluralistic views of the various religions. Exposure to many conflicting beliefs, especially if they are superficially or inappropriately presented, can be confusing or miseducative to the immature mind. If religious-related information is presented at the elementary level, shall it be mandatory or optional? Assuming parents could elect not to let their children participate, how should these children be protected from the usual treatment unfortunately accorded those who are considered different?

The number of questions is not significantly reduced nor the answers made any clearer by delaying religious-related instruction until secondary school. Again, many educators question whether the typical high school student is sufficiently mature for a serious study of various religious veiws; therefore, some recommend that course enrollments be restricted. The most frequently suggested standard for admission is the student's grade point average. Should this be the only or even major criterion for restricting enrollment in classes related to religion? Is a student's grade point average indicative of the openness and mental maturity re-

quired to function effectively in studying a sensitive subject
like religion?

Finding qualified teachers to staff religion courses
would be a very difficult problem, and to begin a program of
this type without properly prepared teachers could be disas-
trous. Teacher education institutions are not currently offering preparation in this field, and the use of clergy could
open the schools to overt religious proselytizing. The use
of current teachers prepared in related fields such as the
social sciences is not recommended because of the sensitive
nature of religious topics.

Assuming teachers were to be prepared, what consideration, if any, needs to be made of the teacher's religious
background? Can a religiously faithful person be open and
objective in teaching about other religions? How would parents react to a Jew, agnostic, Muslim, Christian Scientist or
Jehovah's Witness teaching about religion in the typical
heterogeneously populated school? The writer finds it difficult to believe these people would be employed no matter how
well they were qualified.

Another serious problem related to teaching courses in
religion is the lack of teaching materials. Currently the
amount and quality of prepared textbooks and teacher materials
is very limited, and those which exist are Western oriented.
In addition, what types of teacher materials will be admis-
sible? Will teachers be allowed to use the actual printed
doctrines of specific religions, for example, the Koran, Bible
and Ten Commandments? If so, how does a teacher utilize such
information without appearing to be promoting a particular
viewpoint? Can a teacher be expected to conduct a critical
examination of what some youngsters will be taught is a divinely inspired document?

No course in comparative religion can treat all the
world's major religions except superficially. If, in an
effort to avoid being superficial, the course involved selected religions, can we expect agreement on the criteria to
be used in deciding which shall be included and which excluded? Should the concept of "equal time" apply? Can practical policies regarding visiting ministers, priests, and
rabbis be formulated? With regard to this latter point, for
example, would Reform Jews consider an orthodox rabbi an
acceptable spokesman for the Jewish faith before a class of
sixth graders?

Invariably those who favor including comparative religion and related courses in the public school curriculum stress the necessity of objective teaching. It should be pointed out that in many cases the concept of objectivity is neither wanted nor understood. What is essentially desired by many is an induction into the tenets of their own particular belief system.

Objectivity is a much used word with dual meaning. Does objectivity involve putting aside one's values and being non-partisan in dealing with the issues involved? If so, is it possible to teach religiously related courses in any type of rigorous manner? On the other hand, does objectivity mean openness in revealing one's views combined with fairness and adequacy in explaining the sides and views of all others? If this be the accepted meaning, how much of the American public is mentally prepared for this type of approach to teaching about religions, and how many teachers could ever be qualified to present all sides adequately?

The author contends that objectivity is a practical impossibility when teaching about religious views. If religion is to be learned, it must be experienced; if it is to be experienced in the classroom to the degree that learning will effectively take place, it must be taught rigorously. American students, parents, and religious leaders are not prepared for a rigorous and objective approach to teaching this sensitive subject. To attempt an objective approach to teaching about religion in the public schools could create a clamor and arouse interests which would distract from the subjects which form the basis of the American public school curriculum.

Good teaching will cause changes in behavior. These alterations may be viewed as losses or gains of faith, depending upon the nature of the change and the perspective of the observer. The Supreme Court has established a policy of religious neutrality in the public schools. The schools may not legally act in ways that will either advance or inhibit religion. This means that the school should not seek to cause students to lose or alter their faiths. How then does a teacher design and teach a course about religion in which students effectively learn, and not at the same time run counter to the intent of the laws?

Proponents of teaching about religion in the schools minimize the possible conflict that open debate of religious matters in the classroom situation may generate between students, parents and their religious leaders. Such conflicts may have positive effects on a few students, but certainly not in the case of all who may enroll in such classes. The presentation of differing views on religious beliefs may well lead to the development of biases and prejudices and thereby exacerbate rather than alleviate the problems related to a religiously pluralistic society.

Any serious academic study of religion is bound to reveal a number of beliefs that cannot be well grounded in any academic sense. Students typically are not tolerant of ideas they view as strange or absurd. Students in class who hold such beliefs are going to be embarrassed unless extreme care is exercised by the teacher. Some people argue that these students should be embarrassed and disillusioned if their beliefs cannot stand honest scrutiny. What these individuals really desire is that those who are embarrassed be led to accept their own beliefs. At this point, the author would like to interject the comment: After all, who can tell, maybe these students would be better off holding their strange and absurd beliefs.

Character and Religious Values

One of the arguments frequently projected to justify more religious experiences in public education evolves from the assumption that moral consciousness and character can only be formed in a religious context. Others, however, will point out that morality derives from the experience of social living, and needs no theological base. Morality, furthermore, is superordinate to religion, and evidence to this effect shows up whenever a court gives primacy to one person's welfare rather than another's beliefs. Blood transfusions and regulation of cultic practices are cases in point.

There is evidence that a religious faith, taught as a way of life, accepted and believed in by the student, can influence human behavior. However, the evidence does not support the position that instruction in religion or participation in religious-type exercises is a necessary ingredient for the development of a conscience and morality. The fields of anthropology, sociology and psychology have produced a plethora of facts which indicate that character evolves from experience in the cultural system, religious or otherwise. Observant individuals can recall having known people of outstanding character who did not consider themselves religious. On the other hand, most people have known individuals who were religious and yet demonstrated poor moral concepts and continuously behaved counter to laws.

A prominent current myth is the belief that high moral standards can arise only from a religious faith. A cursory reading of the daily newspaper will reveal that many of the crimes are committed by individuals who attend church and consider themselves religious. Criminologists and penologists know that many inmates of our country's institutions consider themselves religious individuals. Sociologists have provided evidence which indicates there is no positive relationship between church membership and crime rates in the nation's cities.

Given the point that a religious commitment can help in the development of personal qualities which produce healthy character in some students does not prove the generalization holds in all cases. It would be a serious error to assume that a few hours a week of exposure to a course in Comparative Religion or The Bible as Literature will significantly influence character development.

If personalities are to be influenced in ways that will stimulate the development of approved character traits, proper child rearing practices must begin early in life with the family and be consistent throughout the child's environment. Experiences which illustrate and stimulate socially approved character traits must be provided by all the socializing agents which influence the child. The school through courses which teach about religion cannot expect to develop what the family, the church, the peer group and the mass media have failed to develop.

Are Christian Tenets Essential to the Democratic Ethic?

Another frequent argument used to justify and promote religious-associated activities in the schools stems from the assumed relationship between Christian and democratic principles. This position asserts that the roots of the democratic ethic emanate from the basic tenets of Christianity. It is assumed that democracy can be nurtured only among those who subscribe to Christian principles. In other words, the fundamental principles necessary to democracy can only be derived from Christian doctrine.

On the surface this thesis may appear reasonable to some, but a closer examination indicates this is not the case. The Christian belief in the supreme value of the human soul is closely related to the democratic view emphasizing the worth and dignity of the human being. However, one should be very careful about making a causal relationship and concluding that democracy has evolved from Judeo-Christian principles and can only be developed among those who embrace such a system of beliefs. Believing in Christianity does not guarantee democratic forms of behavior. The Christian beliefs in the dignity of the soul and the concepts of brotherhood and equality have frequently been used to rationalize very undemocratic forms of behavior. There are many examples in history where the prevailing social philosophy, based on Christianity, has been used to justify a hierarchical society composed of rigidly stratified social classes, all ordained by God. The author has been intrigued for a long time by the inner workings of a human mind which believed deeply in the Christian faith, while at the same time operating a plantation system based on slavery and participating in an organization advocating the principles held by the Ku Klux Klan.

It is true that Christianity has made many vital contributions to the development of democratic traditions in the Western view of the term. On the other hand, it is not correct to believe Christianity is a precondition for democracy. The first organized and widely practiced democracy existed in Athenian society and appeared long before the development of Christianity. Democracy is indebted to many sources both secular and religious for its rich traditions and views on freedom and dignity.

Is Religion the Answer to Conflict in International Relations?

Many advocates of a more religious orientation to public education do so on the basis that religion includes principles of behavior which will lead to peace and goodness in the world if adopted by all people. Unquestionably, all religions embrace tenets which could assist in bringing about peace and kindness if practiced on an individual and intergroup basis. Immediately one must pose the question: Which religion should be utilized for such purposes?

The world has never enjoyed a common religious faith. For example, Western civilization, and more specifically the United States, contains hundreds of theological groups. Unfortunately, the fact that a religion provides the tenets for proper behavior does not guarantee the followers will behave according to religious principles. The present situation between the two Irelands is a case in point. In addition, the history of Europe is especially illustrative in regard to this case. The story of this part of the world is awash with bloody wars, many of which were fought in the name of religion. These conflicts usually continued until all but one of the rivals were destroyed or capitulated, only to have the victor's religious beliefs imposed upon them by very ruthless means. Consequently, a very cursory review of history indicates that few religious groups have displayed any degree of flexibility or tolerance on religious issues. The writer has serious difficulty believing that the current cleavages which exist among religious groups will vanish in the foreseeable future.

Assuming that a system of standards for directing international relations could be developed from one or more religious orientations would not necessarily solve the problem of establishing guidelines for international relations. It would be quite naive to believe the Communists could be dealt with through policies established on religious principles. It might be more accurate to assume that the Marxists would exploit this type of situation to their own advantage by becoming much bolder and more expansionistic in their international behavior.

There is no question that the contemporary world is in desperate need of higher standards with which to guide international behavior. Also, there is no question that the Judeo-Christian orientation, in addition to many others, has much to offer for the improvement of this beleaguered situation. Nevertheless, it seems unlikely that any compromise will develop among the various religions of the world that could provide a set of criteria for governing international relations. In fact, the opposite could prove to be true. Using the current Middle Eastern dilemma as an example, it seems reasonable to assume that any attempts at religious compromise between Muslim and Jew would be apt to inflame tempers and further compound the problems of the area. The evidence of history and the current world situation does not indicate that any specific religion or combination thereof offers the type of flexibility necessary to provide a basis for governing human behavior throughout the world.

Conclusion

The teaching about religion in American public schools is a very complex and delicate issue which has persisted throughout our nation's history. Religion tends to be an emotional, inflexible and socially explosive subject which creates a great amount of concern for student welfare and restricts the potential good that could accrue from a more religious orientation to educational practices in American society. Efforts to encourage more religious-related experiences in the public

56

schools provoke many complex and unanswered questions. In addition, many of the assumptions held by advocates of such a move will not stand up under scrutiny.

The Constitution and subsequent Supreme Court decisions severely restrict the type and nature of religious-related experiences schools may offer students. Religion is a concept difficult to define, thereby making it difficult to formulate criteria for decisions necessary to establish content of religious-related courses. The problems related to the teaching of religiously oriented courses are astronomical. The assumption that religious experiences are necessary for development of individual character and political democracy are invalid, and the generalization that religion can provide the answer to problems in international relations is not borne out by history.

It is by no means certain that if the American public schools were opened up to a more religious approach to instruction organized religion would regain any of its former influence in American life. It would be very tenuous to assume that traditional religious beliefs would be strengthened and encouraged through the limited amount of religious instruction which could legally be afforded in the schools. The contention that the diminishing influence of the church, mosque and synagogue is attributable to the secularization of life is a very simplistic answer to a complex problem. Social forces, such as the scientific revolution, which originated centuries ago, have gradually eroded religious influences. These forces are still present and rapidly gaining in strength. The notion that the introduction of religious studies into the curriculum will cause them to disintegrate through better character development and improvement of international relations is very debatable. Consequently, opening up the public school curriculum to more religious-oriented courses is not recommended at this time.

PART THREE -- TUITION TAX CREDITS

Should tax credits be granted in response to the payment of tuition to a non-public school?

The question of tax credits is but one of several church-state issues in the area of education. Heated disputation takes place on constitutional, economic, educational, and even moral grounds. Support for this form of tax relief by the Reagan administration encouraged proponents to continue the legislative efforts begun in the 1970s. A Supreme Court ruling in 1983 on Minnesota's tax credit law opened the door for more activity on the state level. That decision, however, being inconsistent with one exactly ten years earlier, left still uncertain the status of tax breaks for those using tuition-charging schools.

The first article examines five charges levied against tuition tax credits: cost, federal control, state control, constitutionality, and elitism. The authors conclude that none of these has sufficient merit to justify denying financial relief to those who, for a variety of reasons, have opted for private education. Tax credits, furthermore, are consistent with existing educational tax allowances and with judicial precedent going back over half a century.

The second article views tax credits as in reality aid to private schools, many of which are church-related. Thus credits are of questionable constitutionality. While non-public schools may exemplify a form of educational freedom of choice, from the financial perspective they make little economic sense. Increased public expenditure, such as through tax credits, would only exacerbate the financial problem. Furthermore, mild as an initial credit might be, passage of any aid bill would in time lead to even greater public funding.

REV. JOHN A. THOMAS is Superintendent of Schools for the Roman Catholic Diocese of Toledo, Ohio, a position he has held for eight years. He received his doctorate in education from the University of Michigan. EDWARD J. NUSSEL is an Associate Dean and Professor in the College of Education and Allied professions at the University of Toledo. He taught nine years in the Detroit Public Schools. His doctorate is from Wayne State University, and his specialization is sociology of education.

AMERICANS UNITED FOR SEPARATION OF CHURCH AND STATE is an educational organization dedicated to preserving the constitutional principle of church-state separation. National offices

59

are located at 8120 Fenton Street, Silver Spring, Maryland, 20910.

THE CASE FOR TUITION TAX CREDIT

Rev. John A. Thomas and Edward J. Nussel

In their quest for financial relief, supporters of private schools continue their efforts at promoting legislative action for tax reform. A number of proposals for tuition tax credits have been attempted. Tuition tax credit legislation would amend the Internal Revenue Code to permit a taxpayer to claim a credit for educational tuition payments made for himself, his spouse, or his dependents. This would add to the number of educational tax allowances which already are available under the law. One such proposal was the Tuition Tax Credit Act of 1977 and was promoted in the Ninty-fifth Congress by Senators Packwood and Moynihan. The proposal, if passed would have provided a credit of 50 percent of tuition up to $500 per child. However, even though compromise measures were discussed in both houses, House-Senate conferees dropped tuition credits from their tax bill. Since that time the debate has persisted. Why has there been such pressure by private school interests to achieve a tuition tax credit law?

Clinchy and Cody cited a number of factors including the prestige of private education, religious values, a desegregation escape, avoidance of problem children, and the obvious financial benefit. But the authors insisted that the most persuasive reason for the willingness to defect from the public school is that "far too many parents ... feel themselves to be at the mercy of a remote and unresponsive bureaucracy. They feel -- and too often quite rightly -- that the decisions about what the school system will be like, how it will be run ... are made at levels far removed from the individual parent, child, and school."[1]

A major legal basis for an escape from this public school control was established by the landmark Supreme Court decision in Pierce vs. Society of Sisters. In this decision the Oregon Act of 1922 requiring public school attendance was struck down because it "unreasonably interferes with the liberty of parents and guardians to direct the upbringing and education of children under their control."[2] Paying twice for this right for those who can afford it is a continual annoyance. Then there are those who can't afford to exercise the right and at the same time feel the powerlessness mentioned by Clinchy and Cody. The seeds of discord are thereby sown.

The critic of such movements is quick to point out that separate schools promote divisiveness and selectivity and that supporters of such a cause ought to be willing to pay for their self-styled exclusion. On the other hand, Coons argues that families of means are able to select particular public schools based on their ability to choose.

> Those who lack the means (or the church
> subsidy) must go to the government schools
> where they can afford to live.... This system
> of tax supported schools is "public" only in
> the vapid sense that it is a creature of the law.
> Viewed in terms of its structure and functions,
> it is simply a monopoly reigning over the
> education of the non-rich; and it is a unique
> monopoly making an offer an ordinary family
> can't refuse.[3]

Most big cities have their exclusive, stereotypic, surburban communities with one high school. These "public-private" high schools are college preparatory, academic institutions and are more alike than different when compared to their private counterparts. So when the controversy surrounds control and exclusiveness, the arguments quickly heat up.

Five Issues

Let us turn now to five major issues surrounding the implementation of tuition tax credits as proponents strive to find a legal means of exercising parental rights without violation of the law.

1. The first issue is based on the notion that tuition tax credits are too costly.

In examining the cost of tuition tax credits a careful analysis of a particular piece of legislation is necessary. For example, the Senate Finance Committee's Subcommittee on Taxation and Debt Management held public hearings on June 3 and 4, 1981 regarding S. 550, the Tuition Tax Relief Act of 1981 (Packwood-Moynihan). In connection with those hearings, the staff of the Joint Committee on Taxation prepared an analysis of the legislation. The concluding section of that analysis, setting fourth the "revenue effects" of Packwood-Moynihan (S. 550), is reproduced here.

VII. REVENUE EFFECT [4]

The provisions of S. 550 are estimated to reduce budget receipts by $99 million in fiscal year
1982, $2,691 million in 1983, $5,160 million in
1984, $6,308 million in 1985, and $6,857 million in
1986.

The following table gives a breakdown (for
fiscal years 1982-86) of the estimated revenue cost
of the credit attributable to elementary and secondary education and the cost attributable to college
and other post-secondary education.

ESTIMATED REVENUE EFFECT OF S. 550, FISCAL YEARS 1982-86
(Millions of Dollars)

Item	1982	1983	1984	1985	1986
Elementary and Secondary Education	−40	−1,082	−2,030	−2,198	−2,276
College and other post-secondary ed.	−59	−1,609	−3,130	−4,110	−4,581
Total revenue effect of the bill	−99	−2,691	−5,160	−6,308	−6,857

The $7 billion figure used by some opponents of tuition
tax credits is apparently based on the $6.857 billion figure
projected by the Joint Committee on Taxation. However, several important distinctions need to be made. Most of the opposition to tuition tax credits centers on providing benefits
to parents of students in elementary and secondary schools.
As indicated by the Joint Committee table set forth above the
"$7 billion" figure includes Packwood-Moynihan tuition tax
credits for parents of students in private elementary and
secondary schools and for parents of students (and self-sup-
porting students) in colleges and other post-secondary
schools. Of that "$7 billion" total -- which is the "high"
total projected for 1986 -- approximately one-third, or $2.276
billion, would be attributable to students enrolled in elementary and secondary schools.

References to reduced budget receipts, or to what the Joint Committee labels the "Revenue Effect" of Packwood-Moynihan, include two components:

1. Reduced federal income tax payments from taxpayers whose federal tax exceeds the amount of their credit, who will be able to reduce their tax payment to the federal government by the amount of their credit; and

2. A "refundable tax credit" for taxpayers who have no federal tax liability or whose liability is less than the amount of their credit, entitling them to receive payment from the federal government in an amount equal to the difference between the amount of their credit and their tax liability, if any.

The Joint Committee did not provide a breakdown of its "Revenue Effect" figure showing what part of the $6.857 billion total would result from tax reductions and what part would result from refundable tax credits, i.e., federal payments or expenditures. However, it is clear that Packwood-Moynihan would not "cost" the federal government $7 billion in new expenditures.

A much different cost analysis is presented if more recent legislation is examined. In 1983, the Office of Tax Analysis of the Department of the Treasury presented the following information relative to Senate Bill 528/H.R. 1730.

Estimated Revenue Effect
S. 528/H.R. 1730 as Introduced
Fiscal Year 83 - Fiscal Year 88

1983	1984	1985	1986	1987	1988
0	245	526	753	779	763

On February 1, 1984 new OTA estimates were released showing costs of $337 million in Fiscal Year 1985, $594 million in Fiscal Year 1986 and $853 million in Fiscal Year 1987 with effective dates moved back one year.[5]

There is some fear that private schools will raise tuition from year to year and thereby drive up the annual "cost" to the federal treasury. However, this shouldn't happen because Congress routinely uses rate schedules, dollar limits and similar devices to control the impact of tax and related legislation. That is precisely what it did in fashioning the recently adopted tax reform legislation, including those provisions which provided huge tax benefits to the oil companies.

The last argument surrounds President Reagan's recently adopted tax reform program which provided a wide range of tax relief, including tax credits, exemptions and reductions for the oil industry that, by conservative estimates, will "cost" the federal treasury approximately $4 billion annually by 1986. Oil and other natural resources are important national assets, but our children and private schools are equally important -- or more important -- national assets. The President and his supporters have demonstrated their willingness to provide tax relief, with its attendant "cost," to preserve and promote the former. The President has indicated his willingness to provide the same kind of relief for the latter, but some of his supporters have not.

2. The second major issue poses opposition to tuition tax credits based on "federal control."

In examining this issue it is important to underscore that tuition tax credits provide tax relief to parent-taxpayers, not to private schools. Some opponents of tuition tax credits claim that they will benefit the schools because (1) they will enable parents, who might otherwise be unable to do so, to keep their children in private schools, and (2) they will enable the private schools to increase the tuition charged those parents. The appropriate responses to these claims are two in number.

i. Insofar as the first of these two statements is accurate, it describes a benefit to parent-taxpayers who wish to send their children to private schools but find it increasingly difficult to do so because of financial pressures, e.g., inflation and increasingly heavy taxes.

ii. With regard to the second of the two statements, the tuition charged by private schools is determined primarily by operating costs, such as teachers' salaries, supply costs, and fuel and utility costs. The availability of tuition tax credits will not affect those operating costs. Such credits will benefit the parent-taxpayers who must ultimately bear those costs.

Consider, for example, "child care expenses," which were allowable federal income tax deductions prior to 1976 and for which a tax credit has continued. These tax credits enable a parent, who might otherwise be unable to do so, to place his or her children in the care of others who charge for that service or care. Similarly, a tax deduction or a tax credit for

65

home insulation enables a homeowner, who might otherwise be unable to do so, to insulate his or her home. Although these tax benefits to parents and homeowners have stimulated the child care "business" and the home insulation industry (manufacture, distribution and installation), they have not been criticized on the ground that they amount to "granting private child care operators or the home insulation industry the benefit of federal tax credits," nor has it been demonstrated that they have caused increased child care or home insulation charges to the consumer-taxpayer who receives the tax credit.

Any attempt to distinguish private schools from private child care providers and the private home insulation industry must be carefully considered. Some private child care providers have religious affiliations, but that has not been seen as a basis for challenging the tax credit for child care expenses or characterizing it as "granting private child care providers the benefit of federal tax credits." Are private schools sufficiently different to warrant such a characterization of the tuition tax credit proposals? If so, what are the differences?

It is also important to recognize that federal tax and expenditure legislation is not regulatory in character and does not necessarily require or result in federal regulation or control. Federal tax laws (deductions, exemptions, credits, etc.) and federal spending laws are basically fiscal, not regulatory, measures. That is not to say that Congress, in drafting and adopting such legislation, cannot or does not include such qualifications, limitations and restrictions as it deems necessary and proper. For example, Packwood-Moynihan legislation would provide a tax credit only for tuition and related educational expenses paid to a private school that (1) has properly qualified as a not-for-profit entity, and (2) does not exclude students on account of race, color, or national or ethnic origin. Such qualifications, limitations and restrictions do not constitute undue federal regulation or control of such schools.

Millions of Americans received educational benefits -- federal expenditures -- under several versions of the G. I. Bill of Rights. That legislation included a wide range of qualifications, limitations and restrictions, but it resulted in little or no federal regulation of the schools attended by the beneficiaries. Some individuals even studied for the ministry under G.I. grants. Thus, the question of federal regulation or control included in or flowing from tuition tax credit legislation rests initially with Congress. More generally, a concern with excessive bureaucratic regulation or

66

control is hardly an argument against doing that which is otherwise in the public interest. That is especially true in the case of a Republican administration that has advocated broad "deregulation" and is committed to "getting the government off the backs of the people."

3. The third major issue poses opposition to tuition tax credits based on "state control."

Some opponents of tuition tax credits claim that it "could lead to some form of governmental control over private schools ... perhaps regulation of curriculum and admission policies." These opponents apparently fear some excessive state control through state departments of education. An examination of recent court decisions show that their fear is unfounded. Several courts in the past several years have considered the restrictions on state education agencies in attempting to impose administrative rules non-public schools.

In 1976 the Ohio Supreme Court held in State v. Whisner, that:

> Where the "minimum standards" promulgated by
> the State Board of Education are so comprehensive
> in scope and effect as to eradicate the distinction
> between public and non-public education, application
> of these "minimum standards" to defendants, parents
> of children attending a non-public religious school,
> abrogates their fundamental freedom, protected by the
> liberty clause of the Fourteenth Amendment to the
> Constitution of the United States, to direct the up-
> bringing and education, secular or religious, of
> their children. [6]

That case, which was decided under the present Ohio Minimum Standards, endorsed a "hands off" doctrine of "masterly inactivity" by the state in matters of regulating religious schools.[7] Justice (now Chief Justice) Celebrezze, writing for the Whisner majority, found those Minimum Standards to be "so pervasive and all-encompassing that total compliance with each and every standard by a nonpublic school would effectively eradicate the distinction between public and nonpublic education."[8] The decision found that these Standards effectively gave the state education department power "to control the essential elements of nonpublic education."[9] This produced "absolute suffocation of independent thought and educational policy, and the effective retardation of religious philosophy," according to the court.[10] Since no criminal charge was involved in Whisner, the defendants were discharged, but the standards were not expressly invalidated.

More recently the Kentucky Supreme Court prohibited its own State Board of Education from setting educational standards for nonpublic schools in Kentucky State Board of Elementary and Secondary Education v. Rudasill.[11] The judicial trend expressed by the Ohio and Kentucky Supreme Courts toward minimum standards is complemented and reinforced by statutory action May 1, 1979 by which the North Carolina legislature deregulated private education in that state. The North Carolina deregulation statute removed substantive educational requirements previously used by that state to regulate nonpublic schools. The consistent trend throughout the past few years, in both the judicial and legislative branches, is toward lesser or simply no control by state departments of education over nonpublic schools. Opponents of tuition tax credits are conjuring up an imaginary obstacle when they argue that state control of nonpublic schools may follow enactment of a credit program. Any efforts at control, as reviewed above, would simply be stricken as contrary to well-established constitutional law principles, which have been repeatedly and recently applied to the consistent rule that the state is severely limited in imposing any control over any nonpublic school policies.

4. The fourth major issue poses opposition to tuition tax credits based upon "unconstitutionality."

Much of the opposition to tuition tax credits has been based, in major part, upon a contention that such credits amount to an unconstitutional grant of government aid to religion. As pointed out in the preceding discussion of the "federal control" issue, the opposition argument on that point is usually premised upon a characterization of tuition tax credit legislation as "granting private schools the benefit of federal tax credits." That characterization is significant in any discussion of possible "federal control," but it is even more significant in any discussion of "unconstitutional aid to religion."

Over the past 35 years, the Supreme Court of the United States has struggled with the issue of "aid to religion" in a variety of cases dealing with the state or federal legislation that resulted in some benefit to religiously affiliated schools, to the children who attend those schools, or to the parents of those children. The decisions in those cases have not produced a clear and reliable distinction between legislation which is constitutional and that which is unconstitutional.

In more recent years the Supreme Court has developed three guidelines for assessing constitutionality in such cases:

1) Does the aid program have a secular purpose? Is it directed by some aim other than the advancement of religion.

2) Does the aid program bring about excessive entanglement of government and religion through administration of the program or create some kind of political division along religious lines.

3) Is the primary effect, or any principal effect, of the program an aid to religion? The primary effect can neither advance nor inhibit religion.

Attempting to ascertain the "primary effect" of advancing religion is not always easy. Two recent cases are frequently cited in an effort to clarify the question. In the Nyquist case [12] a New York State law authorizing tax deductions for tuition payments to private schools was declared unconstitutional. Although the majority in Nyquist concluded that the tuition reimbursement plan had both the purpose and the effect of encouraging attendance at private schools, and was therefore unconstitutional, the opinion expressly reserved the question of whether or not a genuine tax deduction or tax credit for tuition actually paid would satisfy the requirements of the First Amendment.

The second of these recent decisions, was the Supreme Court ruling regarding a Minnesota law that allows tax deductions for the cost of public, parochial and other private education. This decision was rendered on June 29, 1983 in a 5-4 decision by the Supreme Court. [13] One of the reasons that the court was willing to approve the Minnesota law was that it aided all students. This makes it "vitally" different from Nyquist. In that decision, the grants were given only to private school students, most of whom were Catholic. But the Minnesota law appears to be more neutral because it provides benefits to a "broad spectrum of citizens" and therefore "is not readily subject to challenge under the Establishment Clause."

5. The fifth major issue poses opposition to tuition tax credits based on an argument that it benefits the wealthy.

Using 1978 census data Jacobs concluded that: "tax credits would primarily aid children from the most disadvantaged families."[14] Her data reveal that 29 percent of the elementary and 21 percent of the secondary students attending private schools come from families with an income of less than $15,000. Of these 92-93 percent are Caucasian. Since 1978, however, a continuing trend seems to be persisting because more recent information indicates that Hispanic and Black enrollments in parochial schools are each about 8 percent, lowering the white percentage to 84.[15] Are these figures so small that they place the major benefits of tax credits on the wealthy?

We have already witnessed changes in other tax laws which benefit the upper classes. Why can't persons who are middle income or poor benefit from tutition tax credits? Returning to a point made earlier in the paper, why can't inner-city people have a choice of schools especially when they believe that their local public school is inferior or does not teach proper values?"

Conclusion

The issues surrounding tuition tax credits are indeed complex. Perhaps the Minnesota case goes the farthest in attempting to unravel some of the problems. It might still be possible to legislate the issue at the national level but perhaps the best hope of all is that people will respond in terms of what is best for children.

Notes

[1] Evans Clinchy and Elisabeth Allen Cody, "If Not Public Choice, Then Private Escape," Phi Delta Kappan, LX (December, 1978), 271.

[2] Pierce vs. Society of Sisters, 268 U.S. 510 (1925).

[3] John E. Coons. "Making Schools Public," in Private Schools and the Public Good, ed. Edward McGlynn Gaffney, Jr. (South Bend, Indiana: University of Notre Dame Press, 1981), 92.

[4] U.S. Congress, Joint Committee on Taxation, Description of S.550 Tuition Tax Relief Act of 1981 (Washington: Government Printing Office, 1981), p. 17.

[5] "Tuition Tax Credits." Issue Brief, No. 1B81075, updated February 1, 1984. (Washington: Congressional Research Service, Library of Congress, 1984), p. 11.

[6]State vs. Whisner, 47 Ohio St. 2d 181 (1976).

[7] Board of Education v. Minor, 23 Ohio St. 211, 249 - 251 (1872), cited with approval in State vs. Whisner 47 Ohio St. 2d 181-210 (1981).

[8]State v. Whisner, pp. 211-212.

[9]Ibid., p. 215.

[10]Ibid.

[11] Kentucky State Board of Elementary and Secondary Education vs. Rudasill, 589 S.W. 2d 877 (October 9, 1979), cert. denied, 48 U.S. L.W. 3731 (May 13, 1980).

[12] Commitee for Public Education vs. Nyquist, 413 U.S. 756 (1973).

[13]Mueller vs. Allen, 51 U.S.L.W., 5050 (June 29, 1983).

[14]Martha J. Jacobs, "An Update: Who Would Benefit from Tuition Tax Credits?" Phi Delta Kappan, LXI (June, 1980), 681.

[15]Issue Brief, p. 10.

TUITION TAX CREDITS: THREAT TO RELIGIOUS
LIBERTY AND CHURCH-STATE SEPARATION

Americans United for Separation
of Church and State

President Reagan on April 15, 1982, announced his support for a tuition tax credit plan to aid parochial and other private schools. Addressing an enthusiastic audience at the annual meeting of the National Catholic Educational Association in Chicago, the President proposed that families with an annual income of $50,000 or less be given a federal income tax credit of up to $100 in 1983 for each child in a non-public elementary or secondary school. The credit would increase to $300 in 1984 and $500 in 1985. Families earning between $50,000 and $75,000 would be entitled to partial credits. Though the U.S. Senate tabled a modified version of this plan late in 1983 by a 59 to 38 vote, proponents are certain to try again.

There are several reasons why this plan should be utterly rejected by Congress. In short, it is constitutionally suspect, fiscally irresponsible, and politically unwise. An examination of previous decisions by the U.S. Supreme Court shows that the tuition tax credit concept is of dubious constitutionality. In its 1973 PEARL v. Nyquist ruling the High Court struck down a similar New York state tuition tax reimbursement scheme. In that decision, the justices noted that the real recipients of tuition tax credits are not private school parents, but private schools themselves. The credits are geared directly to the amount of tuition the parents pay. Though the route is indirect, the result is the same. Tax dollars due to the federal treasury are funneled into the bank accounts of private schools.

Because the overwhelming majority of private schools are religious in character, such financial support violates the First Amendment's ban on government aid to religion. (Sixty-five percent of the students enrolled in non-public education attend Roman Catholic schools, while most of the remainder attend the schools of less than a dozen other faiths. Only fifteen percent of the non-public students are in secular schools.)

But beyond the unconstitutionality of the plan, tuition tax credits are bad public policy for a number of reasons. Chief among these is the fact that they undermine the public school system. Throughout the history of the United States,

73

we have upheld the principle that all Americans should be allowed the pursuit of happiness and opportunity to develop their full potential. Essential to that principle is the availability of a good education for every person regardless of station in life. Consequently, we have constructed, after much struggle, a nationwide system of public schools, open and free to all without respect to financial ability or other qualification. The nation's advance toward that goal has sometimes been slow and uneven, but the desirability of the goal has remained.

For the first time, however, it seems conceivable that our government could turn from that principle. The Reagan administration has enacted cuts in federal aid to public education, while proposing new federal programs of assistance to private and parochial schools. It is a change in principle which a nation adhering to equal opportunity for all can scarcely tolerate.

To assert that a strong public education system is essential is not to denigrate in any way the contributions of the nation's private schools or to question their right to operate freely. In the nation's early years those schools were often the only source of education, though their availability to the public was often limited by financial and other considerations. Today, private schools offer an agenda of religious education and other specialized programs for those who prefer such.

Those who operate and use private and parochial schools should join with the public school and religious liberty communities to oppose tuition tax credits. Indeed, many have. Government aid invariably brings government controls. The much cherished independence of private education may very well disappear if substantial public support of such schools become a reality.

A further reason for opposing tax credits is simple economics. The tuition tax credit plan would wreak havoc with the Reagan administration's effort to balance the federal budget. With current private school enrollment, a credit such as the one proposed by the President would cost an estimated $4 billion during its first few years of operation. If the credit encouraged more parents to move their children from public to private schools, as some fear, the cost would increase further. In addition, Congress and the administration would no doubt be pressured to increase the size of the tax credit in subsequent years. In short, the cost of such a program once initiated would be open ended and almost impossible to control.

The economic argument for tuition tax credits rests on unstable ground. Catholic school proponents have been fond of claiming how much money their schools save the public. The usual procedure is to determine the per pupil cost of public schooling in a community by dividing the total cost to the taxpayers by the number of pupils enrolled. Then this per pupil cost is multiplied by the number of youngsters enrolled in the non-public school to reveal the "savings" to the public. This is a beautiful example of misuse of data. Every time a new youngster enrolls in the public schools the cost to the taxpayers does not increase by that average per pupil cost. As parents in communities with declining school enrollments have frustratingly found out, lower enrollments do not lead to lower costs.

Where duplication of school facilities is the result of the existence of both public and non-public schools, we have an unsound expenditure. This approaches the level of absurdity when two schools, one public, one non-public, lie a few blocks (or even across the street) from one another, each with partially used science laboratories, music equipment, libraries, and instructional materials. In a time of declining school age population, tuition tax credits could well serve to exacerbate this situation.

The American people have repeatedly and uniformly opposed public tax aid to private and parochial schools by considerable margins. Many public opinion polls across the country have reported that view. Direct voter referenda in twelve states over the past 15 years have confirmed that principle. In the District of Columbia in 1981, the voters rejected a tuition tax credit scheme by a nine to one margin.

Advocates of tax aid for parochial schools -- through tuition tax credits, vouchers, or some other method -- like to use the argument that they are enhancing "freedom of choice" in education. Upon close examination, however, "parental choice" through parochiaid is more myth than reality. The argument that tuition tax credits will provide choice rests on a highly questionable assumption. The argument assumes that parents, given some financial benefit, will remove their children from one local school (likely the public one) and enroll them in another local school (likely a non-public one). Non-public schools are not found everywhere, however. They will be found in large population centers and in those relatively few smaller communities where one religious group, largely for historical reasons, has maintained a parochial school.

What makes the "choice" argument ring even more hollow is that even where a non-public school or school system does exist there is a particular religious or social class orientation which makes that school unacceptable to many who supposedly would use it. So, for example, tax credits such as advocated by the Reagan administration, will not provide much choice for a fundamentalist Christian family looking for an alternative to the public school in a community where there are only public schools and Roman Catholic ones. The many publicized cases of parents trying to teach their children at home is vivid testimony to the unavailability of the particular non-public school such parents may be seeking.

The argument for choice rests on other equally tenuous assumptions. One is that the absence of credits or some other monetary gift prevents parents from sending their youngsters to a non-public school. The hypothesis that financial concerns prevent many families from using non-public schools has been extensively researched. Studies such as those conducted in Philadelphia, St. Louis, New York City, and New York state all conclude that tuition costs are an insignificant factor influencing non-public school enrollment. One conclusion which can be drawn from the results of such studies is that parents are exercising their choice -- the choice of deciding whether to spend money on private school enrollment or on something else. The tremendous drop in Roman Catholic school enrollment in the 1960s occurred at a time when tuition to Catholic schools was minimal.

At the present time, and under any parochiaid scheme likely to be acceptable to non-public school interests, the ultimate "choice" in parochial or private school admission is in the hands of their school administrators. Preference is normally given to children of members of the religious body which operates the school. Non-public schools also may, and often do, "choose" to admit or retain only students likely to do well academically, or whose discipline is beyond reproach, or who are all members of the same sex. Parents may "choose" a non-public school for their children, but it is the school which "chooses" whether or not to admit the child. (Public schools, of course, have very little freedom to "choose" students. They must take all applicants, including those rejected or expelled by parochial and private schools.)

"Choice" is also limited by the nature of a parochial school's curriculum and philosophy. Would many Christian parents "choose" a Jewish School? Would many Jewish families "choose" to send their children to a conservative Christian school? How many people would "choose" an Amish school? Non-

76

public schools may exercise much greater choice than public schools in matters of courses, course content, and emphasis. They may "choose" to permeate their programs with the doctrines, tenets, and values of a particular religious body. Public schools, serving an unchosen and therefore quite pluralistic constituency, and operating under the First Amendment, may not "choose" to deviate from a benevolent neutrality with regard to religion and religious values.

So, too, with teachers! Non-public schools may choose teachers whose religious beliefs and affiliations are acceptable to the school's owners. This largely explains why discussion of sensitive issues -- such as religion -- generates less concern among school managers and parents in non-public schools than in public ones. There is more confidence in the teachers' orientation and "loyalty." (The "loyalty," of course, is reinforced by the fact that non-public school teachers have far less job security than their public counterparts.) As for the public schools, they may not even inquire of a teacher or prospective teacher about his religious beliefs or affiliation.

Finally, we the people "choose" the boards of local citizens and parents who run our local public schools. We have no voice in "choosing" who will run parochial and private schools. Yet there are those who want to "choose" that all taxpayers will be made to support parochial and private schools, who would deny the right of all Americans to "choose" which religious institutions each of us will support.

There are many choices that can be made in public education. Students, especially in secondary schools, have varying amounts of freedom to "choose" elective courses. If the people of a community "choose" to expand the variety of courses, programs, and modes of education in their district, they can create additional choices for students and parents within our existing public school systems. Of course, we then sometimes have to "choose" to spend more money to allow for such expanded "choices."

The parochiaiders' "parental choice," then, is largely a myth. They also tend to ignore the basic American principle that support of religious institutions is and should be a matter of individual voluntary choice. But the right to individual voluntary choice in supporting religions and religious institutions is violated by any law or government action which directly or indirectly diverts public funds, extracted from all citizens of all faiths, to private institutions which exist primarily for religious reasons and purposes.

A cartoonist with a Milwaukee newspaper once put it very well. A parochiaider is portrayed saying, "I choose to operate a sectarian private school. Then I choose which teachers to hire and which kids to admit. Then I choose that all taxpayers will pay for my choice."

The idea of choice, then, should not be distorted for use by those who do not respect the American constitutional principle of separation of church and state, who do not honor the very American idea that religious institutions are to be supported only by truly voluntary donations.

President Reagan's parochiaid proposal is nothing new. Controversy has raged for nearly two centuries in the United States over tax support of sectarian private schools. In the main, however, public support has been confined to public schools. Deviations from this consensus policy have been few and relatively minor.

During the last quarter century, sectarian pressures on Congress and state legislatures for various forms of tax aid for parochial schools -- all of them referred to generically as "parochiaid" -- have been intense. Most parochiaid plans have been defeated in committee or in floor votes. Nearly all of those which survived the legislative process were challenged in court by Americans United and other groups.

In an important series of rulings in the 1970s, the U.S. Supreme Court and lower courts ruled unconstitutional the following parochiaid plans: state payments to supplement parochial teacher salaries; "purchase of services" from parochial schools; tuition reimbursement grants and tax credits; grants to parochial schools for building maintenance and repair; publicly provided instructional services in parochial schools; loans of instructional materials, other than textbooks, to parochial schools; some forms of bus transportation and some textbook loans; assignment of regular public school teachers to parochial schools ("reverse shared time").

As of 1981 the only forms of parochiaid which have been upheld by the Supreme Court are bus transportation, except for field trips; textbook loans, except to schools practicing "racial or other invidious discrimination"; and medical and psychological diagnostic and therapeutic services. Federal aid in the form of instructional services is still being tested in court.

In _Mueller v. Allen_ (1983) the Supreme Court narrowly upheld a Minnesota program of tax _deductions_ for both private and public school costs (though the bulk of the assistance went to parochial school patrons). This may signal a weakening of the Court's adherence to the wall of separation principle as it applies to education. As recently as March of 1984, however, the High Court (in Lynch v. Donnelly) cited the 1973 Nyquist decision as an example of the Court's dedication to the preservation of the First Amendment's Establishment Clause. This would seem to indicate that the Court has not changed its view that a tuition tax credit intended to benefit parochial schools is unconstitutional.

Despite adverse court rulings, advocates of the tuition tax credit parochiaid plan have continued to pressure Congress for passage of such a plan. Until Reagan's announcement of his proposal, its most vocal proponent has been Sen. Daniel F. Moynihan (D-N.Y.). He has expressed the view that congressional passage of a tax credit bill would result in the Supreme Court's reversing its earlier rulings. In 1978 Senators Moynihan and Robert Packwood (R-Ore.) led a major effort to get a tuition tax credit bill through Congress. The measure narrowly passed in the House but was solidly defeated in the Senate.

Tuition tax credits, quite simply, reimburse parents for tuition paid to parochial or private schools. The credit is subtracted directly from the amount of federal income tax owed. The original Packwood-Moynihan bill would have reimbursed 50% of tuition up to a maximum benefit of $500 per student per year. The amount of the reimbursement would be subtracted from the parent's annual federal income tax bill. Tuition tax credits could be designed to reimburse up to 100% of tuition with no upper limit on tuition. And passage of a mild tax credit bill would surely lead to pressure to have the program increase until full support is achieved.

The following objections to that tuition tax credit parochiaid plan were presented by Americans United for Separation of Church and State in testimony before the Senate Finance Committee in early 1978.

1. As applied to parochial schools which enroll over 90% of all non-public school students, a tuition tax credit plan would violate the First Amendment. State legislation quite similar in intent and effect was ruled unconstitutional by the U.S. Supreme Court in Committee for Public Education and Religious Liberty v. Nyquist (1973), Sloan v. Lemon (1973), Essex v. Wolman (1973), Grit v. Wolman (1973), Franchise Tax Board v. United Americans (1974). Tuition tax credit parochiaid clearly violates the "no establishment" clause and is clearly a union of church and state at the financial level.

2. The genesis and promotion of this plan represents a confluence of religious and political interests. As the Supreme Court pointed out in the 1971 Lemon parochiaid ruling,

> In a community where such a large number of pu-
> pils are served by church-related schools, it can
> be assumed that state assistance will entail con-
> siderable political activity. Partisans of paro-
> chial schools ... will inevitably champion this
> cause and promote political action to achieve their
> goals. Those who oppose state aid, whether for con-
> stitutional, religious, or fiscal reasons, will in-
> evitably respond and employ all of the usual political
> campaign techniques to prevail....
>
> Ordinarily political debate and division, how-
> ever vigorous or even partisan, are normal healthy
> manifestations of our democratic system of government,
> but political division along religious lines was one
> of the principal evils against which the First Amend-
> ment was intended to protect.

This plan could so entangle religion and politics that two centuries of progress in our country with regard to religious liberty and church-state separation could be obliterated.

3. Denominational elementary and secondary school facul-ties, student bodies, and curricula tend toward religious homogeneity. Tuition tax credits, by aiding such schools, would be federal government subsidization of sectarian divi-sion and divisiveness in education. The result of this could only be a decline in interfaith and community harmony.

4. While many non-public schools are well integrated racially, in general they tend to serve smaller percentages of minority students than do public schools. Tuition tax credits would in the long run harm the cause of racial inte-gration and worsen public school racial imbalances.

5. According to the National Center for Educational Statistics, 57% of elementary public school parents earn less than $7,500 per year (in 1967 dollars) while only 34% of non-public parents fall in that category. While 45% of non-public elementary parents earn over $10,000 per year (in 1967 dol-lars), only 25% of public school parents are in that category. On the secondary level, public school parents have a median income of $12,300, while non-public school parents have a median income of $15,962, which is 30% higher. Tuition tax credits would exclusively benefit non-public school parents,

who tend to be more affluent, and provide no benefits whatever for generally less affluent public school parents.

6. Since non-public schools are often selective academically, tuition tax credits would enhance the competitive position of non-public schools in relation to public schools.

7. By subsidizing non-public schools which tend to be religiously homogeneous, and to serve proportionately fewer minority and less affluent children, tuition tax credits, would:

    a. Encourage the religious, ethnic, and class balkanization of American society and increase the centrifugal forces in society which have proven so destructive in other countries.

    b. Weaken the competitive position of the democratic, religiously neutral, more open public schools which serve 90% of our children. (This would gradually convert public schools into shrunken "wastebaskets" for poor, minority, and handicapped students. The American dream of a great common school system would be shattered.)

    c. Reduce academic freedom and lessen the educational pluralism and diversity to which the individual child is exposed more in public than in non-public schools.

8. Acceptance of and dependence upon tuition reimbursement tax aid would in the long run diminish the freedom and independence of private schools to pursue their religious or other special missions. Public schools may not hire or fire teachers for religious reasons, and may not impose religious observances or instruction upon students. Should parochial and private schools partially or wholly supported with public funds be allowed to do what public schools may not?

Tuition tax credits would also intrude government and public dollars into the internal denominational controversies not only over tax support but also over whether separate, parochial education should be continued.

9. Public schools are controlled by local boards elected by and responsible to all the people, including those who patronize non-public schools. Tuition tax credits would compel the public at large to support private and parochial schools in whose operation they would have no voice. Our

ancestors fought a war for independence from "taxation without representation."

10. The American people in recent years have repeatedly expressed their views on the subject of government aid for parochial and private schools. They have consistently voted against such aid. Here are the results of the statewide referenda on government aid for parochial and private schools since 1967.

STATE	YEAR	VOTE AGAINST	VOTE FOR
New York	1967	72.5%	27.5%
Michigan	1970	57 %	43 %
Nebraska	1970	57 %	43 %
Oregon	1972	61 %	39 %
Idaho	1972	57 %	43 %
Maryland	1972	55 %	45 %
Maryland	1974	56.5%	43.5%
Washington	1975	60.5%	39.5%
Missouri	1976	60 %	40 %
Alaska	1976	54 %	46 %
Michigan	1978	74 %	26 %
District of Columbia	1981	89 %	11 %
California	1982	61 %	39 %
Massachusetts	1982	62 %	38 %

We understand the problems of parents who choose to send their children to private religious schools. But the preservation of religious freedom, church-state separation, public education, and the independence of church schools surely outweighs any benefits which a minority of parents might receive from the plan. Faith communities, aided by the income tax deductibility of religious donations, surely have the financial and spiritual strength to keep their private educational institutions healthy without government aid or entanglement.

82

PART FOUR -- PERSPECTIVES ON TEACHER UNIONS

What judgments can be made about teacher unions?

One of the most significant educational phenomena of the past few decades has been the rise to influence of teacher unions and their growing militancy. An examination of the questions asked about teacher organizations in the annual Gallup Polls of the Public's Attitude Toward the Public Schools reveals that in general the public has come to accept such unions, and the differing views are now over what rights and bargaining powers they should have. The strength of the unions and the behavior of local and state power structures toward them does vary noticeably in different parts of the country. However, both the National Education Association (NEA) and the American Federation of Teachers (AFT) are now prominent in national politics, and that is not the only thing they have in common. Starting with its power base in industrial urban areas, the AFT has expanded from concern with teacher salaries, fringe benefits, and working conditions to involvement in all phases of the educational enterprise. At the same time, as teachers have gained control over organizational policy-making, the NEA has become strident in promoting teacher interests. Today, in terms of what they do, the two major teacher organizations are more alike than different.

The first of these two obviously partisan articles notes the significant increases in teacher salaries, improved working conditions, and the growing professionalism of teachers. Organized teachers working for these changes made them possible. What unions now need to turn their attention to are upgrading teacher training standards, establishing effective self-policing, implementing better ways to help beginning teachers, and making the occupation more attractive to potential entrants.

The second article examines a problem which arises when unions seeking to speak for all teachers attempt to make the alleged beneficiaries of union activities carry some of the burdens, too. The issue is commonly labeled the "agency shop," which refers to language in contractual agreements which requires even those teachers who do not wish to join the union to pay fees roughly equivalent to the cost of union membership. The issue here is seen as the rights of the individual versus compulsory unionism.

DAL LAWRENCE is president of the Toledo, Ohio Federation of Teachers, Local 250, AFT. He is the author of the city school system's intern peer review plan, which has been cited by the Rand Corporation as one of the four best programs of its kind in the country. For eight years Lawrence was a high school social studies teacher.

EDWARD REMINGTON is a staff member of the National Right to Work Committee and has worked with the Committee's education division, Concerned Educators Against Forced Unionism (CEAFU) for the past eight years. In addition to the issue of forced unionism in education, he has written and worked on a number of issues facing America's public schools. CEAFU is at 8001 Braddock Road, Springfield, Virginia, 22160.

THE ROLE OF TEACHER UNIONS IN EDUCATION

Dal Lawrence

> As long as there are oversized classes,
> too heavy teaching loads, and deficits in
> supportive services, there will be militant
> teachers.
>> David Selden, former president
>> American Federation of Teachers

The development of teacher organizations from an inauspicious eighteenth century beginning has been recounted several times. It is not the purpose of this paper to retrace that history. Teacher unions were not especially powerful as recently as 1960; they are powerful now. What then is their role today and for the future? That is the central issue in this paper.

Presently teacher unions focus their power on the traditional aims of American workers: wages, fringe benefits and working conditions. This is not surprising because teachers traditionally experienced deplorable wages, received no fringe benefits except a retirement system, and had much overrated job protection and nearly impossible working conditions. It was a set of circumstances nearly as old as public schools themselves.

There have been dramatic improvements in teacher salaries. Aside from the economic benefits of affording a more comfortable living, higher salaries have meant that more men and family primary wage earners now choose teaching as a career. Fewer teachers hold second income jobs, thereby affording greater opportunity to concentrate on a teaching career. Teacher unions have laid the groundwork for a career in the classroom free from undue economic deprivation. Until recently relatively few American teachers had the option of planning a lifetime of work in the classroom. The destructive impact on our nation's classrooms resulting from aborted careers, second jobs, and movement into school administration and away from the teacher-learner process has been incalculable but nonetheless real. If better elementary and secondary education rests in part on a stable, professional cadre of teachers, there can be little doubt that teacher unions have bargained into existence the opportunity to achieve this professional status.

One can argue that today's teachers are less capable than the teacher of thirty or forty years ago. There certainly are statistics depressing enough to have us believe that today students are taught by poorly educated, poorly trained teachers incapable of writing the simplest sentences or of performing even the most basic mathematical calculations. Such conclusions are misleading at best. It is not the contention of this paper that higher salaries have brought with them better prepared teachers. Higher salaries have simply given us the opportunity to improve the professional capability of American teachers. The role teacher unions will play in the process of improving professional competence will be crucial and, it is argued, absolutely necessary if the opportunity is to be seized and if the quality of teaching performance is to be improved. We have a wider variety of people from differing social, economic and racial backgrounds at work in our classrooms. They can and do make teaching a career in far greater numbers than even before. I am confident that they will use their unions to raise teaching standards and police their ranks far more effectively than was ever done when school boards begged to get a teacher – any teacher – into the classroom, a condition that was the direct product of shockingly low wages.

Working conditions likewise have improved dramatically. Class sizes have been reduced largely as a result of collective bargaining limitations imposed on school management long before declining enrollments became a factor in the class size equation. Planning time is now the rule, not the exception. Special classes and programs that would have been unthinkable just twenty years ago have been added in every school district. Teacher unions played a pivotal role in obtaining these specialized programs for exceptional students through their lobbying and through the process of negotiation. The result has seen the more difficult student removed from "regular" classrooms at the same time class sizes were being lowered. Certainly the tremendous amount of individualization currently in existence could not have taken place without the specialization so common in our schools today.

Of all the improvements in working conditions, none can be more significant for the future of the teacher as a professional than the new self-image teacher unions helped create. Teachers were never professionals in any realistic sense of that term before they unionized. How soon we forget the humility of teachers underpaid, subjected to administrative harassment and low community esteem. Don't for one second believe that the good old days before picket lines were days of joy and pride for the vast majority of American teachers. They were bitter days filled with the specter of rejection and failure: "Those who can, do; those who can't, teach!" Only those who worked to supplement a spouse's income could afford to ignore the cruel irony of the powerless clinging to a non-existent "professionalism" imposed on them by non-practicing "professionals." The rest drove a bus, sold shoes, or left. America's teachers were the beat generation -- and had been for generations on end.

Much of the criticism of teacher unions today stems from the fact that many people were shocked to see their child's teacher walking a picket line. The media generally covers strikes by public employees to the fullest extent possible. Editorial policy seldom is favorable regardless of the circumstances which produced the strike. Citizens (and taxpayers) find it unpleasant to discover that the money they have supplied to the schools is insufficient. Conditions in the nation's schools had been ignored for years. Even outrageous student drop out rates seemingly went undetected and certainly produced no great public outcry for better schools. Picket lines got the public's attention. Probably there was no other mechanism that could have caught the public's attention and focused it on the quality of education as quickly and as effectively as did the teacher strike. In its broadest perspective, the militancy of teacher unions has created a reservoir of national concern never before present, and it is only after the public gains recognition of a problem that citizens can be galvanized into action. Picket lines have not been in vain although educational problem solving of national significance remains for the future.

A more immediate benefit has been produced by unionization, however. It is through collective bargaining agreements and strikes that classroom teachers have gained considerable control over their profession. Teacher union committees at local schools, armed with contract language, have appeared as a counter balance to the traditional authoritarian control school principals exercised over the lives and "professionalism" of the teacher. Henceforth, the rules of the workplace will not be dictatorial or arbitrary. Superintendents have been stripped of their roles as spokespersons for teachers. Things important to teachers now are expressed collectively and with considerable impact. Teaching staffs have begun looking to their own elected representatives for assistance. The NEA has been taken over by teachers -- finally. People might not have liked it, or understood it, but teachers through their unions are at last standing on their own two feet. No longer will the nation's classrooms be manned by the downtrodden.

Pride is what the teacher has discovered -- pride and the dignity that comes with the realization that things can be changed through collective effort and a willingness to stand up and be counted. The role of the teacher union so far has produced nothing so important as the realization on the part of today's teacher that he has made a better place for himself in society. I would suggest that no change in education is more significant or so necessary to future educational successes than the transformation of the attitude of American teachers from disillusionment and defeat to militant pride and confidence in the ability to build for a better future. Teacher unionization has done that.

What about the future? What needs to be accomplished so that America's elementary and secondary schools produce the best educated citizenry possible? Let's look at the state of the profession itself. Following are four key improvements that I think are needed (listed not necessarily in order of priority):

* Teacher training standards must be upgraded.

* Self-policing of the profession must be established and made effective.

* An internship must become standard in the professional development process.

* Funding for schools must be increased sharply and the tax based altered not only to better service exceptional students, but to establish salary levels which will attract outstanding college students to the teaching field.

These four concerns are central to future improved teaching performance and professional development. Teachers through their unions will at least influence, if not determine, the degree to which each will be improved. All are interrelated. None can be ignored if elementary and secondary schools are to achieve a level of performance sufficient to restore public confidence in public schools.

Twenty years ago there would have been little thought given to the classroom teacher's notions about these issues. Lip service would have been paid as usual, but the basic decisions would have emanated from the major educational bureaucracies: superintendents' associations, school boards' associations (dominated by the administrative associations), state departments of education, administrative staffs, and the

National Education Association controlled as it has been since its inception by its professional staff and various educational management personnel. Teachers had been effectively written out of the decision making equation. Certainly their complicity with the bureaucracy had left them far from blameless.

Conditions and compensation which had been the uncomplaining lot of the farmer's daughter turned teacher were not so readily accepted by the new breed which came to man the classrooms in the years following World War Two. Like other historical movements great and small, when frustrations finally spilled over after years of restraint, the result sent shock waves through society. We noted the public antagonism toward strikes. What has gone unnoticed by the public is the price our nation paid for the years in which the schools were managed without effective input by teachers. Stated bluntly, teachers were bought off. Codes of ethics stressed harmony, and a teacher who could easily be persuaded to "go along" in return for vague hints about promotion or job security was precisely the wrong kind of teacher for a democratic society -- something finally discovered by the nation's youth during the sixties. Teacher militancy, at least in part, ended the age of "friendly persuasion."

But the future generally keeps few promises. The power and influence of teacher unions in shaping the future of schools and the profession is not self-executing. What then lies ahead?

Teacher training standards are obviously important, controversial, and too lax. Much else is not quite so obvious. I cannot in this paper deal with the background or controversies surrounding America's teacher training institutions. They are much maligned, greatly abused, and as often as not, deservedly so. What has to be kept in mind, however, is that no state has training standards that are the products of significant influence by teacher unions - or teachers. Why would any professional want to establish entrance or training standards so low that the profession becomes a target of scorn and the butt of jokes?

There are reasons, of course, and one of the biggest is monetary in nature. Historically our schools have been underfunded, and traditionally an academic education has been suspect. Management personnel charged with the responsibility of keeping schools open for a society notorious for its suspicion of taxes and politicians had little incentive to sacrifice their careers on the altars of higher teacher pay, so necessary to achieve higher teacher standards. The public demanded neither, at least not when presented in taxation terms, and leverage against the public was not possible while teachers were unorganized or, if organized, not in possession of a collective bargaining contract.

Training standards have yet to be included as a topic for teacher picket signs, but the power to influence standards does for the first time exist. Just as important, teachers are beginning to see that it is not in their long range interest when trainees consistently score embarrassingly low on standardized tests in competition with other college students. Constant public ridicule of the mental capabilities of classroom teachers cannot escape even the dullest teacher. Teacher union leaders have already seized on such criticism in an effort to overhaul standards and upgrade the quality of those entering the profession. The American Federation of Teachers advocates entrance exams for teachers and internships for all new teachers. State departments now regularly go to teacher unions for nominees to committees investigating a host of standards and ways to improve them. Today there is greater input than previously, but that input is still greatly diluted by the input of non-teachers on the same committees. Compromise is the name of the game, and training standards for teachers will probably remain an illusive goal, buried in the layers of bureaucracy at state government levels.

If there is any dramatic improvement, such as a requirement for college trainees to pass a series of academic competency tests to remain in the education curriculum, it will be teacher unions that ultimately force the changes spurred on by the continuing public clamor for better teachers. The traditional associations of administrators, board members and college professional educators still lack incentive to make the changes, and still view their self-interest in the perspective of careers much too threatened to act decisively. Traditional leadership has failed, and it will continue to do so here. Only teachers have incentive enough to turn public criticism of how teachers are prepared to their long-term advantage; and it is only the unionized teacher that is insulated enough from career threatening pressures to demand real, hard-nosed changes in teacher preparation. It will not be easy.

Self-policing could be construed as much too close to the self-interest of teachers to hold forth much hope that their unions will be effective in weeding out incompetent teachers. The arguments advanced against the effectiveness of traditional leadership organizations in the area of preparation standards most certainly apply now to teacher unions.

Self-governance by professionals, in fact, has been largely suspect in medicine and law if its purpose is maintaining uniformly capable physicians and lawyers. The case against teachers in this instance is far from closed, however.

First, there is the obvious need to eliminate the poorest teachers to curb the damage they are doing not only to students but to their colleagues -- a need far more urgent and obvious than in medicine or law. Although it is not generally understood, teachers themselves invariably support the elimination of the obviously incompetent. Furthermore, the school establishment has failed miserably in maintaining an acceptable level of competence despite having ample legal authority to do so as well as generous motivation. Unions have been blamed for preventing or making it more difficult to remove terrible teachers, but the truth is that management has been so lax and so incompetent in the techniques of evaluation and firing that most of the blame for this failure must be placed squarely at the feet of school principals and personnel divisions. If anything, unions have forced school authorities to improve their capabilities in the areas of procedural and substantive due process, not an altogether bad idea for those charged with the responsibility of passing along to future generations in a democratic society these cornerstones of individual rights.

What then can teacher unions realistically be expected to accomplish? I would suggest that at the very least unions will insist that teachers hired at the local board level be required to pass basic competency examinations in their teaching areas as well as being required to demonstrate acceptable communications skills. It is shocking to think that few school boards have such requirements, especially in view of the criticism of the overall quality of teachers in training. This pressure at the local level could lead to reinstituting statewide teacher exams, reversing a trend of several decades. Better teachers mean fewer removals later on.

Self-policing is a necessary part of achieving a professional status. In Toledo, Ohio we are experimenting with a device we call "intervention." Briefly, intervention means that a teacher is identified as performing at an unacceptable level. A successful teacher is assigned to that teacher on a full-time basis for a period of several weeks to identify weaknesses and prescribe corrective techniques. Ultimately, the "consulting teacher," as he is called, issues a "status report" recommending a course of action that could lead to dismissal or retention of employee. The recipient of intervention does not have a choice. Intervention is instituted only after agreement between the principal and the union committee and once this is done the message to the teacher is clear: "Improve or face dismissal." Note that the mechanism is triggered only after agreement between school management and the union. Obviously, it is possible for a variety of reasons to abort intervention in cases where it is sorely needed and this has happened. But the process has been used successfully -- successful in that some teachers have been helped, and some have found other occupations. Intervention is being accepted by the teachers because for the first time there is an awareness that it is through their own elected representatives that self-policing is initiated and accomplished. Management is pleased because it too recognizes the need -- as well as the dismal track record -- to eliminate incompetent teachers; and support of the union itself is found reassuring especially since antagonisms between labor and management are allayed at the outset.

Admittedly, total self-policing such as is found in medicine or law is not probable anytime in education's foreseeable future. An institution so inextricably bound up with the public interest realistically cannot expect to achieve total professional control over hiring or firing. Indeed, I would admit that such control is in the interest of neither the public nor the professional. However, experience has shown the education family that procedures and techniques must be implemented which allow teachers a far greater voice in this crucial matter than has ever existed in the past. To do so will increase effectiveness in policing experienced teachers no longer performing satisfactorily, and it will vastly reduce tensions and strife between teachers and school management when it becomes necessary to "police the ranks." It is an unexplored area fraught with danger for all concerned, but it is reasonable to expect that teacher unions and school management will perform much better as allies than as antagonists.

No discussion about the role teacher unions will play in the coming years can be complete without looking at internships as part of the future professional development process. We need not argue whether present teacher training programs are adequate, or how satisfactory or unsatisfactory they may be. What is important as far as teacher unions are concerned is that a first year experience as an intern can improve the new professional's level of competence, greatly ease the adjustment from college student to full-time employee, and give the union an effective voice in who should continue teaching. The public is happy because screening of new teachers can be very effective -- maybe for the first time. Teachers are happy because they can negotiate a role for themselves in the

92

internship. Older models for teacher evaluation and growth are at the very least called into question. Even more likely, a dramatic change in whole evaluation and professional growth processes can be expected to take place.

There is a hitch, of course. Vested interests of school administrators who traditionally have held sway over teacher evaluation stand in the way. Principals fight to prevent being taken out of their evaluation role even for a year, arguing that to do so would dilute their authority to manage a school. However that may or may not be, teachers through their unions will either share or control all or part of the evaluation process in the years ahead.

In Toledo teachers have bargained control over the first year. Evaluations are the province of specially trained "intern consulting teachers." Consulting teachers are released from teaching duties for a year at a time to work with six to eight first year interns. Principals merely file a summary form indicating the intern's attendance record, relations with parents, and observance of local school rules. All professional classroom work of the intern is the sole responsibility of the consulting teacher. Even the principal's summary form must be filed with the consulting teacher who in turn has the discretion to use it as he sees fit. Evaluation standards are jointly developed by the union and school management. The intern program is governed by a nine member "panel of review." The union names five members of the panel. All evaluations by consulting teachers must be approved or disapproved by the review panel after the final March evaluations are completed.

Does it work? This is the third year for the program. Four interns were denied contract renewals in the first two years. This year it appears that three more interns will be screened out of the profession. In the six years immediately preceding the intern program, only one new teacher was denied a contract. I suggest that internships not only will give teachers considerable authority to police their own ranks and upgrade professional competence, but they also will meet with acceptance by the public. Traditional lines of authority in this key process will slowly fade as unions move to take greater control of their profession.

Funding for schools will continue to be a source of friction between public school interests and those who seek to hold down taxes. Teacher unions have traditionally played important roles in lobbying efforts for increased state aid and in campaigns to increase local taxes. The significance of this role in the future will be determined by whether the two major unions, the NEA and the AFT, merge. Lobbying already seen as effective in statehouses and in Congress, will be even more intense in the future if merger can be achieved.

Tax reform will more and more attract the efforts of teacher unions. Reform of state aid formulas and efforts to shift the school tax base away from property taxes would seem to be the major focus. Again, successes will directly benefit students and parents as well as teachers. Within the educational family, teacher unions have emerged as the most effective spokesmen for tax reform and changes in distribution formulas. Part of this effectiveness is attributable to sheer numbers, but a greater level of sophistication in lobbying and in attracting media attention is also evident. Coalitions are the norm in today's legislative scene. While no educational organization is excluded from these coalitions, the principal participants in and instigators of coalitions are the unions. Such efforts only enhance the influence of local teacher organizations within their respective districts.

The four areas discussed in this paper are not meant to be all-inclusive as far as the future of education is concerned and the role teacher unions will play in that future. They do, however, go directly to the major problems that plague schools today: low public confidence, inadequate performance, low self-esteem among teachers, and inadequate funding. It would be difficult to imagine any solutions or improvements in these areas without critical roles being played by teachers through their unions and their new found power. The advent of teacher power, even teacher militancy, can only be seen as a positive force for improvement of our nation's schools over the long pull.

Those who view teacher unions as a cause of educational problems or as barriers to reforms and improvements fail to understand not only the dynamics of collective teacher action but the nature of the problems teachers face in the classroom as well. Teacher dissatisfaction with being excluded from the making of decisions that most directly affected them and their students was a major reason for the growth of teacher unions. Teachers' futures, and the future of public education, are forever linked to their unions.

COMPULSORY UNIONISM: AN EDUCATIONAL TRAGEDY

Edward Remington

> The "agency shop" funnels large sums of money
> into union treasuries from people whom that union
> has not sold sufficiently on the "benefits." They
> are unwilling to become members and pay dues. An
> "agency shop" is an admission by the union of its
> inability to sell its services. It, therefore,
> resorts to forcing itself upon workers. [1]
>
> Educator Joy Davenport in
> response to NEA demands that
> she be fired for refusing
> to pay forced union dues

It all started in 1978. Joy Davenport stood before students at Massachusetts' Greenfield High School teaching supervised studies. It was October and the start of another school term for the twenty-year veteran and, like years hence, the fall brought renewed vigor from the summer respite. But this year was different. An affiliate of the National Education Association-union (NEA) had rammed an "agency shop" provision into the contract, forcing all nonunion educators to pay forced union fees for representation they neither voted for or even wanted. And that's what got Joy Davenport and others in trouble.

Ms. Davenport did not want union representation. To her, it was a matter of choice; she wanted to represent herself and stand before her employer to discuss the conditions of her contract. Neither did she wish to support the political and ideological goals of the union -- goals she could not in good conscience agree with. After weighing the matter, Ms. Davenport took a stand for freedom and fought for her right to support organizations of her own choosing.

However, Ms. Davenport's stand drew the ire of the NEA officials. In fact, the union demanded that she and the other dissenting nonmembers of the union be immediately fired. The NEA-union even filed prohibited practice charges with the state labor relations commission against the Greenfield school board for failing to take quick action against the highly regarded teachers. The NEA hierarchy pointed to the state "agency shop" law the union had pushed through the state legislature which authorized the firing of any educator who wouldn't bankroll the union.

It didn't stop there. The NEA agents further told the independent-minded teachers that if they did not want to finance the union's political goals they would have to appear before an internal union procedure, in other words, a kangaroo court. But Ms. Davenport shrugged off the union's threats. She enlisted the aid of the National Right to Work Legal Defense Foundation and fought back. She refused to be cowed by the NEA's assertions that little or no dues money had been expended on political and ideological causes.

Ms. Davenport was right. After a three-year legal battle, the Supreme Judicial Court of Massachusetts upheld a lower court decision stating that the teachers could not be forced to finance political activities against their will. Ms. Davenport was fortunate. Unlike many of her colleagues throughout the nation, she had the Foundation behind her. Still, to this day, preserving individual freedom of choice in Greenfield's public schools is a never-ending battle -- and a battle the community's teachers must wage to preserve one of our most basic and fundamental rights -- freedom of choice and association.

The Union Official Catch 22

Sadly, Joy Davenport's fight for her freedom of choice is far from unique. In fact, a majority of the nation's three million educators are confronted daily with having to sacrifice their academic and individual freedoms by having to pay union dues in order to keep their jobs. For some educators, joining a union represents their personal interests. But for others -- including thousands of individual educators presently embroiled in court suits to protect their freedom of choice -- forced union membership is an anathema to the very basic American right to academic freedom.

To pinpoint the reason why Joy Davenport and others are locked into forced union membership contracts is a simple matter of state law. In Massachusetts, officials of the National Education Association and the American Federation of Teachers successfully strong-armed the state legislature in 1978 into enacting a compulsory "agency shop" measure against the Commonwealth's teachers. The "agency shop" requirement, long a top goal of the NEA and AFT union officials, forces educators to pay union fees equivalent to membership fees for unwanted representation and the privilege to be a "nonmember" -- or more aptly termed, a captive passenger. Educators who refuse to pay dues can be, and are, fired legally at union official demand.

The Massachusetts "agency shop" authorization, like other similar teacher union official-backed state laws, is firmly entrenched with the three P's: politics, power, and protection. Like their counterparts in the private sector, the NEA and AFT union officials have borrowed a page from the National Labor Relations Act (NLRA) of 1935. The NLRA and its federally authorized provisions for compulsory unionism have been scaled down by teacher union officials as a model for state legislation. Although a federal "agency shop" law over teachers remains a top priority of the NEA and AFT officials, the Big Labor hierarchy has been blocked from mandating forced membership nationwide.

Predictably, the NEA and AFT officials have poured their political warchests into state campaigns to wrestle compulsory unionism authorizations from the state legislatures. To date, sixteen states have been snared by the union hierarchy. Two states, Hawaii and Rhode Island, actually require teachers to pay forced "agency shop" fees to teacher union officials before they can even enter the classroom. In Minnesota, school boards are forced to levy forced "agency shop" requirements at the request of the union bargaining agent. Eleven states (California, Conecticut, Illinois, Massachusetts, Montana, New Jersey, New York, Ohio, Oregon, Washington, and Wisconsin) permit negotiations for forced dues although elected school board officials have the right to reject their adoption.

However, Big Labor officials often succeed in tempting school officials with the false promise of "labor peace" in return for the power to collect fees from teachers. They also accept vastly lower salary increases in return for their own protection -- forced fees. In Alaska, Pennsylvania, and the District of Columbia, teacher union officials are empowered to negotiate "maintenance of membership" agreements, forcing educators who join the union to remain members for the duration of a two to three-year contract. But the vast majority of the state legislatures have refused to buckle under to NEA and AFT demands for compulsion. Thirty states have strict prohibitions against compulsory unionism for their public employees; twenty have enacted popular Right to Work laws, which prohibit the "agency shop" and protect individuals' rights to decide for themselves whether or not to join a union. Another nine states are currently driving towards enactment of freedom of choice legislation.

In fact, the tide is turning and the Right to Work movement is gaining more and more momentum throughout the country. Too many school officials have had to fire outstanding teachers whose only crime was their refusal to pay forced "agency shop" fees. In those states that have acceded to compulsory unionism legislation, the teacher union officials' defense of forced fees has become much too transparent and a lesson to be learned by other state legislatures considering the NEA and AFT-backed "agency shop" scheme.

The argument offered by the teacher union hierarchy in defense of compulsory unionism is less than convincing. To a large degree, NEA and AFT apologists rely on the claim that educators who don't pay up are "free riders." What the union officials don't say is that they were the ones who waged an all-out lobbying blitz to extract the power to be the "exclusive" or monopoly bargaining agent of all teachers in a bargaining unit -- even over those who voted for another union or no union at all. Once designated the monopoly bargaining agent, the union invariably returns to the legislature with the hollow argument that it is burdened by monopoly representation privileges and that it is only just for all teachers to pay up or be fired. What unions refuse to "remember" is that the privilege of monopoly bargaining is joined by an obligation, one they lobbied for, to represent members and nonmembers "equally and without discrimination."

However, an increasing number of lawmakers see the monopoly bargaining scheme for what it is: a teacher official Catch 22, purposely designed to rob individual educators of their right to choose whether or not they want union membership. Under monopoly bargaining, individual educators have no right whatsoever to represent themselves individually before their employers. In fact, they are prohibited in some circumstances, from even discussing the terms of their contract with their employer. And in _every_ instance where legislation has been introduced to relieve teacher union officials of their so-called burden of representing nonmembers, the proposals have been vigorously fought by those same union officials! Thus, monopoly bargaining is becoming widely regarded as a blotch on the First Amendment's guarantee of freedom of association.

Another ill-conceived and weak attempt to justify compulsory unionism by teacher union officials is that forced fees are levied against nonmembers through a "democratic" election. Again, what teacher union officials fail to point out is that they are private organizations, not sovereign governments. Under our republic, the power to tax is rightfully and strictly limited to governments of, by, and for the people. If other private organizations were to rely on compulsion, all farmers would be forced to join the Farm Bureau;

98

all veterans, the American Legion; all manufacturers, the National Association of Manufacturers, and so on. If majority rule were to be truly applied, no one in America would be permitted to join a union since a full 80% of the nation's workforce have opted not to join a union.

Aside from a misapplication of the union role as a government, "agency shop" elections are hardly democratic -- and any insinuations that they are simply aren't true. A case in point is Rutgers University in New Jersey, where officials of the American Association of University Professors-union (AAUP) recently rammed a forced fee authorization into the faculty contract without a vote of those at whom the "agency shop" clause was directed -- the non-AAUP members. In this blatant manipulation of the Rutgers' faculty, the AAUP hierarchy permitted only union members to vote on the forced-fee levy, thus assuring themselves that all Rutgers' faculty members would be forced into their union. As a result, 2,752 faculty members who did not belong to the AAUP-union were shut out of their right to vote and the union minority of 1,351 rammed into the unwanted master contract a provision requiring all faculty members to bow to AAUP demands for tribute -- or be fired.

If the teacher union officials' notions of majority rule weren't enough, the last and most spurious argument they espouse is that compulsory unionism is necessary to ensure a strong union. Samuel Gompers, the father of organized labor, rejected compulsory unionism out of hand when he laid down the founding principle of the American trade movement. Speaking at his last AFL convention, Gompers stressed: "I want to urge devotion to the fundamental principles of human liberty -- the principles of voluntarism. No lasting gain has ever come from compulsion. If we seek to force, we but tear apart that which, united, is invincible ... I want to say to you, men and women of the American labor movement, do not reject the cornerstone upon which labor's structure has been builded -- but base your all upon voluntary principles and illumine your every problem by consecrated devotion to that highest of all purposes -- human well being in the fullest, widest, deepest sense." [2]

Teacher Officials Reject Freedom Plank

But reject it they did. Since its inception, the entire teacher union movement has been built upon that which Samuel Gompers felt strongest against -- compulsory unionism. And today, the NEA, AFT, and AAUP-union officials have erected a stronghold of compulsion over the teaching profession which has prompted the spiraling decline in the quality of education for the last fifteen years. Over a short span of two decades, the nation's three teacher unions evolved from professional, dedicated associations devoted to enhancing the quality of education in the United States to militant labor unions which have admittedly placed individual freedoms and the education of our youngsters far behind their efforts to become the dominant political force in our nation.

The NEA led the transformation, making its first moves to take over American education in the early 1960's. It was during this time that a militant faction within the association launched a successful coup to steer the NEA on a path of compulsory unionism. With a coercion-minded leadership at the helm, the new NEA officials initiated a "unification" scheme. Under the "unified" system, every educator who joined a local education association also had to join and pay dues to the state and national NEA affiliates. By instituting the unification drive, the NEA top brass assured themselves of a massive influx of dues money to use in the political arena.

In 1970, the NEA bosses had their sights solidly fixed. Proclaimed then-NEA president George Fischer during a speech at the union's annual convention: "We are determined to control who enters, who stays, and who leaves the profession. Once this is done, we can also control the teacher training institutions."[3] Just two years later, NEA president Catherine Barrett reiterated Fischer's promise, stating that "We [NEA] are the biggest potential political striking force in this country and we are determined to control the direction of education." Even then, Barrett promised to have ten million dollars on hand for the 1976 presidential elections, adding that NEA would not "only be competitive with any existing political force, but would be the greatest of political forces."[4]

By 1976, the union's officials poured an estimated $100 million into the presidential elections, in both direct campaign contributions and "indirect" or "soft" services, such as running massive phone banks and voter registration drives, and employing full-time lobbyists in each of the 435 congressional districts. Leading up to the 1980 presidential elections, the 1.5 million member NEA sent 435 delegates to the Democratic National Convention -- the largest block in history.

In comparison, the 550,000 member American Federation of Teachers-union (AFT) is smaller -- but no less militant. Affiliated with the AFL-CIO, the AFT-union's raw strength lies in the large urban cities, such as New York, Baltimore, Chicago, Detroit, and Washington, D.C. During the early 1960's, the AFT and its president, Albert Shanker, took on the NEA for supremacy over the nation's teachers. Brazenly candid about forced dues scheming, AFT representative John Schmind laid down his union's guiding edict in 1971, ordering his underlings to "organize all the teachers, clerks, and semi-professionals and get a closed shop."[5] Ever drifting away from professionalism in teaching, AFT president Albert Shanker declared just four years later that a "professional is the closest thing to a propped-up dead body" he knew of. In 1980, the leader of the AFT political machine launched a campaign to usurp the NEA blockade, ordering his representatives to organize all NEA members. "Everyone of those teachers who is not a member in our local makes us weaker," he said. Then he added that "anybody who thinks teachers should go it alone deserves a visit to the psychiatrist."[6]

While smaller than the NEA and AFT-unions, the 75,000 member AAUP-union is the principal abductor of higher education faculty throughout the nation. Once a professional organization, the union has now placed forced fees and coercion ahead of the so-called defense of academic freedom. One such example recently occurred in Michigan where the militant AAUP officials called an illegal strike at Eastern Michigan University where the AAUP hierarchy was demanding the power to fire any faculty member who refused to cough up "agency shop" dues. Now the union has begun to run joint organizing campaigns with both the NEA and AFT officials, sharing in the spoils of collecting "agency shop" dues.

Political Power Fueled By Forced Fees

Because NEA, AFT and AAUP-union officials derive their political power from compulsory unionism, individuals who are forced fee payers are faced with a double-barreled infringement of their freedom of choice and association, and even their own right to contribute to political causes of their own preference. But as Big Labor officials carry out their merciless plot to tax and control employee freedoms, union and non-union members alike are rising in resistance to protect individual liberty. Spearheaded by a handful of courageous men, the National Right to Work Committee, organized in 1955 by forced union members of the Brotherhood of Railway Trainmen, works for the enactment of freedom of choice laws to protect the American work force. Since the committee's inception, twenty states have either passed or solidified a strong commitment to freedom of choice for their employees with Right to Work laws. Another ten state legislatures have laws on the books protecting individuals from compulsory unionism in varying degrees. Many more new state Right to Work laws can be expected within a few short years.

Aside from statutory protection against compulsory unionism providing individuals with the right to join or not join a union, Right to Work laws are a proven economic boost to the American economy. According to statistics compiled by the U.S. Department of Labor, states that have had the foresight to enact Right to Work laws have led the nation in the creation of new jobs, have the highest per capita disposable income, and the lowest unemployment rates for the past ten years. The reason for the economic boom in Right to Work states is that freedom of choice laws offer a conducive business environment and curtail abusive, runaway union power. For example, in Idaho, a non-Right to Work state, Big Labor recently forced an entire business to close down. The Bunker Hill Company, a mine and smelter complex, was facing bankruptcy. An investor group agreed to help save the company and 1,500 jobs in exchange for wage and seniority concessions. The company's rank and file overwhelmingly voted in favor of the proposal, but Pittsburgh, Pennsylvania-based officials of the Steelworkers International refused to sign the contract and forced the plant to go out of business in early 1982.

Yet, union officials continue to ignore the economic incentives of Right to Work laws, claiming that forced union members achieve higher earnings. That is a blatant untruth. According to recent statistics compiled by the World Report of the First National Bank of Chicago, employees in Right to Work states have a per capita disposable income of $4,606 compared to forced union members in non-Right to Work states who average $4,601. Furthermore, statistics released by the U.S. Department of Labor show that the Right to Work states created 677,000 new manufacturing jobs between 1972 and 1982. During the same time, the non-Right to Work states lost more than 789,000 jobs.

Forced Unionism Injustice Fought

In an effort to combat union officials in the legal arena, and to secure precedent-setting decisions safeguarding employee freedom of choice, the National Right to Work Legal Defense Foundation was established in 1968. Providing free legal aid to victims of compulsory unionism, the Foundation has acted in concert with Concerned Educators Against Forced Unionism (CEAFU), the education division of the Committee, to advance individual liberty in the teaching profession.

102

In 1976, CEAFU Advisory Board member, Dr. Anne B. Parks, a renowned Detroit, Michigan, high school guidance counselor, was fired for no other reason than her refusal to bankroll the local affiliate of the AFT-union. Steadfast in her belief that no individual should be forced to contribute financially to political causes against her will, Parks enlisted the aid of the National Right to Work Legal Defense Foundation and fought the AFT-union officials all the way to the U.S. Supreme Court. While she remains fired and barred from school grounds for refusing to support the AFT-union, the High Court ruled unanimously that educators cannot be forced to support unwanted political causes and ordered the militant teachers union to refund forced-fee money to educators who don't agree with the union's heavy-handed political crusades.

In another challenge over the use of forced fees for politics, the National Right to Work Committee took the NEA-union to task in 1978 for using an insidious "negative check-off" scheme to force educators to pay compulsory political contributions against their will. Under the scheme, NEA officials had local boards of education automatically deduct the forced-fee payments from teachers' paychecks without their consent -- a massive violation of the Federal Campaign Act of 1971. Despite the blatant illegality of the NEA's "negative check-off," the union netted nearly one million dollars from the operation and funneled the money to federal candidates during the 1976 and 1978 congressional elections -- chiefly to candidates who pledged themselves to the union's compulsory unionism demands. Filing a lawsuit on behalf of the nation's teachers, the Committee forced the Big Labor-dominated Federal Election Commission (FEC) to take actions against the NEA. The FEC, then chaired by former assistant general counsel to the AFL-CIO, Thomas E. Harris, had no recourse but to condemn the "negative check-off" scheme. In the fall of 1980, the NEA-union officials admitted to using the illegal collection scam and paid a $75,000 fine -- a mere wrist slap considering much of the tainted money could not be returned.

Until employees are freed from the shackles of forced union support, Big Labor officials will continue to ignore the wishes of employees because the offense far outpays the punishment. Consider the recent sampling of legal battles that CEAFU activists, with the aid of the Right to Work Foundation, have waged:

Item: Throughout the state of New York, AFT-union officials are attempting to sidestep state law by not providing a refund system to teachers who want forced political fees returned. Furthermore, teachers have waited more than a year to receive a political refund of 76¢ -- an amount AFT officials claim proportionally represents how little they are involved politically.

Item: In Illinois, Susan LaVine, a tenured, outstanding foreign language teacher in Lyons township, was fired at NEA demand for refusing to pay forced "agency shop" dues. Because state law did not authorize "agency shop" firings in 1978, LaVine was vindicated. But she remained unemployed because her position had been filled.

Item: In Michigan, two CEAFU activitists, Paul and Lori Chamberlain, were threatened with firing by NEA officials over their joint refusal to pay a $75 strike fee to finance a strike in another school district. The Chamberlains, with the help of the Foundation, had to go to court to have NEA officials blocked from imposing the illegal requirement.

Item: And in Simi Valley, California, NEA officials threatened the community with mass dismissals to teachers who refused to pay forced "agency shop" dues. Two teachers were actually served subpoenas in their classrooms for not supporting the NEA-union officials.

If the teacher union officials' flagrant attempts to dictate the political and ideological leanings weren't enough, yet another tragic consequence of compulsory unionism upon the teaching profession is its suppression of the educators' academic freedom. Said CEAFU Advisory Board member Carol Applegate when she decided to fight Grand Blanc, Michigan, NEA officals who had her fired for refusing to pay forced tribute in 1968: "I vowed to test in any way possible the validity of a system that demands, 'You either pay dues to the teacher union or you will be fired.' I did this because I could not in good conscience stand before my class and say 'think' when I was being denied the right to think myself."7

No less adamant on the importance of academic freedom, renowned educator and scholar Russell Kirk states: "So I come full cycle, back to academic freedom -- which is freedom from ideology, freedom from obsessive political activism, freedom from centralized power over the intellect, freedom to teach and study and think. Being treated as if he were one of an unthinkable herd, incompetent to make his own decisions -- is the ultimate insult to a man of learning."8

In fact, the teacher union officials have admitted that their takeover attempts are directly tied to a bent creed of treating teachers like "beasts." In 1976, when the NEA-union officials were caught stealing political money from teachers via the illegal "negative check-off" system, the union's general counsel tried to justify the scam by stating: "It is well recognized that if you take away the mechanism of payroll deduction, you won't collect a penny from the people, and it has nothing to do with voluntary or involuntary. I think it has to do with the nature of the beast, and the beasts are our teachers who are dispersed all over cities who simply don't come up with money regardless of the purpose."[9]

The nation's students aren't treated any differently. Said a top official of the NEA's state affiliate in Oregon in early 1982: "The major purpose of our association is not the education of children, rather it is or ought to be retention and/or preservation of our members' rights. We earnestly care about the kids and learning, but that is secondary to the other goals." Just as vocal as to where students stand with teacher officials, the AFT hierarchy recently ordered Florida organizers to install a compulsory unionism curriculum in Dade County schools. In a bulletin issued to its members, the AFT officials demanded that young children sing "Solidarity Forever" in music class, that problems which union officials have with management be used to illustrate everyday math problems, and that slanted union periodicals fill the library shelves.

Polls Confirm: Let Individuals Decide

There is little, if any, disagreement among the American taxpaying public and the academic community that the teacher union officials' plan to take over education must be stopped. Every Gallup, Roper, and Opinion Research poll for the past ten years has consistently shown that 70% of the American citizenry -- including a majority of union members -- favor the elimination of compulsory unionism with the adoption of Right to Work laws. In education, the 1981 <u>Instructor</u> magazine poll, which was conducted among 225,000 subscribers, found that 82% of the nation's educators are adamantly opposed to forced unionism. More telling, 72% of the respondents were members of the NEA and AFT unions.

According to Kurt Hanslowe, a member of the Cornell University faculty, the coercive interests of union officials are diametrically opposed to the wishes of the American citizenry. Says the former assistant counsel for the United Autoworkers union (UAW):

[T]he union shop in public employment has the potential of becoming a neat mutual backscratching mechanism, whereby public employees, representatives, and politicians each reinforce the other's interests and domains, with the individual public employee and the individual citizen left to look on, while his employment condition and his tax rate and public policies generally are being decided by entrenched and mutually supportive government officials and collective bargaining representatives over whom the public has diminishing control.[10]

That union officials are out of step with the American public and the education profession is beyond dispute. The only remaining question is when will every individual in the nation be afforded Right to Work protection. Since the advent of compulsory unionism in all areas of employment, the nation's lawmakers and elected school officials have learned the hard way that union-demanded firing of such employees as Joy Davenport and Anne Parks is a price too steep to pay. They know all too well that adherence to union official dictates will result only in the tragic firing of dedicated, outstanding employees whose only "crime" was to stick up for their individual freedoms. Now, our elected officials must remain firm in their commitment to the principles of liberty on which our nation was founded. To do otherwise will only ensure union domination over the individual in the workplace.

Notes

[1] Statement before the Greenfield, Massachusetts School Committee, May 31, 1979.

[2] Florence C. Thorne, Gompers: American Statesman (New York: Philosophical Library, 1957), p. 61.

[3] Speech made during the 108th Annual Convention of the National Education Association, San Francisco, July 3, 1970, p. 5.

[4] Interview with Catherine Barrett, "NEA Signals New Role of Teachers," Washington Star News, July 2, 1972.

[5] "Must School Boards Force Teachers to Join Unions?" National Association of Educational Negotiators Bulletin (September, 1980), p. 4.

[6] Speech made before the 65th Annual Convention of the American Federation of Teachers, Denver, July 13, 1981.

[7] "Academic Freedom: The Carol Applegate Story," statement by the National Right to Work Legal Defense Foundation, October, 1973.

[8] Russell Kirk, "Academic Freedom and the 'Agency Shop,'" Education (February-March, 1974), p. 198.

[9] "NEA Union Lawyer Calls Teachers 'Beasts,'" Los Angeles Times, March 18, 1979.

[10] Kurt L. Hanslowe, The Emerging Law of Labor Relations In Public Employment (Ithaca, N.Y.: New York State Schol of Industrial and Labor Relations, 1967), p. 115.

PART FIVE -- MERIT PAY

Is merit pay an appropriate basis for teacher salaries?

An examination of salaries and wages in public and private enterprises produces few generalizations other than that compensation amounts tend to be arbitrary, individuals get what they can get, and the salary range in any occupation approaches "what the traffic will bear." Individual expertise, the status of a particular occupation, the nature of the work, the assumed importance of a job to society, the supply of and demand for workers, and the financial condition of the employing enterprise exert varying degrees of influence on a person's remuneration. Teachers in America, for example, historically have demonstrated little expertise, except at the college level, where average salaries have tended to be higher than in elementary and secondary schools. Factors such as lack of expertise, but also the temporary nature of teaching jobs, the relative powerlessness of teachers, and the limited role assigned to the school contributed to low staus during much of our history. The presumed relatively short work day and school year, and the widespread employment of women contributed to the view of teaching as a soft job. Since teachers were working with children, that is, non-productive individuals, their occupation was judged of minor social importance. While it is true that during the years of this nation's most rapid growth more classrooms were being built than teachers were being trained, since somebody could always be found to man those rooms, even supply and demand factors did not work in teachers' favor. Finally, teachers were employed by towns and small communities which had limited financial resources for any public project, and in the Jacksonian tradition held all adults as able to fill any public role or office.

Today schools are big business, responsibilities assigned to them are constantly growing in number, and teachers have organized to promote their own economic interests. An increasing awareness of the importance of good teachers is matched by a concern with getting and keeping good teachers. Compared with other occupations requiring a college degree, however, teaching salaries are low. They are low even when compared with some occupations requiring no training. Assuming there is a relationship between good schools and teacher salaries, how can the latter be improved? On several occasions in our history one answer has been to pay teachers on the basis of assessed performance rather than experience and training.

109

Theodore Lownik Library
Illinois Benedictine College
Lisle, Illinois 60532

The first of the two following articles takes the position that the public schools must adopt merit-based salary approaches if they are serious about attracting and retaining quality teachers for their classrooms. Included in such approaches are incentive pay, master teacher plans, and school-based merit pay. Adopting one or more of these practices can contribute to a restoration of public confidence in our schools.

The second article views merit pay as just one more gimmick suggested by those who fail to consider the complexities of teaching and learning. In the absence of any favorable experience, arguments for merit pay rest upon dubious assumptions. It is even more doubtful that the very problems such proposals seek to meliorate -- inability to attract the best persons to teaching and to keep them in the schools -- will be significantly affected even if a merit plan is adopted.

PHILIP KEARNEY is Professor of Education and Chair, Division of Educational Foundations, Policy, and Administration, School of Education, University of Michigan. Previous positions include Deputy Director of the Institute for Educational Leadership in Washington, D.C. (1977-1980), and Associate Superintendent of Public Instruction for the State of Michigan (1968-1977). His doctorate is from the University of Chicago.

SAM R. SNYDER is Associate Professor of Educational Theory and Social Foundations in the College of Education and Allied Professions of the University of Toledo. For several years he has been engaged in research on the racial ecology of the public schools of Toledo, Ohio. His doctorate is from the University of Michigan. He has also taught in public schools in New Jersey and Ohio.

MERIT PAY: A NEEDED REFORM

C. Philip Kearney

"If we want to achieve excellence, we must reward it....
It's a simple American philosophy that dominates many other
professions, so why not this one?"[1] With these words, spoken
to a recent gathering of state teachers of the year, President
Ronald Reagan added his voice to the growing chorus of Americans advocating merit pay for teachers. Indeed, why not merit
pay? Why not pay teachers on the basis of performance, or on
the basis of differentiated responsibilities, or on the basis
of supply and demand rather than simply on the number of academic credit hours and years of experience they have accumulated? As Tennessee Governor Lamar Alexander, a strong ad-
vocate of a master teacher plan for his state, put it: "Virtually every other important part of the American workplace
has found some fair way to pay more money for doing a good
job. There's absolutely no reason we can't do it in public
school teaching."[2]

Merit Pay: A Centerpiece of Education Reform

Merit pay for teachers is not a new concept. It has
been with us for a number of years. In the early part of this
century merit pay schedules were common. It was not until the
1920's, in efforts to remove inequities in pay between elementary and secondary teachers and between males and females,
that the so-called single salary schedule came into being.
Over the next several decades, the single salary schedule--
under which the only criteria for salary differentials are
academic training and years of service--became the dominant
mode of paying public school teachers. Even so, there were
periodic calls for a return to merit-based approaches, and the
debate waxed and waned.

Now suddenly, in the mid-1980's, the public's attention
again has been focused on this controversial topic as a result
of the flood of national reports that surfaced during 1983
calling for sweeping reforms in American education. The most
visible of these reports perhaps is A National At Risk, the
work of the National Commission on Excellence (later to become the President's Commission on Excellence). The Commission urges that salaries of teachers "be professionally competitive, market sensitive, and performance-based."[3] A second
national report, the Twentieth Century Fund's Making The
Grade, proposes "reconsideration of merit-based personnel

111

systems for teachers."[4] A third major report, <u>Action for Excellence</u>, issued by the Education Commission of the States, advocates development of "ways to measure the effectiveness of teachers and reward outstanding performance."[5] President Ronald Reagan, as we have seen, along with most of the 1984 Democratic candidates for President, has jumped on the merit pay bandwagon. And the same circumstances hold in most states. In Michigan, for example, the Republican Party Caucus issued its own educational reform report which, among its recommendations, proposes a master teacher plan with financial incentives to encourage good teachers to remain in the profession.[6]

But it is not only reformers and policymakers who are calling for renewed efforts to develop and implement merit-based approaches. A great part of the general public is of the same view. Several recent national opinion surveys indicate that better than 60 percent of the public favors including performance as a factor in determining teachers' salaries. The 15th Annual Gallup Poll revealed that 61 percent of the respondents favored paying a teacher "on the basis of the quality of his or her work."[7] Those who were familiar with the report of the National Commission on Excellence were even more strongly in favor of merit-based approaches--with favorable responses increasing to 71 percent. Teachers also joined in the chorus. In a poll conducted by the National Association of School Boards among elementary and secondary teachers, some 63 percent felt that more effective classroom teachers should receive larger salary increments than less effective teachers. Over 60 percent of the responding mathematics and science teachers favored paying bonuses in areas of teacher shortage.[8] Similar attitudes were revealed in a third major survey, undertaken by the Gallup Organization for the U.S. Chamber of Commerce. Sixty-six percent of the interviewees felt that teachers' pay should not be based on seniority but rather on how well teachers teach.[9]

Thus, through national and state reports calling for educational reform, through increasingly favorable views of the general public, and through a complex of other political, social, and economic forces, merit pay has become an issue of central concern to the nation and an item high on the agenda of most public policymaking bodies. For many, be they reformers, policymakers, or general citizens, merit pay is seen as one means of restoring excellence to American public education. Irrespective of one's views on merit pay--pro, con, or undecided--it is an issue that will be with us for some time to come. It has received far too much current attention not to be.

Merit Pay Defined

Like many terms in education, merit pay is not well-defined. It means different things to different people. It is a term rather loosely used to describe any number of financial reward programs for teachers and, sometimes, for administrators. Jordan and Borkow, from the Congressional Research Service of the Library of Congress, suggest that there are at least three identifiable but separate and different kinds of programs that usually are lumped in discussions of merit pay: (1) incentive pay programs, (2) master teacher proposals, and (3) true merit pay programs.[10]

Incentive pay programs provide an additional salary supplement to any teacher who teaches under specific, predetermined conditions--for example, in a school characterized by severe educational disadvantage or in a shortage area such as mathematics or science. In its pure form, the incentive pay program rewards a teacher for the conditions under which she or he teaches, not for how she teaches or the amount of responsibility she is willing to assume. The "Second Mile Plan" of the Houston, Texas school district is a classic example of an incentive pay program. Teachers receive incentive pay if they are willing to teach in a high priority location, if they are teaching in critical staff shortage areas, if they exhibit outstanding teacher attendance, if they complete approved college course work or in-service training, or if they work in a unique school. They also receive an additional stipend if they teach in a school that reaches its learning goals. All teachers in the school receive the bonus in this latter case. However, under our categorical scheme, this is not an example of incentive pay but rather true merit pay. More about that later.

Master teacher proposals generally provide a staged career development plan for teachers, with differential pay for differential responsibilities. Opportunities are available to proceed through the stages, for example, apprentice teacher, journeyman teacher, master teacher, with increasing responsibilities and increasing pay at each stage. Generally limits are placed on the number of teachers accepted in each of the categories. These plans may operate on a state-wide basis, such as Tennessee's, or on a local district basis, such as the one in Charlotte-Mecklenburg, North Carolina. Under the "Better Schools Program" proposed by Tennessee Governor Lamar Alexander, there are four levels of certification: apprentice teacher, professional teacher, senior teacher, and master teacher. For the professional teacher, senior teacher, and master teacher, there are salary supplements geared to each level and, for the senior and master teacher, opportunity to work on a 10-month, 11-month, or 12-month contract. Master teachers who choose to work on a 12-month contract earn up to $7,000 in supplementary pay. The major responsiblity of the senior and master teachers continues to be classroom instruction. Additional responsibilities are above and beyond classroom instruction and include counseling, training, and evaluating other teachers, working on curriculum activities, and the like.

True merit pay programs--as opposed to incentive pay and master teacher proposals--are based on how well a teacher performs. Under a true merit pay approach, the teacher undergoes systematic and periodic evaluation and, if her or his performance warrants, receives additional pay. While true merit pay programs are somewhat rare, they do exist. One of the better known and longer duration programs operates in LaDue, Missouri, a school district in suburban St. Louis. The criteria for evaluating performance were developed jointly by teachers and administrators; the principals conduct the evaluation and assign merit points which form the basis for the merit award. A teacher may receive up to 15 merit points with each point being worth $300. A more interesting, and perhaps more viable, approach is that used by the Dallas, Texas public schools. All teachers and staff in a school in which students perform better than expected on standardized tests receive a merit award--$1,500 for each teacher and $750 for each member of the support staff.

Screens and Magnets

The central problem that advocates of merit pay are attempting to address is, of course, the problem of attracting and retaining excellent if not outstanding teachers for the public schools. Or, put another way, it is the problem of improving and maintaining teaching as a high quality profession. A concept that is useful in sorting out and clarifying the several approaches often advocated to improve the teaching profession is the concept of "screens" and magnets."[11] A screen works to keep undesirable, ill-prepared, or incompetent persons out of the profession, either by blocking initial entry or by ousting a person who has succeeded in gaining initial entry but who is no longer meeting the standards of the profession. The best examples of currently operating screens are state certification requirements, either for initial certification or for continuing certification.

A magnet, on the other hand, works to entice people into the profession and to keep them there once they have entered. Traditionally, one of the strong magnets of the teaching profession has been the opportunity to serve, the opportunity to fulfill altruistic motives. Another has been time-off in the summers to pursue further education or other interests.

Unfortunately, salary has never been a strong magnet for the teaching profession. Even with the advent of collective bargaining and a general increase in salary levels for teachers, inadequate salaries are a major reason why the schools have not been able to attract and retain as many excellent teachers as are desired and needed. While average teacher salaries have increased by 84.1 percent over the ten year period from 1972-73 to 1982-83, the consumer price index has increased by 128.7 percent.[12] Inflation has far outstripped increases in salaries for teachers. Neither has the relative position of teachers' salaries improved. In 1983, the average starting salary of teachers--$12,700--was still half that of computer specialists, engineers, and accountants.[13] Clearly, the teaching profession is in need of some strong salary magnets if it is to compete successfully with other professions and occupations in attracting and retaining quality personnel for American's classrooms.

Needed: Merit-Based Magnets

Some argue that the solution to the problem is to raise teachers' salaries across-the-board to make the profession competitive with other occupations that attract bright, young college graduates. They contend that only in this way will teaching be able to compete in the labor market for the skilled talent necessary to restore excellence to the schools. If the schools want teachers who are as able as computer specialists, engineers, and accountants, then they will have to pay the supply cost which, according to one recent estimate, would mean raising beginning teachers salaries between $4,000 and $10,000.[14]

This, of course, would also lead to across-the-board raises for all teachers--if not by reason of equity than simply by reason of union demands. The resulting new revenue needs would be staggering and probably impossible of attainment, at least in the short run. The most likely consequence would be small, across-the-board increases for all teachers including beginning teachers, but not substantial enough to attract new talent away from the higher paying occupations.

It would be business as usual with a little better overall salary for all teachers.

What is needed is not only to improve the general salary condition of all teachers, but more importantly to attract bright, new graduates away from non-teaching careers and into the classrooms. In the current labor market, the only realistic way to do this is to pay competitive salaries for scarce talent--particularly for new college graduates with degrees in science and mathematics. Why science and mathematics? Because that is where the most critical shortages are. The National Science Teachers Association, in a recent survey, discovered that almost half of newly-hired mathematics and science teachers are inadequately prepared to teach those subjects. Their counterparts, who are adequately prepared, are lured by the high beginning salaries in business and industry --salaries often in excess of $20,000 a year. Teaching, with its beginning salaries of $12,000 to $13,000 a year, doesn't attract newly-graduated scientists and mathematicians.

Attempts have been made to address the problem by providing opportunities for retraining existing staff in these subjects and providing grants and forgivable loans to students willing to acquire degrees in and teach these subjects. However, a good many of those teachers who are retrained and those students who acquire degrees quickly realize that they also are now "scarce" talent. The results are predictable. They too are lured away by the substantially higher salaries in business and industry.

What is not needed are massive retraining programs in shortage areas like mathematics and science, nor tuition and grant award programs to prospective teachers of subjects in shortage areas. What is needed are salary differentials in shortage areas to attract "scarce" talent. The schools must be able to compete in the labor market with business and industry for new graduates in science and mathematics--and in other critical shortage areas that arise. Perhaps the salaries need not be competitive on a one-for-one basis; there certainly are non-pecuniary attractions to teaching. They must, however, be competitive. The substantial difference in beginning salaries of math and science graduates who go into teaching and those who join business and industry must be substantially reduced if not eliminated. Otherwise the schools will continue to be staffed by less than well-qualified teachers. The answer, for any state or local district, is to establish an incentive pay program that provides the special salary increments necessary to attract qualified teachers in critical shortage areas.

As a companion to the incentive pay program, a state or local district also ought to establish some form of a master teacher program that offers added attractions to persons with "scarce" talent. Most, in addition to competitive salaries, will be interested in opportunities for increased responsibilities and for professional development in their subject matter areas and in the art of teaching. Why not provide these opportunities and, at the same time, provide additional salary increments for the person willing to accept increased responsibilities, to work a longer year, to improve her or his subject matter expertise and teaching skills? Such a program, coupled with an incentive pay program, will do much to attract and retain qualified teachers in critical shortage areas like mathematics and science, as well as qualified teachers in other subject matter areas.

The same school systems, state and local, also might well incorporate a true merit pay approach along the lines of the program operating in the Dallas, Texas public schools. Why waste time arguing about and attempting to deal with the problems and difficulties of setting up a true merit pay program that rewards individual teachers and staff members on the basis of performance? Why not move to a program that uses the performance of the entire school—and the performance of all its students—as the basis for awarding merit pay? Wouldn't the prospect of a substantial salary bonus—say $1,000—provide a powerful incentive to teachers and staff in a school to join together in an effort aimed at meeting and exceeding the achievement expectations that the school board, the administration, and the citizens held for all the children in the school?

Our program—a combination of incentive pay, master teacher plan, and school-based merit pay—also will go a long way toward addressing another serious problem, namely, the declining prestige of the teaching profession and the lack of self-esteem among many teachers. When the public realizes that teachers no longer have a sinecure, that increased pay is not based exclusively on academic credit hours and years of experience, that increased pay calls for increased responsibilities, that increased pay demands increased performance, that highly paid science and mathematics teachers have been attracted away from equally high paying jobs in business and industry, then—and only then—will teaching be looked upon as a prestigious profession.

Perhaps then public school teachers will begin to hold themselves in at least the same esteem as their counterparts in colleges and universities, who traditionally have been subject to some form of merit pay. In the typical university situation, beginning salaries are individually determined and based in part on the "scarcity" of talent; and evaluations of performance help determine yearly increases. The master teacher plan also is present. Rather than apprentice teacher, professional teacher, master teacher, the university employs the faculty ranks of assistant professor, associate professor, and professor. Attainment of these ranks is based on an evaluation of performance. Why wouldn't public school teachers who are willing to subject themselves to similar professional criteria be held in the same esteem?

Finally, the acceptance of merit-based salary approaches is a step vital to the restoration of the public's confidence in the schools and, most importantly, the public's willingness to continue to provide the dollars needed to ensure excellence in the schools. We live in an age of accountability. The public is demanding increased accountability in the expenditure of public funds. The public is calling for increased productivity in the schools. The public wants to be assured that teachers are teaching and that, somehow, their salaries are related to the quality of their teaching. An incentive pay program, a master teacher plan, a true merit pay system all go a long way toward providing this assurance. The public simply will not continue to provide money without this assurance.

A Final Word

There are other arguments that support merit-based salary approaches; there are arguments against such approaches. But doesn't the basic concept, in and of itself, have merit? Doesn't the idea that performance ought to be a vital factor in salary determination just make good common sense? Again, as President Reagan noted, "It's a simple American philosophy that dominates many other professions, so why not this one?"[15] So why not this one?

Notes

[1] As quoted in American Association of School Administrators, _Some Points To Consider When You Discuss Merit Pay_ (Arlington, Virginia: The Association, 1983), p. 5.

[2] Ibid.

[3] The Naional Commission on Excellence in Education, _A Nation at Risk: The Imperative for Educational Reform_ (Washington, D.C.: U.S. Government Printing Office, 1983), p. 30.

[4] The Twentieth Century Fund, _Making the Grade: Report of the Twentieth Century Fund Task Force on Federal Elementary and Secondary Educational Policy_ (New York: The Fund, 1983), p. 10.

[5] The Education Commission of the States, _Action for Excellence: Report of the Task Force on Education for Economic Growth_ (Denver: The Commission, 1983) p. 27.

[6] The Michigan State Republican Caucus, _Excellence in Education: A Republican Action Plan for the '80's_ (Lansing: The Caucus, 1983), p. 3.

[7] George Gallup, "The 15th Annual Gallup Poll of the Public's Attitudes Toward the Public Schools," _Phi Delta Kappan_, LXV (September, 1983), p. 45.

[8] Marilee Rist, "Our Nationwide Poll: Most Teachers Endorse the Merit Pay Concept," _The American School Board Journal_, CLXX (September, 1983), pp. 23-27.

[9] Survey Research Center, Chamber of Commerce of the United States, _Consumer Opinion Survey_ (Washington, D.C.: The Chamber, August, 1983), pp. 2, 10.

[10] See K. Forbis Jordan and Nancy B. Borkow, "Merit Pay for Elementary and Secondary School Teachers: Background Discussion and Analysis of Issues," (Washington, D.C.: Congressional Research Service, The Library of Congress, September, 1983).

[11] See Gary Sykes, "Incentives, Not Tests, Are Needed to Restructure Teaching Profession," _Education Week_ (May, 1983).

[12] The Education Commission of the States, "Raising Teacher Quality Levels," _Issuegram_ (Denver: The Commission, June, 1982), p. 2.

[13] American Assocation of School Administrators, <u>Some Points to Consider When You Discuss Merit Pay</u>, p. 6.

[14] Michael J. Murphy, "Estimating the Supply Costs of Ability for Teachers," Paper Prepared for the Annual Meeting of the American Education Finance Association, Orlando, Florida (March, 1984), p. 11.

[15] As quoted in American Association of School Administrators, <u>Some Points to Consider When You Discuss Merit Pay</u>, p. 5.

MERIT PAY: AN IDEA WHOSE TIME HAS COME . . . AGAIN?

Sam R. Snyder

Merit pay is evidently one of those ideas whose time has come and gone and come again. In a New York Times editorial of 1859 a merit pay proposal is referred to as "stupid"and "unjust."[1] About a hundred years later a philosopher of education concluded that the true profession, built upon a sound theory, "requires of its practitioners a theoretical competence, and, having established its status and value in the eyes of the public, rewards its practitioners on the basis of professional merit."[2] Another quarter-century has passed and the banner is raised once again: merit pay for teachers.

Where does this idea originate, and why does it capture the popular imagination? The thesis of this paper is that the appeal lies in the simplicity of the proposal. It appears to be a simple solution to a simple problem. The reality is that the problem is extremely complex, and the so-called simple solution is no solution at all. As one author has pointed out, pay is one-dimensional and human behavior is multi-dimensional.[3]

Cast in its simplest terms, merit pay is the application of the principles of behavior modification to teachers' behavior. In order to improve teacher performance, one has to positively reinforce appropriate classroom behavior and at the same time negatively reinforce inappropriate classroom behavior. Application of the technique assumes that (1) teachers will do virtually anything for more money, (2) we can identify appropriate teacher behaviors, and (3) we can identify inappropriate teacher behaviors.

The techniques themselves are not new, of course; teachers have been urged to use them on children for years. Nor is their application to teachers a new concept. In one school district in Ohio prospective teachers were told that if they did not join the teachers' union they would receive an additional $200 per year in their pay. This suburban district was a bastion of anti-unionism for years, not because teachers will do anything for money, but because the district attracted teachers whose values were compatible with that prevailing ideology. Like the school district in western Pennsylvania that rewarded teachers with extra compensation for being head of household, for living in the community, for owning one's own home, school districts tend to set policies which will reward appropriate behavior and not reward inappropriate behavior by the professional staff.

Let us assume for sake of argument that assumption #1 is true, that is, teachers will do virtually anything for additional pay. Let us further assume that we can readily identify appropriate teacher behaviors. We can now proceed with our task. What we want our teachers to do seems straightforward enough. We want them to teach our children and young people competence in academic subjects, good study habits, and habits of responsibility and good citizenship. Therefore it should not be too difficult to develop criteria to measure whether or not those goals have been attained.

Academic achievement can be determined by scores on academic achievement tests such as the Iowa Test of Basic Skills. If a teacher is effective, it certainly should have some effect on student achievement. It is reasonable to expect that each student will achieve nine months growth in each subject from one academic year. In all fairness, we must remember that students do sometimes regress over the summer. Therefore, standardized achievement tests should be given twice a year, once in September and again in June. The tests in September can be used as base-line data and merit pay can be distributed based upon the growth exhibited by students on the tests given in June. A formula can be worked out whereby X number of dollars is rewarded for each student who gains more than nine months growth and an equal amount of merit pay is subtracted from those who fail to meet the nine-month growth criterion.

The next step in the process would be to observe those teachers who was successful in raising the scores of their students on standardized achievement tests. Those procedures which seemed to be productive could then be isolated and catalogued and inservice sessions could be held to inculcate those techniques into the repertoire of the other teachers. The unsuccessful teachers could also be observed and inappropriate procedures could be identified. Procedures could then be set up to have these progressively extinguished. Eventually we would create a cadre of supervisors who would be rewarded for modifying the behavior of classroom teachers who would be rewarded for modifying the behavior of students, or so goes the rationale.

It is not difficult to predict the results from this point. There would be no rewards for the students, just the listlessness, apathy, and boredom that comes from performing stupid, repetitive, and intrinsically meaningless tasks. We have enough collective experience with assembly line workers to predict that consequence with some accuracy. The discipline problems created by such a system would require the establishment of the school as a police state, and no citizenry is going to allow itself to be taxed to send its children to jail in the name of education.

A second result would be competition among teachers for different classes and pupils. No one would want the apparent non-learners. To the extent that an individual teacher was sensitive to the school's pay system, she would be spending unnecessary time and energy deciding which students she would want for the next term, influencing individuals to take one of her courses, and pressuring the administration to assign her particular classes. Teacher morale would have to be adversely affected, and cooperation between members of the instructional staff would probably come to an end. These are far from unrealistic claims. They are reasonable hypotheses based on human nature.

In any given school district there are likely to be some excellent teachers and some incompetent teachers, with the majority falling somewhere in between those extremes. It has been argued that if teaching is a profession, then teachers should be paid on the quality of their performance, and better performance should be recognized with greater financial rewards. What better scheme than to institute a pay system which rewards the excellent teachers, encourages the mediocre teachers to excel, and discourages the incompetent teachers from remaining in the system.

Is the behaviorist learning model really appropriate, however? Are standardized test scores truly evidence of the quality of teaching? Both questions clearly have to be answered in the negative. Students may learn much that is not readily demonstrable, especially on paper and pencil tests. Bright students may run with an idea thrown out to the class by the teacher, and in so doing miss all the detail which will show up on the test. A teacher's well-planned and well-executed lesson may have no impact on the youngster whose parents separated the previous day. How meaningful is a test of convergent thinking administered to a highly creative youngster accustomed to quickly milking a point and moving on? Finally, if tests become the determinant of quality, how do we prevent the deadening "teaching for the test"?

Virtually no one objects in principle to merit pay for meritorious service. The idea of rewarding merit is not a new idea, and it is not restricted to education. The federal bureaucracy has had a long history of using merit ratings. However, the way the system works in practice is not always what the designer had in mind. When any department is threatened by budget cuts, administrators always threaten to cut essential personnel to save middle management jobs. The army cuts combat troops; school districts cut teachers. What one soon learns is that meritorious service is a function of loyalty to an administration. What one becomes concerned with is dedication to one's own career, and all other activities become subordinate to personal promotion. In the armed services, it is referred to as "ticket-punching." At the university level it takes the form of pursuing high visibility goals such as short-time research and publication, both to the likely detriment of teaching and advising students. Productivity, in terms of teaching and learning stands to suffer.

If merit ratings and merit pay have not increased productivity and efficiency in public service, perhaps a better model can be found in private industry. Here, too, the record is far from encouraging. It has been observed that most white-collar workers want merit pay until they get it, and then they do not want it at all. The idea behind merit pay is that by rewarding efficiency one will increase productivity among workers. Yet, in a study done at a General Electric plant, 90% of the workers felt that their performance was in the top 50% in productivity.[4] Obviously, in such a situation, no matter how the merit pay pie is cut, almost half of the workers are going to feel disgruntled, disaffected, and dealt with unfairly. There is no evidence to suggest that lower morale and heightened animosity between management and labor increase productivity. In a study using accountants, 37% felt they were in the top ten percentile in performance. Again, this kind of one-dimensional thinking assumes that there is a simple causal relationship between productivity and pay.

If there is not an appropriate model in either public service or private industry, certainly there are some school districts in the United States which have experimented with merit pay. San Marino, California, is one such district. Its merit pay plan had an evaluation form which included instructional skills, pupil relationhips, parent and community relationship, classroom responsibilities, professional growth, and personal factors. San Marino recently dropped this plan, which had been in effect for twenty-five years.[5]

The Charlotte-Mecklenburg, North Carolina school district and the states of Tennessee and Kansas have all studied at

length the fundamental premises of merit pay. All have empha-
tically discarded the idea. California has also been considering a state-wide plan. The estimate is that this plan
would take eight years to become operational and that the cost
would be $30 million the first year. Florida was the first
state to adopt a state-wide plan, but about 10% of the 16,000
school districts in the United States have experimented with
merit pay. Most plans have failed within the first few years.[6]

In virtually every case where merit pay has been seized
upon as a panacea, it has fallen short of expectations. While
many lay people tend to support it, many professsional educators are extremely wary. Most of the "quick-fix" plans are
not well thought-out or well researched. They tend to be
divisive, difficult to communicate, cumbersome to administer,
time-consuming to evaluate, expensive to operate, and ambiguous in their results.

If merit pay for teachers has a record of demonstrated
failure, why does the idea persist? Developing a pay-for-per-
formance plan is deceptively difficult. The analogies between
productivity models such as those used for salesmen and teaching performance soon break down because teacher performance is
not easily gauged by objective standards. If there were a
one-to-one relationship between teaching and learning, then
the problem would be as simple as our original illustration
with the behavior modification schemes of supervisors and
teachers. That is, if teaching were like selling, then if
teaching occurred, someone had to learn, just as when selling
takes place, someone has to buy. Conversely, if learning has
taken place, then someone had to teach. Unfortunately for
those who value simplicity as a supreme value, teaching remains more like fishing. One can devote his day to doing it
without tangible results.

Some merit pay plans, in an attempt to get around the
troublesome problem of subjective evaluation, have devised[7]
standards which measure teacher results, not their methods.
It has been noted however that high tests scores, which may
please parents and principals, are neither the goal of education nor even necessarily the mark of a good teacher. The
idea of using students' scores on standarized tests for
teacher evaluation has come mainly from business leaders who
do not understand the nature of the problem. Performance-
based pay in both the private sector and education has been at
best mixed and inconclusive. What the empirical evidence
seems to suggest is that there are things that merit pay can
and cannot do. What it cannot do is (1) improve the morale of
teachers, (2) entice new teachers into the schools, (3) pre-

vent talented veterans from leaving, or (4) help weed out tenured incompetents. [8]

What merit pay has done historically is break down relations between administration and staffs and be used as an excuse for school boards to perpetuate low salaries; principals to play favorites and discriminate against women, minorities, and union activists; and teachers to suspect their colleagues and superiors of nefarious doings. [9] The historical record, furthermore, disputes the assumption stated early in this paper, namely, that teachers will do virtually anything for more money. That fortunately many highly competent people stay in the classroom is undeniable. The percentage who opt for administrative posts or meet the requirements to teach in college remains small. "Money-oriented" persons do not go into teaching. Even those teachers who militantly pursue a better wage package such as through union activity are not trying to leave the profession.

One writer has predicted that four events will occur wherever merit pay plans are put into effect: (1) money will be lost, (2) teachers will be disaffected, (3) the public will be cheated, and (4) children will pay the price.[10] There have been some merit pay plans that have succeeded, but these have tended to be in congenial school districts characterized by strong, dynamic leadership, teachers and administrations cooperatively working out the plan, moderately respectable salaries for all, and significant bonuses. The most promising alternatives to merit pay recognize that the only way to get better teachers is to improve the conditions under which they teach, and to upgrade the status of the profession itself.[11]

The consensus of opinion seems to be that any scheme imposed upon teachers by administrators, school boards, or state legislatures has more disadvantages than advantages. While there is no evidence that merit pay promotes excellence in teaching, it is generally conceded that the best way to reward outstanding teachers is to offer them expanded responsibilities and opportunities to develop professionally. Experience at the college level beautifully exemplifies this. Professors usually put a higher premium on laboratory and library facilities, on research assistants, and on secretarial help than on a limited increase in financial compensation.

All professions and all crafts form voluntary organizations for the mutual benefit of their members. The purpose of such organizations is threefold: (1) to set standards of workmanship or professional expertise, (2) to control entry into the field, and (3) to control wages and working conditions. Educational organizations have had limited success in these areas. Merit pay arrangements, by tying practitioners more closely to those who will determine merit, will not contribute to a strengthening of the profession. There are, furthermore, no compensations for this limitation. Merit pay will not increase salary money; it will merely redistribute it. Indeed, while we can do little more than guess at people's motives, it is reasonable to surmise that merit pay advocates from outside education see such a system as a means for making teacher pay more attractive without increasing the financial burden of the public.

What is needed in the area of fair and equitable compensation for teachers is not another gimmick such as merit pay, piled on top of an already dysfunctional system. What is needed is a reorganization of public education by professional teachers for the benefit of the American public. What this reorganization might look like can only be conjectured at this point, but to the extent it facilitates the educational process and establishes conditions which make teaching a more attractive occupation there will be little reason to introduce the "quick fix" and the gimmick in the first place.

Notes

[1] New York Times editorial of 29 September 1859.

[2] Hobart W. Burns, "The Merit Plan: Boon or Bane?" in Philosophy of Education: Essays and Commentaries (New York: Ronald Press, 1962), p. 415.

[3] Daphne S. White, "Can Merit Pay Work in Education?" American Educator, VII (Winter, 1983), p. 8.

[4] Ibid.

[5] Dorothy Wickendon, "Merit Pay Won't Work," The New Republic, November 7, 1983, p. 12.

[6] Patti Breckinridge, "Florida Merit Pay," Education Week, 28 March 1984, p. 7.

[7] Wickendon, "Merit Pay Won't Work," p. 13.

[8] Ibid., p. 12   [9] Ibid.

[10] Susan Moore Johnson quoted in _Education Week_, 28 March 1984, p. 15.

[11] Wickendon, "Merit Pay Won't Work," p. 13.

PART SIX -- GOVERNMENT AND EDUCATION

Is governmental involvement, especially that of the federal government, an overall benefit to education?

The United States is rather unique in its educational development. Unlike the experience in most countries, its schools were created by local initiative rather than resulting from the imposition of a national system. This has led to definite benefits, but also shortcomings. On the positive side, the local community regarded the schools as its own, willingly financed them, and became involved in their activities. In return, the schools have been responsive to the needs and wishes of the community. On the negative side, sensitivity to community control has often resulted in schools adopting practices and programs of dubious educational value, has placed the educator at the mercy of local pressure groups and even individual parents, and has resulted in less than adequate funding where local property taxes generated insufficient revenue.

Throughout the twentieth century state governments have come to play a more active role in school financing. The federal government, especially since Sputnik in 1957 and the Elementary and Secondary Education Act of 1965, has also assumed a prominent role. He who pays the piper calls the tune, and along with the dollars allocated to local systems by the state and federal government have come policies, programs, directives, regulations, and requirements. Are our schools really better because of, for example, the increased federal activity relating to education? What should be that federal role in the future?

The first article sees a growing resolve, principally during the years of the Reagan administration, to limit, perhaps abolish altogether, the federal government's role in the maintenance and improvement of public education. Examination of past and present federal support suggests a need to continue federal categorical aid, so characteristic of President Johnson's "Great Society" and "War on Poverty" programs, as a chief means of encouraging excellence in American education.

While recognizing the increasing dependence of local school systems on outside money, the second article sees the policies which accompany such funding as for the most part harmful to education. Government controls interfere with teaching, contribute to expensive and inefficient bureaucracy, depersonalize what should be a very personal operation, and

129

inhibit the development of professionalism. It is in the development of an educational profession, however, that hope for real improvement in school programs lies.

MALCOLM B. CAMPBELL is Professor of Education at Bowling Green State University, Bowling Green, Ohio. A frequent contributor to educational journals and recipient of a Lyndon B. Johnson Foundation grant-in-aid, his research interests include comparative higher education and federal education policy studies. His doctorate is from the University of Michigan.

LEO D. LEONARD is the Dean of the School of Education at the University of Portland, Oregon. He is heavily involved in the politics of education in Oregon, having served on a number of state education planning committees. At this writing he is President of the State Council of Deans of Education (OACTE). His doctorate is from Utah State University.

THE FEDERAL GOVERNMENT AND THE PUBLIC SCHOOLS:
A NEED FOR CONTINUED CO-OPERATION

Malcolm B. Campbell

Article the Third. Religion, Morality and knowledge,
being necessary to good government and the happiness
of mankind, schools and the means of education shall
forever be encouraged.

An Ordinance for the Government
of the Territory of the United
States North-West of the River
Ohio

Two months prior to the adoption of the United States
Constitution, the Continental Congress of the United States,
sitting in New York City on July 13, 1787, passed the Ordinance of 1787. The Third Article of this Northwest Ordinance,
following its predecessor, the Land Ordinance of 1785, which
stipulated that the sixteenth section of public lands become
rectangular townships reserved "for the maintenance of public
schools within the said township" upon sale of the lands,
inaugurated a tradition of federal government support for
public education. This tradition, however controversial, continues to the present day. Of supreme importance to the vitality of public education in the decades ahead is the question of what forms federal support for public education will
take. The resolution of that question depends on whether the
federal government and the public schools can forge a necessary partnership in the provision of education for an increasingly heterogeneous American public. If not probable,
this necessary partnership is possible. In good measure, that
partnership rests on an understanding of federal support, past
and present, together with speculation on the future.

The Past: Establishment of Categorical
Federal Aid as Principle

Federal support for public education is an American tradition long on rhetoric and short on implementation. Ambig-
uously reserved for the states by the Tenth Amendment to the
United States Constitution (December 15, 1791), control of
educational provision and support of educational opportunity
were sharply debated issues in the early national period.

While the founding fathers and specific essayists on the subject, for example, Samuel Knox and Samuel Harrison Smith, rhetorically supported the notion of national support, they were unwilling to include provisions for a federally controlled national system of education in the United States Constitution. By default, the knowledge necessary for the republican assets of representative government, liberty, and virtue would be shaped in schools financed and organized by the states.[1]

Acting on an earlier suggestion of General Henry Knox that American military officers receive systematic training, the Congress established the United States military academy at West Point in 1802. By this act a tradition of federal support for specific educational purposes was initiated. Coupled with the earlier Land Ordinance policies granting federal lands to the states for educational purposes, this tradition not only resulted in the expansion of American higher education, for example, the creation of the land-grant college movement in the late nineteenth century occasioned by the Morrill Acts of 1862 and 1890, and federal aid to predominantly black colleges evidenced in the Higher Education Act of 1965, it also established a scattered federal involvement in education when special circumstances warranted that presence. Examples of this federal presence in the twentieth century are numerous: the Smith-Lever Act of 1914, which created agricultural extension programs for farmers; the Smith-Hughes Act of 1917, providing federal funding of vocational teachers' salaries; the literacy education of 40,000 illiterate young men sponsored under the Emergency Conservation Work Act of 1933; and the Servicemen's Readjustment Act of 1944.[2]

In the 1950s and 1960s federal involvement in American education continued to support specific circumstances by providing "categorical" financial aid to public education. Two specific circumstances received top priority in the burst of federal legislative activity from 1958 to 1965: the perceived need (occasioned by the dominance of vocationally-oriented students in an expanded high school enrollment, Dael Wolfe's study of the American reserves of specialized talent, and the Soviet thrust in space with the orbiting of Sputnik) to provide increased educational opportunity for the highly talented, together with the realization (announced in the Brown v. Board of Education of Topeka, Kansas, Supreme Court decision, the Carnegie Corporation-commissioned Slums and Suburbs, Michael Harrington's The Other America, the Civil Rights Movement, and President Lyndon B. Johnson's War on Poverty) that the poor had been neglected in American public schools. Federal support followed rapidly to meet these concerns. The National Defense Education Act of 1958 provided federal aid to secondary and higher education with the aim of extending educational provision in science and technology and accenting the teaching of foreign languages for highly capable students. A constellation of congressional acts in the mid-1960s targeted federal support at the poor. The Economic Opportunity Act of 1964 provided enrichment programs (so-called Head Start) for pre-school children. The Civil Rights Act of 1964 requested a survey (known as the Coleman Report) "concerning the lack of availability of equal educational opportunities for individuals by reason of race, color, religion, or national origin in public educational institutions at all levels in the United States." The Elementary and Secondary Education Act of 1965 (E.S.E.A.), provided federal financial assistance to local educational agencies serving concentrations of children from low-income families "to expand and improve their educational programs ... which contribute particularly to meeting the special educational needs of educationally deprived children."[3]

The Elementary and Secondary Education Act of 1965 encouraged a more direct participation by the federal government in the administration of education programs at the local and state levels. From its inception as a Department of Education on March 2, 1867, the U.S. Office of Education (U.S.O.E.), variously housed in the Department of the Interior, the Federal Security Agency, and (after 1953) the Department of Health, Education, and Welfare, functioned as an autonomous and low-profiled "forgettable federal agency," with major responsibilities for collection and dissemination of information, coordination of educationally targeted relief programs, foreign visitors, support of land-grant colleges, and vocational education. This disbursement of massive federal aid mandated by the Elementary and Secondary Education Act of 1965 to abolish inequities in educational opportunity across the nation, established U.S.O.E. as a major center of influence in the determination of American educational policy.

While Title V of E.S.E.A. provided funding to strengthen state departments of education, local agencies were encouraged to apply directly to the U.S. Office of Education for the funding of supplementary educational services and centers (Title III) as well as for the support of research, development, and dissemination projects. Dangers to national security and perceived threats to national welfare, chief catalysts for federal aid to education prior to congressional authorization of funding levels in E.S.E.A., were replaced by the "child benefit" theory. This notion that the ultimate beneficiaries of federal involvement in American education are children, not schools, is a view of public funding enunciated in the Cochran v. Louisiana State Board of Education case (1930) where the United States Supreme Court permitted Louisiana to distribute free and nonreligious textbooks to children in parochial schools, and in the Everson v. Board of Education of Ewing Township ruling (1947) when the Court affirmed free bus transportation for parochial school children in New Jersey as constitutional.[4]

The recent past of federal support for American education has been given to aiding localities and states in the extension of educational opportunity. In the main that support has been given to compensatory education programs for students deprived of that opportunity, for example, the Bilingual Education Act (1968), later to become the Comprehensive Bilingual Education Amendment Act (1973), providing categorical aid to improving the education of children fron non-English speaking homes with special emphasis on Asian-American, native-American, and Spanish-speaking students. Moreover, the contemporary history of federal legislation has underscored the right of every child to educational opportunity, for example, the Vocational Rehabilitation Act (1973), forbidding the use of a handicapping condition as a basis for exclusion from schooling, and the Education for All Handicapped Children Act (1975), requiring local and state compliance with the provision of a "free appropriate public education" for each handicapped child. These are legislative embodiments of a judicial precedent established by federal district court decisions in Pennsylvania Association for Retarded Children v. Commonwealth of Pennsylvania (1972) and Mills v. Board of Education of the District of Columbia (1972).[5]

Federal initiatives in supporting the extension of educational opportunity and guaranteeing individual right of access to "free appropriate public education" have occurred within the context of two principles of federal aid to education: "supplement not supplant" and "maintenance of effort." Federal funding of educational programs, in other words, is an auxiliary to local and state financing of educational provision, not a substitute. Additionally, local and state authorities are to maintain their funding levels for public elementary and secondary education and not reduce those levels in view of the federal presence. These two principles, coupled with the categorical nature of federal aid and the quest for local autonomy and participation, have created tensions which are evident in the United States at present.[6]

The Present: Challenges to the Principle of Categorical Aid

The strong consensus of the mid-1960s and early 1970s in support of a strengthened federal involvement in American public education to deal with problems of a national scope, for example, "disadvantaged youth," became increasingly fragile, even elusive, in the late 1970s and early 1980s. Ironically, this demise of consensus occurred at the very time that education was receiving greater prominence through the efforts of the Carter Administration to create a cabinet-level Department of Education. On May 2, 1980, President Jimmy Carter signed Executive Order 12212, creating the Department of Education with cabinet status in the Executive Branch of the federal government. He viewed the new Department as a means of combining approximately 150 federal education programs into a more efficient and responsive use of federal funds targeted at education. Carter was insistent that the presence of a Department of Education would not result in a presence of federal control in American education.

> The Department will give education a stronger
> voice at the Federal level, while at the same time
> reserving the actual control ... of education to
> states, localities, and private institutions ....
> The Department will cut red tape ... to make the
> flow of Federal dollars to school districts ...
> more efficient, thereby providing students and
> educators with more benefits per dollar of Federal
> funds. [7]

During the Carter and Reagan administrations the question of how best to maximize effective use of federal funding for education became a central issue at the federal level.

The enlarged scope of the federal thrust is clearly visible in the increased proportion of the total costs of American education funded by the federal government. During the 1961-62 school year, federal funding totalled 4.3 percent; by fiscal year 1980, it had more than doubled: 9.8 percent. These percentages, however, mask persistent disparity in federal aid to the fifty states and the District of Columbia. The persistence of this disparity in funding occurs, for example, in the federal contribution to revenue per pupil for public elementary and secondary education in the fifty states. During the 1975-76 school year that contribution ranged from 23 percent (New Mexico) to 4.2 percent (Massachusetts). In fiscal year 1980, the percentages were respectively: 25.1 (Mississippi) and 5.6 (Wisconsin and Wyoming). While federal funding helps to increase educational opportunity in areas with low tax bases and high concentrations of poverty, federal aid's effectiveness in compensating for unequal state and local funding redistribution to areas with concentrations of low-income children is questionable. Given this concern, the nature of federal aid to American education is controversial.[8]

Debate on the nature of federal aid is three-dimensional: Is federal funding most appropriately delivered in the form of categorical grants, block grants, or general aid to states and localities? From the Johnson-O'Malley Act (1934) establishing the principle of federal "Impact Aid" designed to compensate local school districts for the children of parents living on federal property and not paying property taxes, to the Omnibus Budget Reconciliation Act (1981) authorizing federal aid to elementary and secondary education programs through block grants to state educational agencies, the predominant form of federal funding has been the categorical grant. Categorical funding is targeted at specific clientele and issues, given directly to local educational agencies, and regulated by federal government agencies. As both federal agencies and federal regulations grew in the unprecedented expansion of federal categorical aid in the 1960s and 1970s (from 1960 to 1980 the Code of Federal Regulations increased nearly five-fold, 20,036 pages to over 100,000), the block grant approach became a popular alternative means of federal funding.[9]

President Gerald Ford recommended a block grant approach to the federal funding of over 27 education programs (inclusive of Title I, Elementary and Secondary Education Act) in fiscal year 1976. While the 94th and 95th Congresses rejected the block grant concept, the 97th Congress enacted block grant federal funding in the Education Consolidation and Improvement Act of 1981, combining into a single authorization of grants to states, for example, programs previously categorically funded in the Elementary and Secondary Education Act, the Alcohol and Drug Abuse Education Act, the Higher Education Act, the Follow Through Act, and the National Science Foundation Act, "which will eliminate burdensome, unnecessary, and unproductive paperwork and free the schools of unnecessary Federal supervision, direction and control."

Block grants are a form of federal aid which combines the funding of programs targeted at a particular clientele, for example, educationally deprived children (Title I of the Elementary and Secondary Education Act of 1965, and the Head Start - Follow Through Act, originally funded categorically in Title V of the Economic Opportunity Act of 1964), or programs aimed at the same general sector of education, for example, the 1976 amendments to the Vocational Education Act (1963) applying to persons of all ages in vocational education, work-study, cooperative education, energy education, industrial arts, and residential vocational school programs. Given due recognition of the principles of "maintenance of effort" and "supplement, not supplant," the state educational agencies have sole responsibility for the administration of federal block grants. The most appropriate means of federal funding, however, remains unresolved.[10]

It is especially noteworthy that in Titles V and VI of the Omnibus Budget Reconciliation Act of 1981, federal financial assistance to local educational agencies with high concentrations of children of low-income families (originally, Title I, Elementary and Secondary Education Act of 1965) and Head Start (developed as an enrichment program for preschool children aged four through five years) remain as categorically funded programs under the administration of the Secretary of Education and the Secretary of Health and Human Services (the new designation of the Department of Health, Education, and Welfare following the creation of a separate Department of Education in May, 1980), respectively. The federal government has been reluctant to channel funding to states and localities entirely through the block grant mechanism. Thus, the largest federal participation in compensatory education programs targeted at disadvantaged youth and based on economic need (Title I of the Elementary and Secondary Education Act of 1965, as amended) remains closely regulated by the Department of Education on a nation-wide competitive categorical grant basis. While there is no unanimity on the appropriateness of the block grant approach to federal support of American education, neither is there agreement on a third means of delivering that support, general aid. [11]

Since President Lyndon B. Johnson's 1964 Task Force on Education recommended the abolition of inequities in state and local per pupil expenditure, the principle of general federal aid to education has gained favor. Interest groups, for instance, the National Education Association through its backing of the American Defense Education Bill, argue that the federal government currently spends $8.6 billion, less than 1.4 percent of its total revenues, on elementary and secondary education. Federal spending priorities on American education need to be revised upward. The National Education Association claims this revision optimally occurs through Congressional enactment of a principle of general federal aid to education. As usually defined, this aid to education would consist of the distribution of federal untied grants, based on a single funding formula (perhaps based on current per pupil expenditure), to state and local authorities. These grants of aid would be utilized as general revenue for education and would necessitate no further federal control over funding use. Support for a principle of general federal aid to education is, however, lukewarm. [12]

Advocates of general federal aid to education point to three advantages of this funding principle: (a) simplicity through an elimination of complex federal program accountability, (b) a reduction of resentment targeted against federal regulations at the state and local level, and (c) a reduction of the need to categorize students and teachers for federal program elibility. Critics of general federal aid to education stress three objections: (a) the necessity of earmarking funds to ensure that moneys are actually spent on federal concerns in American education, for example, disadvantaged students, (b) the likelihood of a dilution of resources in the implementation of federal goals in American education, and (c) the possibility of requiring substantial increases in federal expenditures to ensure that programs, for example compensatory education, and students, for example the handicapped, benefit to the extent they do now. A continued federal thrust in American education, however, cannot be taken for granted. In the pouring rain of a late spring Republican presidential campaign in Cleveland, Ohio, Ronald Reagan stated that "Federal aid to education has become federal interference." It was a theme that was to characterize not only presidential hopeful Reagan's campaign stump speeches but his administration's posture as well. [13]

The revolt against big government, symbolized by California's Proposition 13 and occasioned in part by a substantial increase in the federal education budget together with the enforcement of regulations governing treatment of the impaired and women during the Carter administration, characterized President Reagan's efforts to dismantle the newly created Department of Education, propose education budget cuts and reduce the federal regulation of educational programs. President Reagan frequently voice his preference for curtailing a federal responsibility in American education. His preference was rooted in his assumption that

> ... education is the principal responsibility of
> local school systems, teachers, parents, citizen
> boards, and state governments. By eliminating the
> Department of Education less than 2 years after it
> was created, we cannot only reduce the budget but
> ensure that local needs and preferences, rather

than the wishes of Washington, determine the education of our children.[14]

As a recent student of American educational policy since the Second World War, Diane Ravitch, put it, President Reagan's preference would give rise to "tasks that were easier said than done."[15]

The Future: Essential Continuance of Federal Categorical Aid

The Reagan administration has defined the federal role in American education as that of fostering excellence in the nation's schools. This drive for excellence rests on the attainment of three priorities: (a) the production of a highly literate society, skilled in the discipline of basic English; (b) a mastery of basic mathematics and scientific laws governing the natural world; (c) a thorough command of the social studies, grounded in a mastery of citizenship education.[16] These three priorities, as President Reagan announced on December 8, 1983, at his administration's "National Forum on Excellence in Education," convened by Secretary of Education Terrell H. Bell in Indianapolis, Indiana, are to occur within the context of six educational reforms: (a) the enactment of stricter discipline codes in the schools, (b) the ending of alcohol and drug abuse, (c) the development of higher academic standards, (d) the encouragement of excellence in teaching through the use of competency-based testing and merit pay incentives for teachers, (e) the restoration of local control in the fostering and implementation of educational policy, and (f) a renewed accent on teaching the basic subjects traditionally associated with academic excellence: English, mathematics and science.[17]

These reforms are gradually becoming operative at the local and state levels by means of enacting a longer school year, an increase in merit pay for teachers deemed "superior," and more rigorous high school graduation requirements. To date the only federal initiative in this nationally diffused reform effort has been to create a President's Commission on Academic Fitness Awards Program, closely modeled on the Physical Fitness Award Program established during the presidency of Lyndon Johnson. The spate of federal initiatives that characterized the Johnson administration is conspicuously and regrettably absent.

The future of federal support for American education, especially public education, is not, however, a gloomy one. In the current national debate on the status of education, a

139

debate energized by a spate of reports on public education initiated by the Paideia Group in 1978, and concluded in January, 1984, with the appearance of the National Association of Secondary School Principals and National Association of Independent Schools-sponsored <u>A Study of High Schools</u>, there is a strong plea that the federal government must form a necessary partnership with the nation's schools. In these reports the future federal role includes but is not limited to: identifying the national interest in education, emphasizing the need for better schools and a better education for young Americans, assisting economically depressed localities with concentrations of immigrant and/or impoverished groups, promoting and supporting English proficiency and scientific literacy programs, ensuring access to equal educational opportunity, providing student financial assistance, and supporting teacher training in areas of shortage or key national need.

Likewise, these reports underscore a need for federal fiscal support in American education. Ambiguous as to whether that support is rendered appropriately by general aid or block grant measures, the National Commission on Excellence in Education; the Twentieth Century Fund; the Education Commission of the States; the National Science Board Commission on Precollege Education in Mathematics, Science and Technology; and the Carnegie Foundation unanimously favor the continuation of federal categorical funding of educational programs at local and state levels, devoted to national interests and/or specific clientele. This unanimity is welcome. [18]

While a broad national trend to shift educational reform efforts from a concern for national policy-making to an analysis and improvement of individual schools is urgent, the federal role as defined in terms of a necessary and vital relationship with the nation's schools is absolutely essential. The role should be a dual one -- the federal government should take the initiative in identifying the national interest in education. As Stephen K. Bailey has noted elsewhere, we desperately need to form broad-based national political coalitions for public education which will coalesce on grounds other than majority pressure and minority pressure.[19]

The school-reform effort of recent years has come primarily from outside the teaching profession. The federal government in the foreseeable future must take the initiative in establishing proschool coalitions which are inclusive of the many publics involved in American education rather than exclusively centered on the special interests of corporate leaders and state governors, no matter how altruistic those interests may be. Secondly, the federal government should maintain and enhance categorical fiscal support for the nation's schools and, concurrently, reduce the administrative paperwork which traditionally has been part and parcel of federal categorical aid. The advantages of categorical fiscal aid in contrast to block grant and general aid are three: (a) earmarking of funds is essential in the determination of whether those moneys have been spent as actually intended; (b) categorical funding arrangements provide a means for building constituencies of support for programs targeted at those who have been denied equality of educational opportunity, for example, the economically disadvantaged and the handicapped, and ensuring that action is taken; (c) in times of budgetary restraint or shortage, categorical aid is less vulnerable than block grant or general aid, one reason why the Reagan administration efforts to reduce the federal fiscal commitment to American education have been relatively miniscule to date.[20]

Presidential hopeful Jesse Jackson recently announced that his first-year federal budget revisions for 1985 will include $10 billion to strengthen the availability and quality of American education. Clearly, the 1985 federal budget must contain fiscal evidence that the federal government is contributory to and mindful of a restoration of purpose in American education. If this evidence occurs, it will place contemporary federal initiatives in American education within the tradition of establishing necessary federal partnerships with local and state education authorities.[21]

One example of the need for federal initiative is the current thrust for excellence in American education centers on the maintenance and improvement of school- and university-based programs in international education. In February, 1966, President Lyndon B. Johnson urged passage of the International Education Act of 1966. This act would have established a center for Educational Cooperation in the Department of Health, Education, and Welfare as a focal point for leadership in stimulating the development of international studies programs in elementary and secondary schools. As President Johnson said at the time, "no child should grow ... in America without realizing the promise ... of the world beyond our borders."[22] Congress, unfortunately, passed authorizations for funding under the act, yet never appropriated funds for the authorization. Immediately prior to President Jimmy Carter's administration, Stephen Bailey, Vice President of the American Council on Education, asserted that the federal government has a "logical imperative" to assume responsibility for three dimensions of international education: advanced foreign and international affairs research, general public understanding of international interdependence, and increasing support of educational exchange.[23] The report, <u>Strength Through Wisdom</u>, of the President's Commission on Foreign Languages and International Studies added a fourth part of international education in need of federal support and leadership: foreign language instruction.[24] In its recent report to Secretary of Education Terrell H. Bell on <u>Critical Needs in International Education: Recommendations for Action</u>, the National Advisory Board on International Education Programs, while commending Title VI of the Higher Education Act (the only major piece of legislation supporting international study programs), urges that a new federal initiative be established "to increase the understanding and skills of teachers ... in foreign languages and international studies." This is an especially noteworthy recommendation when one realizes that foreign language enrollments in high schools have declined from their peak of 36 percent in 1915, to 15 percent in 1980.[25]

The National Advisory Board on International Education Programs, while recognizing that local and state initiatives are sorely needed to place foreign languages and international studies alongside the five "basics" of English, mathematics, computer science, social studies, and the natural sciences as chief components of a sound education, urges the Reagan administration to marshal the leadership and resources necessary to realize a marked improvement "... in the state of our nation's knowledge of the language, history and culture of foreign countries." The National Advisory Board, moreover, urges the research arm of the Department of Education, the National Institute of Education, to encourage research in new methods of language study contributive to fostering excellence in foreign language instruction. While it has most definitely not been the policy of the federal government in recent administrations to support the cultural interests of the nation's ethnic groups, clearly, the federal government's experience in funding the development of teaching materials in 68 languages under the Comprehensive Bilingual Education Amendment Act of 1973, could be invaluable assistance in reversing the national decline of foreign language instruction in American education.[26]

The federal government's role in promoting the endeavor and other public interest issues in our nation's schools is categorically undeniable. It should be realized with federal categorical support, both financial and programmatic, in the near and distant future.

Notes

[1] Excellent discussions of federal contributions to American education in the early National Period are found in: R. Freeman Butts, _Public Education in the United States: From Revolution to Reform_ (New York: Holt, Rinehart and Winston, 1978), pp. 24-65, and Carl F. Kaestle, _Pillars of the Republic: Common Schools and American Society, 1780-1860_ (New York: Hill and Wang, 1983), pp. 3-12.

[2] On the specifics of federal aid to higher education see John S. Brubacher and Willis Rudy, _Higher Education in Transition: A History of American Colleges and Universities 1636-1976_ (New York: Harper and Row, 1976).

[3] A superb summary of federal education programs of the 1960s targeted at the economically disadvantaged is given in Organization for Economic Co-operation and Development, _United States: Federal Policies for Education for the Disadvantaged_ (Paris: O.E.C.D., 1981), pp. 13-24.

[4] A succinct commentary on the "child-benefit" theory is given in Diane Ravitch, _The Troubled Crusade: American Education, 1945-1980_ (New York: Basic Books, 1983), pp. 29-30. The reference to the Department of Education as "a forgettable federal agency" occurs in Butts, _Public Education_, p. 158.

[5] See S. Alexander Rippa, _Education in a Free Society: An American History_. Fifth Edition (New York: Longman, Inc., 1984), pp. 393-395.

[6] For discussion of the principles of "maintenance of effort" and "supplement not supplant" see Organization for Economic Co-operation and Development, _Educational Policy and Planning: Compensatory Education Programmes in the United States_ (Paris: O.E.C.D., 1980), pp. 217-218.

[7] Jimmy Carter, "The State of the Union – Annual Message to Congress," January 21, 1980, in _Public Papers of the Presidents of the United States: Jimmy Carter 1980-81: Book 1 – January 1 to May 23, 1980_ (Washington, D.C.: United States Government Printing Office, 1981), p. 136.

[8] For the persistence in federal funding disparity to the fifty states and the District of Columbia see Organization for Economic Co-operation and Development, _Educational Policy and Planning: Compensatory Education Programmes in the United States_, p. 131; and Lee R. Wolfe, _Revenues and Expenditures for Public Elementary and Secondary Education FY 1980_ (Wash-

ington, D.C.: National Center for Education Statistics, 1982), p. 16.

[9] For a concise, yet in-depth, discussion of federal funding principles see Organization for Economic Co-operation and Development, United States: Federal Policies for Education for the Disadvantaged, pp. 87-95; Organization for Economic Co-operation and Develoment, Educational Policy and Planning: Compensatory Education Programmes in the United States, pp. 156-157. The reference to the Code of Federal Regulations occurs in Theodore H. White, America in Search of Itself: The Making of the President 1956-1980 (New York: Harper and Row, 1982), p. 129.

[10] See the Omnibus Budget Reconciliation Act of 1981 in Public Law 97-35 August 13, 1981 (Washington, D.C.: United States Government Printing Office, 1981), 95 Stat. 464-501.

[11] Ibid.

[12] For the current National Education Association posture on federal funding of American education see National Education Association, Local, State and Federal Roles (Washington, D.C.: National Education Association, December, 1983), pp. 4-5.

[13] Organization for Economic Co-operation and Development, United States: Federal Policies for Education for the Disadvantaged, p. 91. Ronald Reagan's campaign remark is quoted in White, America in Search of Itself, p. 307.

[14] Ronald Reagan, "Address to the Nation on the Program for Economic Recovery," September 24, 1981, in Public Papers of the Presidents of the United States: Ronald Reagan, 1981: Book 1 - January 20 to December 31, 1981 (Washington, D.C.: United States Government Printing Office, 1982), p. 833.

[15] Ravitch, The Troubled Crusade, p. 320.

[16] Terrell H. Bell, Suggested Priorities and Goals for American Education (Washington, D.C.: United States Department of Education, December 8, 1983), pp. 1-2.

[17] President Reagan's documentation of six key reform initiatives in American education was delivered to his version of the traditional (since the Hoover administration) White House Conferences on Education, the National Forum on Excellence in Education, Indianapolis, Indiana, December 8, 1983.

[18]Congressional Research Service, Comparison of Recommendations from Selected Education Reform Reports (Washington, D.C.: The Library of Congress, September 23, 1983), pp. 9-10.

[19]See Stephen K. Bailey, "Political Coalitions for Public Education," Daedalus, CX (Summer, 1981), 42.

[20]Organization for Economic Co-operation and Development, United States: Federal Policies for Education for the Disadvantaged, p. 91.

[21]Jesse Jackson, "Tax Reform and Public Jobs," New York Times (April 22, 1984), p. 2F. Walter F. Mondale, Democratic Presidential candidate, would have the federal government "help ... with affordable college education, equal educational opportunity, and increased investment in our teachers and schools." Walter F. Mondale, "First, Cut the Deficit," New York Times (April 29, 1984) p. 2F.

[22]Lyndon B. Johnson, Message from the President of the United States Relative to International Education and Health Programs, 89th Congress, 2nd Session, House of Representatives Document No. 375 (Washington, D.C.: United States Government Printing Office, February 2, 1966), p. 3.

[23]Charles C. Bergman, The Reorganization of International Activities of the Department of Health, Education and Welfare: An Important Opportunity for the United States in Domestic and World Responsibility (New York: Institutes of Religion and Health, 1976), p. 15.

[24]President's Commission on Foreign Language and International Studies, Strength Through Wisdom: A Report to the President from the President's Commission on Foreign Languages and International Studies (Washington, D.C.: United States Government Printing Office, 1979).

[25]National Advisory Board on International Education Program, Critical Needs in International Education: Recommendations for Action - A Report to the Secretary of Education by the National Advisory Board on International Education Programs (December, 1983), p. 11.

[26]Ibid., p. 8. Diane Ravitch in her superb history of the post-World War II decades in American education suggests the possibility that proponents of bilingualism might identify, indeed "merge their interests," with the "larger public concern" regarding the low status of foreign language instruc-

tion in American education. Ravitch, The Troubled Crusade,
p. 280.

PERSPECTIVES ON GOVERNMENTAL CONTROL OF EDUCATION

Leo D. Leonard

From the time of our earliest public schools, government has been involved in the control and management of the educational system. At first such control was at the local and county levels, then later at the state level. Today we experience considerable federal control, even though school systems maintain their own boards of education, and legally control of the local system resides with the state legislature. Control in brief takes the form of prescriptive standards of operation that include how the money is to be obtained and how it is to be spent. Government dictates what subjects are to be taught, in some states what textbooks are to be used, and what requirements teachers must meet.

In point of fact, there is very little that the federal or state governments do not control in the educational system today. Local public boards find themselves increasingly responsible for interpreting an ever-growing complex of federal and state regulations, regulations which have to be complied with in order to insure the continuation of funded programs and the avoidance of litigation. It is the contention of this article that state and especially federal control in education, no matter how well intentioned, is an obstacle to the efficient and effective delivery of educational services. Furthermore, state and federal control of education tends to inhibit the development of an educational profession.

The bureaucracy now ubiquitous in education can be traced to governmental (state and federal) requirements. It is often heavy-handed and impersonal -- in an institution which by its very nature and purposes calls for sensitivity and an emphasis on the individual. It would be reasonable to describe this bureaucratic system as the core of contemporary problems rather than the cure. Yet, many people espouse control and ever more control over the nation's schools and colleges. The belief, in short, is that educators have not done a good job and that if the job of education is to turn out educated individuals then the schools have failed and the educators are responsible. There is little recognition that the schools have been so politicized that if they fail, it is because they have merely done what they were told or asked to do. Schools have been asked to promote all students, to act as a holding pen for students desiring to enter the work force when there are no jobs, and to water down the curriculum to meet contemporary permissive attitudes towards rights and responsibilities.

The arguments in favor of governmental control are usually based on five general reasons, which can be labeled coordination, efficient delivery, monitoring, equalization, and standardization. With the growth in size of school systems, with increasing enrollment, it has become necessary to coordinate the use of resources and facilities. More people are becoming involved in the teaching process, and if optimal use is to be made of their capabilities, their time and activities have to be coordinated. This leads to the second broad reason, the need for efficient delivery of services so that no one's time, dollars, or effort are wasted in any aspect of this process. It is assumed that administrative levels are necessary to assure efficiency in delivery of educational services.

To assure that there is coordination between the many parties involved in the educational enterprise and that the system operates efficiently, monitoring the entire process has been deemed necessary. Monitoring is necessary for review, evaluation, and recommendation. Of course, those who do the monitoring constitute still one more level in the bureaucracy. Equalization is concerned with dividing resources and services among the participants in like amounts. Equal opportunity is the popular notion of equal resource sharing. The unstated assumption here appears to be that without external control the teaching act would become confined to a relationship between the teacher and a relatively small number of selected students.

The final reason for bureaucratization is to standardize instruction, facilities, and resources. This is the antiseptic approach to learning - the need to insure that everyone takes science in roughly the same square footage of space, using the same standard textbook, and meeting the same set of standard criteria. It is easy to find merit in standardization, as it is for efficiency, and coordination, to mention but two of the other general reasons. However, when attempts are made to act on the basis of these factors, the result is the creation of an additional layer of bureaucracy. Once created, the bureaucratic levels are often given additional justification in legalistic, ethical, and even moral terms.

The bureaucracy spawned by increasing governmental activity may be part of the explanation for the appearance of the romantic critics whose popularity was most noticeable in the 1960s and 70s. Exemplifying the romantics' views were

Ivan Illich's Deschooling Society, John Holt's How Children Fail, and Paul Goodman's Compulsory Mis-Education. In opposition to the growing impersonal atmosphere in the computerized classroom with its increasingly federally mandated programs the romantics called for at least informal face to face relationships with education based on student interests, and teaching unencumbered by regulation and bureaucratic trivia. (At the most the critics called for an end to formal schooling.)

In retrospect, the critics had an impact opposite to what they sought. If they influenced the artificiality of some standards, the general public reaction was that standards were lowered. If they managed to get the traditional lock step methods replaced with personalized learning, the result was viewed as the replacement of learning objectives with non-focused activities. If they exposed the limited accomplishment occurring in schools, the result was a call for more stringent governmental control over programs. An excellent example of this public control and overkill in education can be found in the state of Oregon. In order for a program in a college of education to be accepted by the state of Oregon the program must go through four different state agencies before final approval is received. In many states a similar program need only go to one state agency. It takes two years in Oregon to process a program through the various state bureaus. The failure to comply with state procedures would bring serious academic sanctions against the school violating the statutes. It is this kind of overmanaging that has inhibited development of creative alternative programs.

When we look at true professions such as medicine or law it is immediately obvious that they have little similarity to education in terms of district, county, state, or federal control. As true professions they govern themselves. They do this through appointed or elected councils or bodies which not only set standards but control access to the profession, establish accreditation criteria, and determine licensing procedures for members. Such professional bodies operate a sanction system for those individuals and institutions who violate the established principles. Education has no such equivalent. It is true that education has established some semi-autonomous associations such as teachers unions and professional associations. These associations go through the motions of setting standards and establishing procedures but in point of fact such associations have no authority under law and at best can only be viewed as recommending bodies to state and local education agencies.

Education started out as something less than a profession. The teaching act has never been viewed as sacrosanct. Historically, education has been managed, governed, and politicized by one or more groups acting through legal channels of the county, state, or federal government. These special interest groups' stated purpose is to create a better learning environment for children. An example of this would be a special interest group that controls or at least influences acquisition of library books. Such a group would limit the professional responsibilities of the trained staff. This limiting of the professionals would be done ostensibly for the best interest of the students. Special interest groups have proliferated across the nation and the ebb and flow of their impact has, at times, been most noticeable in the school system. When these groups don't control education, the state does. The state intervenes to dictate policy on teacher qualifications and in general legislate for education in numerous ways. The "state," however, is but the system, albeit legally sanctioned, in which the various special interest groups labor -- sometimes competing with one another -- to have their views given the authority of law.

Community control of the schools is usually traced back to colonial New England. When public schools, as we understand the term were opened in the nineteenth century, and no longer derived their funds from a per student charge or philanthropy, the tradition of community control not only remained, but grew stronger because of the dependence of these schools on the public treasury. Several factors reinforced the trend. Communities grew in size, some of them very rapidly. Government by town meeting was replaced by representative democracy, and the "representatives" doling out funds to the schools continued the practice of laymen controlling who teached, what they taught, and what materials they used. Also, throughout much of the country there was a populist suspicion of educators -- people who taught school because they could not do much else. As the educators themselves received more schooling prior to assuming control of the classroom, they were increasingly viewed as intellectuals, and thus became even more suspect. As for the teaching itself, inconsistent though it may sound in view of the point just made, there was a wide-spread belief that anyone could teach.

The teacher, at best, was an extension of the community. As such, he was to teach what the community wanted taught. It is a logical step from that view to the one that a special interest group from the community can best determine what books and authors should be in a public library. If one can accept the first point it is logically easy to accept the second.

150

Further, the coercion or influence goes far beyond library books; in fact, such influence permeates all levels of decision making.

State and federal control remains in part because the public doesn't trust intellectuals. It certainly doesn't trust the teaching profession to police itself or to provide the necessary services. Unfortunately, there is some evidence to support this distrust. The widespread publicity which accompanies the adoption of new fads seldom, if ever, is followed by news of successes resulting from the innovations. The militancy of teacher organizations often feeds the flames of public discontent. To the extent that some segments of the public feel they are losing control of their schools, they may be increasingly inclined to favor increasing control of those schools by their elected officials -- by government.

Where the negative effects of state and federal control quickly become apparent are in the areas of certification and accreditation. The monster that has been created is at its worst in these two areas. Certification refers to a form of licensing at the conclusion of a teacher training program. A student, after graduating, usually applies to a state agency and subsequently receives his basic or first certificate, in other words, a license to teach. The state, in effect, endorses a person as competent to teach in a given subject area. So far, so good. The problem is that most states have unique courses, laws, and regulations governing certification. This is compounded by the fact that many states have no reciprocity. States refuse to recognize the certificate or credentials of a teacher from another state. Students graduating from an Ohio institution seeking employment in Oregon, for example, will probably have a minimum of one semester of course work to be completed at an Oregon university before they will be granted a certificate to teach. It really doesn't matter what degree they have, the state of Oregon has a number of unique courses that the state legislature has mandated that must be a part of a teacher's program before he will be permitted to have a basic teaching certificate. Oregon has no reciprocity with any other state in the union, so, in theory Oregon could simply refuse to recognize any teacher education program that wasn't completed in the state of Oregon. In practice, this doesn't happen, but it is not easy to be certified to teach in Oregon. California is a similar case. The unique requirements in California make it extremely unlikely that a graduate of an Ohio or Oregon institution will be permitted to teach in California without further education.

What has happened, in effect, is that there may be as many as fifty different certification regulations governing fifty different states. The current trend is for each state to go its own way with its own course requirements and basic skills tests. Yes! Not only are course requirements different, but now students must pass tests in mathematics, reading, and English in order to be certified. This means that a student from New York desiring to teach in Oregon will have to meet Oregon course requirements and a basic skills test. A New Yorker desiring to teach in California will have to pass a different set of courses and a different basic skills test. At this rate of proliferation, someone in a few years will demand that the federal government take over certification and testing in order to standardize the system. Once this happens, education will, for all intents and purposes, be nationalized.

What certification is to the teacher, accreditation is to the school. Almost all public and many private schools are accredited by some kind of agency. Accreditation by a state agency varies from a virtual "carte blanche" to a very prescriptive evaluation of entire programs by the elementary or secondary. A good example of the latter is what occurs in the state of Oregon. Oregon was one of the first states to develop a state teacher accreditation board, the Oregon Teacher Standards and Practices Commission, or TSPC for short. TSPC was established close to twenty years ago to review and accredit teacher education institutions. The Commission looks at a school's governance, faculty, students, resources, and evaluation procedures as part of its accrediting process. Standards and substandards in each of these areas must be met for a school to receive accreditation. The state is not in the least interested in whether the school holds some other form of accreditation. What this results in is duplication of effort for those schools which seek both state and national accreditation. Since national accreditation is by a professional body, the National Council for the Accreditation of Teacher Education, the state is denying that the education profession as a profession has any standards or measures to control and govern itself.

Schools like the University of Portland which are regional in nature need the national accreditation in order to compete for the best students. Since Portland students come from all over the nation, the students leaving Oregon must have national accreditation (whether Oregon recognizes it or not) in order to compete nationally for jobs. As a result, the university is put in the position of having to seek both state and national accreditation. In addition, special programs

152

such as psychology and religious education require additional professional accreditation. Again, the state is little interested in any type of specialized accreditation but only in the accreditation which it administers. Large universities, such as the University of Oregon, are continually preparing for one kind of accreditation or another. Faculty are assigned, on an almost semi-permanent basis, to prepare reports for the next accrediting visit. This results in everyone being overworked with little positive result except the development of prolific, if not competent writers. In order to get out of this mess one might say we should have the federal government take over accreditation. The problem is that the process then would become even more highly bureaucratized, not to mention heavily politicized. We could expect, for example, that the optimal time for a prominent institution to let itself be examined for accrediting purposes would be an election year.

It is not unreasonable to contend that federal funding is political rather than educational in purpose. Recently the hue and cry was raised by educators and within Congress itself as a result of highly questionable grants to a number of universities. Grants to Boston College, the University of New Hampshire, Catholic University, Harvard and most recently Pepperdine were strangely reminiscent of rural electrification and dam building projects over the past half century, projects so located as likely to be of considerable benefit to particular congressmen come the next election. Several critics viewed the procedures whereby these universities got their special allocations as high-handed and clearcut evidence of favoritism.

A school cannot be run like an automobile assembly line. Educating children is not analogous to building a car. No two children are alike, and we can never predict with certainty how any one student will react to any series of educational stimuli. The good teacher needs to be adaptable, and able to react to unexpected conditions. In brief, she needs to be able to rely on her own initiative in many circumstances. External controls can only serve to inhibit such initiative. To the extent that an individual or even an entire school district has to comply with regulations imposed from outside the system, it is reasonable to expect that the teacher or the system will less adequately serve the best interests of youngsters and their parents.

A constitutional issue also can be raised. The position here is that the first ten amendments to the Constitution have the effect of reserving education to the states, thereby prohibiting the federal government's interference. The tenth amendment states, "The powers not delegated to the United States by the Constitution nor prohibited by it to the states, are reserved to the states respectively or to the people." Senator Barry Goldwater pointed out in a speech before Congress in 1961 that "No constitutional amendment to extend federal power or responsibilities over education has ever been considered. If proposed, it would be overwhelmingly rejected." It is interesting to note how Congress has already sought to overrule state educational regulations. Missouri, for example, has a strong state constitutional prohibition against the allocation of tax moneys for church-related schools. To get around this prohibition, Congress re-wrote the Elementary and Secondary Education Act so that it could by-pass state agencies.

Public funding obviously is crucial to the existence of public schools. It is quite likely that a federal role in such financing is here to stay. Just as state-wide funding has become the established response to the inability of some communities to adequately finance their schools, so federal funding will be the response to discrepancies in financial resources among states. Is there, however, a way to direct the federal financial support so that it will have a minimal impact as a factor controlling schools? Of course, there is no guarantee that controls will be not established separate from the funding. The ways financial assistance is allotted may determine the ease (or lack of it) with which the federal government can control education.

We can take as an example the Servicemen's Readjustment Act, commonly known as the G.I. Bill of Rights. Federal moneys, instead of being sent to state agencies or schools, can be given directly to students or their parents, and then used for educational services as the recipient sees fit. Such allocations could be based on academic performance, long-term job goals, or work services provided on a part-time basis. We have had experience doing this at the college level. It may be time to attempt it at the high school level. Even elementary school students could receive assistance based on completing individual education plans based on learning objectives. Those who do not work or produce or don't want school get to vacate the classroom and make room for those who do. This policy would be true for students at all levels. Many would-be students would drop out of school and clog the streets. That may be and it is unfortunate. The American schools, however, should not continue to be gatekeepers, adolescent day care centers, and dumping grounds for societies' flotsom. Society will have to create alternative places for these non-students. The schools should be reserved for those who want to learn.

Much of the blame for state, i.e., governmental, control of education has to be laid at the feet of the educational profession. Too many educators have engaged in self-deception regarding the usefulness of the largesse made available, such as through federal programs. Concern with governmental allocations has got in the way of concern for what contribution is really made by the allocation. Much of the public money from both the state and federal government is used in administration and never gets down to the program delivery level. In general, the public education budgeting process is wasteful. Aside from control, too much money is often allocated with too little return on the dollar. This is largely because educators in public schools frequently have the belief that there will be more money from the same source as long as they do the state or federal government's bidding. Added to this is the recognition that the public moneys must be used up by the end of the fiscal year or the next year's allocation will be smaller.

If control over funding largely explains why governmental agencies rather than the educational profession control schooling, the question then is what steps must the profession take to offset or balance out that control. Part of the answer is easier to state than to implement. If money is to be accepted by the schools, then educators should insist that government leave the operation of the school to the professionals. When schools have accepted public money they have foolishly made bedfellows with whomever has held the money pot. This has led to the increasing public view of educators as little more than academic hucksters. In short, there are many educators, including this author, who believe that education over the last hundred years has been its own worst enemy. We have been too quick to lower our standards, too quick to agree with whomever will supply us with funds, and all too willing to change our values and our morals to reflect the current popular thought.

As if this were not enough, teacher education has traditionally let anyone who sought admission become a teacher. The result has been the recognition among professional colleagues that the least gifted students in colleges and universities often are education majors. When these same majors become the public school teachers the public is reinforced in its belief that teacher education must have external control in order to keep a less gifted and frankly less capable person under control. In short, educators have not made any serious

155

effort to make themselves a profession or to police themselves. Some educators believe that instead of less control we should have more. Instead of state or local control, federal control is sought.

Part of the answer to the question of professionalism also lies in accrediting organizations which are independent of governmental agencies. Serving all school levels are a number of regional bodies, the most prominent of which is the North Central Association of Colleges and Schools. More specialized, but nation-wide in operation, is the National Council for the Accreditation of Teacher Education, whose name indicates its area of concentration. NCATE, as this latter organization is popularly called, has been able to make an agreement with better than 20 states to accept each other's credentials and to permit free flow of teachers moving between states. This is a positive beginning; however, NCATE has come under a lot of fire for applying too stringent a standard to a number of universities, some of whom lived off their good name, as opposed to good program. Denying accreditation to major universities has encouraged some people to argue for doing away with a national professional accrediting body for one controlled by a state or federal body, or have no accreditation at all. If this should happen, certification and free movement across borders could be further limited.

Finally, the hypothesis can be developed contending that much of the dissatisfaction with, and even flight from, public schools is directly related to increasing federal governmental control. People who long supported the public schools have come to feel that they no longer exert control over these schools, but rather have seen federal incursions which have effectively removed the local community from control. Forced bussing is the most obvious case in points. Even proponents of bussing admit that the practice is politically motivated. Critics have used similar wording: bussing is a political rather than an educational solution to unequal educational opportunity.

In conclusion, this writer was one of those who bought all the promises of the great federal programs of the 1960's only to sit back as the years passed slowly coming to the realization that the promises couldn't be delivered. Throwing money at social problems doesn't make the problems go away. Federal and state control of education hasn't bought the solutions we thought it would. Governmental control of education has raised more problems than have been solved; more importantly, such control has inhibited educators' ability to make decisions which call for the expertise only educators have. Nineteenth century teachers may have lacked both the training and expertise needed to improve the educational institution. This condition is no longer the case. Obviously governments are not going to voluntarily relinquish the control they now have over education. It remains for educators to constantly publicize the inability of government to resolve educational problems, and to exert pressures similar to those exerted by the medical profession so that educational decisions which call for expertise will be made by those who have such expertise -- the educational profession.

PART SEVEN -- PARENT RIGHTS AND TEACHER RIGHTS

How should we handle conflicts which arise as a result of different views of education held by parents and teachers?

In an age now past, much of this country consisted of relatively homogeneous small cities and towns where one grew up, went to school, and settled down. The community controlled its schools, staffing them with its graduates, and the school quite naturally reenforced the values of the community. Parents knew their children's friends and teachers, and found the values of all compatible with their own. Today school programs are dictated by the federal bureaucracy; teachers come from other communities and backgrounds; classmates transported by bus from areas distant both culturally and geographically bring different interests, dialects, and values; and instructional materials are produced by publishers thinking not of preserving community tradition, but of meeting myriad demands for relevance, a broadened curriculum, ethnic studies, an international outlook, and an end to racism and sexism in school and society.

As the schools have changed due primarily to political pressures and changing ecological patterns, many of those who hold traditional views have sensed a loss of control over the educational institutions operated with their tax dollars. In attempting to re-assert some of this control they come into conflict with an educational staff increasingly oriented toward decision-making based on professional training rather than local traditions. How are differences between the two to be resolved? What solutions are most likely to be in the interests of a democratic society which values individual freedom and fair play?

The first article notes the changing orientation of the schools, and sees in this process an inadequate sensitivity to parental concerns. Educators seeking to stem the trend of deteriorating national test scores cannot do so without parental support, but this support will not be forthcoming so long as educators remain insensitive to parental values and rights. Education is primarily a parental responsibility, and where the educational profession fails to act in accordance with this fact it runs the risk of losing students to alternative schools.

The second article contends that the real conflict lies in differing views of what constitutes quality education. Quality is not just a matter of opinion. It can be assessed

159

objectively, and achieved only when the complexities of teaching are acknowledged and the expertise needed for dealing with those complexities accepted. To the extent that they understand the nature of human development and learning and the content-process methodologies of the academic disciplines, teachers are in the best position to provide that expertise.

JAMES RICCITELLI is a pastor and Director of the Center for Biblical Studies, Toledo, Ohio. Possessing degrees in sociology and theology, he served in the Christian Missionary Alliance in Upper Volta, West Africa for 18 years. He has taught at Adrian and William Tyndale Colleges.

JOHN R. CRYAN is Professor of Early Childhood Education at the University of Toledo. He received his doctorate in Early Childhood - Teacher Education at Syracuse University. DAVID TAVEL is Director of the Division of Educational Foundations, University of Toledo.

PARENTS' RIGHTS VS. PROFESSIONALS' RIGHTS IN EDUCATION

James M. Riccitelli

Not many years ago, professional educators were respected and praised by parents. But that was the day when authority was a more cherished value than equality. Having traded authority-at-the-expense-of-equality for equality-at-the-expense-of-authority, the public schools today suffer the consequences, and parents tend to hold responsible the professionals who, to keep peace, according to Broudy,[1] are rapidly being forced to adjust to every constituency that has sufficient political power to make itself heard. To a list that includes minority rights, rights of the poor, rights of teachers, and so on, we must add the rights of parents, of children, and of professionals.

Man is considered to have rights that are inborn and no government may deprive him of such rights. Fundamental human freedoms find their roots in the Bible and in Greek and Roman civilizations.[2] In its simplest definition, a right is something one may properly claim as his. Laws guarantee rights, but when rights clash, legislation is sought to provide clarification if not peace. New laws protecting children's rights are being proposed; the Family Protection Act which includes among other things, parents' rights to review public school textbooks (approximately 22 states have textbook adoption procedures), has already found a number of sponsors in Congress.

From Boston to Los Angeles, vandalism, arson, stolen equipment, and violence have required taxpayer-parents to contribute additional millions of dollars in taxes to keep school systems operating. Phrases like "the cancer in our school system," "the cities are being murdered by their schools," and "public schools are dead" are being heard among parents, authors, columnists, and some university professors. Author Elmer L. Towns, a former Bible college president, published his research in 1974 and entitled it, Have the Public Schools 'Had It'? Chapter One, "The Smell of Deterioration," begins this way:

> Some educators are nervously whispering
> in private what was never discussed 20 years
> ago -- specifically, that public education
> has "had it." R. W. Seltzer has done more
> than privately talk about it; he published

an article titled, "Public Education: Is Its Demise Near?" in The Clearing House magazine: "At present rate of deterioration, public school education as it exists today will be dead and buried by the year 2000." Liberal columnist Stewart Alsop agrees, noting, "Public education is in danger of collapse."[3]

Reacting to the public's more insistent finger-pointing, William A. Bort, a professional in the field of education (Virginia Commonwealth University), published an article entitled "Educational Chickens Come Home to the Accountability Roost" in the Fall, 1978 issue of The Urban Review.[4] Bort draws three conclusions:

(1) Education cannot take sole responsibility for national social ills.
(2) Specific limits on what schools can do must be set for them.
(3) Aided by educators, parents must assume major responsibility for their children's education.

Bort seems to be a bit defensive in (1); he implies in (2) that schools have taken on more than they can handle; and in (3) he calls for clarification of the roles of educators and parents. Bort, it seems to me, offers nothing startling or new; one would assume all three statements were part of a traditional view of public school education. In practice, however, parents have been made to assume the major responsibility for the payment of their children's education, while feeling more and more powerless when it comes to challenging changes evident in the philosophy of education. Approaches like behavior modification and values clarification are not interpreted by parents as programs that will strengthen parent-child relationships. (Values clarification, for example, suggests that parents' values are only one set of values that the child must pay attention to whereas parents have traditionally felt that children ought to have a set of values derived from their parents which they may test and revise for themselves when they are older.) Evolution (taught as fact) and its philosophical underpinnings of secular humanism make many parents uneasy. It would seem, in light of the development of alternate schools throughout the 1970's, that some parents have become downright hostile. Since "he who pays the piper calls the tunes" is not true in public education, a trend since the days of John Dewey (a signer of the Humanist Manifesto I in 1933), "he who pays" will quit paying.

162

This is precisely what has been happening all over the country for the last decade. A number of public school systems have had to shut down since they have run out of money. Before profesionals cry "Shame!" they ought to ask the question, "Who set the pattern?" It was public school teachers themselves who first shut down systems in wage disputes! Somehow the halls were no longer "hallowed" after that! Today, if teachers or parents perceive their rights are being violated, the "business" is shut down for a while. Parents... teachers... school boards... a "triangle of tension" to borrow a term from Briault.[5] It is obvious parents are registering protest against the professionals at the ballot box. Since this has caused more frustration than change, parents are now challenging school boards directly on such issues as textbook content, sex education, morality, Christmas celebrations, evolution, secular humanism, and the philosophy of science. The professionals are countering with cries of censorship[6] and with calls for a more rigid separation of church and state.

Are parents being intimidated by professionals who "know better" than parents how to run a school system? The answer is no. Parents are now organizing for a more sustained battle. Local "concerned citizens" groups of parents are developing and in turn encouraging the development of resource groups such as the National Educators Fellowship,[7] L.I.T.E.,[8] The Creation Research Society and the Creation-Science Research Center.[9] Books are also being published on the popular level, such as Towns' volume noted above and Hefley's Are Textbooks Harming Your Children? Hefley's book is the story of Norma and Mel Gabler, a Texan couple, who took advantage of the Texas law giving parents the right to review textbooks before they were adopted by the state's selection committee.[10] In the first chapter titled, "Parents Have Rights, Too," Hefley reports the Gablers found that Texas law permitted review but no one seemed to know how the system worked. When they pursued the matter, nobody seemed to know if or where the books were available for screening. In addition, they received the distinct impression that some educators were "resentful" of their questions. According to Hefley, a newspaper story helped explained why:

> The Texas Society Daughters of the American
> Revolution (TSDAR) and a group called Texans
> for America (TFA) had been appearing before
> the State Textbook Committee in Austin pro-
> testing new school texts. The article quoted
> them as saying the new books were anti-American,
> and gave short shrift to patriotism, morality,

free enterprise, individual and states' rights --
while promoting federal programs, economic
determination, secular humanism, dirty literature under the guise of "social realism,"
the United Nations as an agent for world
brotherhood, and many left-wing ideas.

The writer further noted that the TFA had
dug up a requirement in Texas law stipulating
that publishers and authors must sign a non-
Communist oath before their books could be
purchased by the state. This, along with
protests of book content, had publishers
and educators crying infringement on academic freedom by "book burners" and censors.
The tumult was so great that the Speaker of
the Texas House of Representatives had
appointed a five-member committee to in-
vestigate textbooks; public hearings were
to begin in January, 1962.[11]

Hefley's findings were originally published in hardback
as Textbooks on Trial and eventually, since they could not
be ignored, became required reading for salesmen of major
textbook publishers, according to the back of the paperback
edition which was an updated version published in 1979. The
book was a Conservative Book Club selection in June, 1977,
and was condensed in various magazines. Newspapers, magazines and educators' journals reviewed it. As a result, by
the mid-seventies, the Gablers were receiving telephone calls
for help from various parents' groups all over the country.
The Gablers also made a six-week tour of New Zealand and
Australia in response to requests from parents there who
wished to take action.

So we have another "triangle of tension" which includes
parents... publishers... and professionals. Is this much ado
about nothing? Only a few examples can be given here of
material Norma Gabler, a concerned parent, found in prominent
textbooks. In Inquiries in Sociology, published in 1972 by
Allyn and Bacon, she found on page 37: "It's tactless, if
not actually wrong, not to lie under certain circumstances."[12]
This excerpt clearly supports situation ethics and an ethical
posture of secular humanism. It undermines the traditional
Judeo-Christian position.

Before the Texas textbook commission Norma Gabler summarized a section on child training from pages 254 and 255 of

Holt's 1969 text <u>Introduction to the Behavioral Sciences: The</u> <u>Inquiry Approach</u>.

> We find that children who are taught obedience, respect for rules, and parental authority are prejudiced children: whereas, a child who is disobedient, has no respect for authority, or his parents, doing whatever he wishes, is not prejudiced, but develops basic ideas of equality and trust. [13]

This, too, undermines the Judeo-Christian position as well as the religious tenets of Shintoists, Buddhists, and Hindus, for example. It suggests that equality is more important than authority, and the individual is more important than the corporate group, values that complement one another because each brings balance to the other.

On pages 32 and 33 of the <u>Teacher's Guide</u> to the above textbook, Gabler found the following.

> As they do this exercise, the student [sic] should be developing the concept of cultural relativity -- the idea that "rightness," "goodness," or "badness" of a particular kind of behavior can be judged only in terms of the culture in which it is found. For instance, it is "bad" for people to eat the flesh of other human beings, as people do in a few societies which practice cannibalism? Why does this seem so horrifying to most people in our society and so natural to people in those societies which accept the practice? Why do many people in our society find it reasonable and logical to cook people in electric chairs after they have committed certain kinds of crimes? (Cook them, but not eat them.) [14]

It is obvious that this excerpt deals with moral issues, and it is just as obvious that the persuasion (or is it bias) of the author shows through. On what philosophy does he base his opinions? The Gablers, and apparently thousands of other parents, respond, "Not mine or anything like mine." Norma Gabler concluded, after reviewing the Holt book, "If I want my child's behavior changed, I will do it at home."[15]

In 1973, six of the eight books the Gablers objected to were withdrawn and not used in Texas, a seventh was adopted by the State Textbook Commission with minor changes and the eighth had to be extensively rewritten to meet Texas standards. One of the six rejected books, Psychology for You (published by Sadlier), was quietly dropped after first being accepted when it was drawn to the Commission's attention that the text recommended a sex comic written by the author. The Commission procured a copy of the sex comic, Ten Heavy Facts About Sex, and frowned on the provocative drawings of young women, and the explicit captions calling pornography "harmless" and fears of homosexuality "a waste of time."[16]

The battle for the textbooks goes on and the cries of censorship grow louder. This battle of words has given way to something more ugly such as what occurred in Kanawha County, West Virginia, which witnessed "the most prolonged, intense and violent textbook protest this country has ever seen."[17] This protest began in 1974 when Alice Moore, a first-term member of the Kanawha County Board of Education, rejected the Board's traditional policy of routinely accepting the recommendations of the Textbook Selection Committee. The national media carried stories that it was the poorly educated "fundamentalist," rural, coalmining "creekers" who were protesting schoolbooks in opposition to better educated professional and business people in Charleston.[18] In time, 12,000 county residents in the 44,000 student school district signed petitions requesting the removal of certain textbooks. Included in the list of books to be removed was one of the Interaction high school series published by Houghton Mifflin. In the book was a descriptive poem containing more explicit references to sex then would have been permitted on television; the poem dealt with sex orgies on a bus. With charges and countercharges, the protest got out of hand and resulted in strikes, shootings, threats, fire bombings, dynamitings and arrests.

Since there has been no lack of articles both in journals and in popular magazines on "Johnny" who can't read, can't spell, can't add, and can't handle college textbooks when he gets there, few parents would disagree with the observation that public schools have been deteriorating. Since results on SAT tests show a decline over the years in both verbal and math skills, even educators must agree that there has been deterioration. Educators become superdefensive, however, in the wake of Towns' frontal assault:[19] "Educators have simply failed the trust that has been given them."

Many parents, it would seem, have agreed with Towns, and the result is a startling growth in the Christian School movement. Dr. Tim LaHaye, president of Christian Heritage College (El Cajon, California) and prolific writer, has reported his findings on the Christian school movement to regional conventions

of the Association of Christian Schools International (ASCI).[20]
He noted the growth pattern went from one new Christian school
every day during the early seventies, to two new schools in
the mid-seventies, to one new school about every seven hours
today.

The growth of the ASCI itself has been phenomenal. This
association reports approximately 18,000 educators associated
with it. Nearly 2000 Christian schools (including a small
number of Christian colleges) have membership in the ASCI,
with a total of more than 300,000 students. The ASCI puts its
philosophy "up front" and this philosophy includes the following statement as a primary purpose: "A oneness of spirit and
purpose to bring honor to Christ through Christian school
education." The Ohio Regional Office of the ASCI reports
over 150 schools in Ohio presently (18 were reported in 1970-
73); the California region reports some 900 Christian schools
today (about 62 were reported in 1965-66). LaHaye observed
that with the present rate of growth, over half the number of
pupils in school by 1990 would be found in Christian schools.
The ASCI is only one of several Christian school associations.
Other major associations include the American Association of
Christian Schools, headquartered in Florida, and Christian
Schools, International, with headquarters in Grand Rapids,
Michigan. Many schools supported by Baptists are associated
with the former, and schools supported by Reformed churches,
the latter. In Ohio, a number of independent churches (often
carrying the name "Baptist") are associated with yet another
association, the Christian Schools of Ohio, based in
Cleveland.[21]

The growth of the Christian school movement seems to indicate that the basic issue from the parents' point of view
relates to the philosophy of education, not the methodology.
In particular, the issue is morality. Parents see the rela-
tivism of secular humanistic morality as both contrary and
hostile to their traditional belief that God has spoken about
certain issues and declared them wrong. Parents have also
awakened to the fact that science cannot prove or disprove the
existence of God (despite the claims of the philosophy of
science); it is simply, by definition, something that is outside the realm of science. Parents find that they do not
wish to expose their children further to a one-dimensional
world (the natural, physical world which science can explore);
they want their children out of an environment where teachers
and textbooks mock the existence of a two-dimensional world,
one that also includes in its definition of reality, the
spiritual world.

Shifting for a moment from the morality issue to legal issues, we find that certain parental rights are already clearly defined by law. In Pierce v. Society of Sisters (1925), the Supreme Court strongly upheld the right of parents to determine the upbringing of their children and further affirmed the right of parents to send their children to parochial schools rather than government schools. In Whisner (Ohio v. Whisner, Ohio Supreme Court, July 28, 1976) the Court stated:

> In three early cases ... the [U.S. Supreme] court utilized the "liberty concept" embodied within the due process clause of the Fourteenth Amendment to invalidate legislation that interfered with the right of a parent to direct the education, religious or secular, of his or her children. Thus, it has long been recognized that the right of a parent to guide the education, including the religious education, of his or her children is indeed a "fundamental right" guaranteed by the due process clause of the Fourteenth Amendment. [22]

In addition, the Ohio Supreme Court cited the following language from Wisconsin v. Yoder:

> The history and culture of Western civilization reflect a strong tradition of parental concern for the nuture and upbringing of their children. This primary role of the parents in the upbringing of their children is now established beyond debate as an enduring American tradition.... [23]

Legally then, the issue of who is responsible primarily for the education of children is clearly established. Bort's third conclusion (see above), when one strikes out his word "major," has clear legal support: "Aided by educators, parents must assume responsibility for their children's education." Such a responsibility is a right supported by law. The textbook issue is viewed by Christian parents as an attempt to subvert this right supported by law. The professionals are fighting back on the basis of another law, that of freedom of speech; they see the issue as one of censorship. Professionals are arguing for intellectual development and against ignorance while parents are arguing that this intellectual development is infringing on their rights to be responsible for their children's moral development. Parents are

168

not objecting to scientific <u>data</u>, but rather to the scientific <u>facts</u> that include both data and conclusions drawn from those data, conclusions that lean on humanistic presuppositions. School boards turn to professionals for advice and tend to turn a deaf ear towards parents who are not "experts." If Christians protest against certain public school policies, they may be labeled "fundamentalists," a term that has derogatory overtones when used by non-Christians. Parents see the professionals as purveyors of immorality and decry the increasing evidence of secular humanism in the public school system. Since he cannot take on the professional either before a court or a school board, the parent, after trying to increase his political strength (petitions, numbers of sympathetic parents present at hearings), simply gives up and turns to an alternate school system more compatible with his beliefs.

Secular humanism was identified by the Reverend Jerry Falwell, a leader in the Moral Majority movement and pastor of the Thomas Road Baptist Church in Lynchburg, Virginia, as the new religion of modern society. His claim is supported in general by contemporary evangelical Christians. Falwell also contended that exposure to higher education, particularly social sciences, leads to a decline in religiosity and increased adherence to humanistic ethics. This hypothesis was tested by Hammond who reported her findings at the 30th Annual[24] Meeting of the Society for the Study of Social Problems. Hammond tested college students in the Campus Crusade for Christ, a conservative evangelical group, and students in college sociology classes. She used discriminant analysis, and found that the two goups were significantly discriminated by 18 variables, including some tenets of secular humanism and attitudes on moral and political issues. She concluded that the striking differences support Falwell's accusations about social science.

Secularism is defined as "the doctrine that morality should be based solely on regard for the well-being of mankind in the present life, to the exclusion of all considerations drawn from belief in God or in a future state."[25] The Humanist Manifesto I was drawn up in 1933 to codify the tenets of secular humanism. In 1973, the Humanist Manifesto II was drawn up as a revision of the first manifesto. In the revised manifesto, there is a paragraph on moral values:

> We affirm that moral values derive their
> source from human experience. Ethics is
> <u>autonomous</u> and <u>situational</u>, needing no
> <u>theological</u> or <u>ideological</u> sanction. Ethics

stems from human need and interest.[26]
(emphasis in original)

Secular humanism is in itself a religion, and this is the heart of the issue from evangelical Christians' point of view. Humanists themselves claim it is a religion in their Humanist Manifesto I. In addition, the testimony of the United States Supreme Court remains uncontradicted. The Court allowed the definition to stand in its opinion handed down in Torcaso v. Watkins, a case in which seven justices concurred. Justice Black wrote footnote eleven in this case in which he stated that "among religions in this country which do not teach what would generally be considered a belief in the existence of God are Buddhism, Taoism, Ethical Culture, Secular Humanism and others...."[27] (emphasis added)

In The Philosophy of Christian School Education, edited by Paul A. Kienel, Executive Director of the Association of Christian Schools International, Hocking lists some "alarming trends" in modern secular education:

1. The retraction of the Bible from society
2. The rejection of the only concrete and personal re-
    velation of God in Jesus Christ
3. The reduction of reality to the natural level
4. The rebellion against the only holy and moral regu-
    lations of the universe as found in the Bible
5. The refusal to accept or recognize the validity of
    religious knowledge and experience
6. The removal of the dignity and worth of man as a
    being created by God
7. The resistance to Christian ethics and teachings as
    being discriminatory to other religious beliefs and
    practices[28]

Hocking goes on to give thirteen principles which form the basis of the Christian philosophy in education, the first of which states, "The Christian philosophy of education is based on the authority, authenticity, and reliability of the Bible as the complete and final revelation of God concerning all matters of faith, truth, and practice." The two main under- lying objections to the books under criticism in the Kanawha County protest, according to Hillocks,[29] were that the books disparaged Christians and/or Christian beliefs and that they reflected undue violence and cynicism." Christian parents in that case as well as other cases throughout the country did not see demands to remove textbooks as an attempt to support censorship in the land; rather, they demanded that the moral protection they are to provide their impressionable children be also provided by the school system which teaches their children several hours per day, five days a week. If the professionals insist their stand on moral issues is neutral, but allow textbooks and teaching with is not neutral, how shall the educators "aid" parents? What aid does one get from an "enemy"?

We have explored parents' rights; what rights do the professionals have? In the light of the discussion on the legal issues, whatever rights the professionals have, such must be delegated by the parents (and supported by the state where necessary). The rights of the professionals are based on their know-how and skills, on their expertise, and on their competence. But it is clear that the willingness of parents to delegate authority to professionals is contingent upon the fact that the professionals' methodology is based on a philosophy and/or morality that can at the least coexist with that of the parents. Evangelical Christian parents, the Amish, devout Catholics and Jews feel strongly about not allowing professionals who subscribe to a different philosophy to teach their children -- perhaps as strong as parents who are secular humanists and support capitalism and the free enterprise system would feel about letting their children be taught in schools dominated by the philosophy of Russian communism.

How such a dilemma of rights will be resolved can only be guessed at right now. Creationists will probably succeed one day in having evolution taught as a theory rather than a fact and already financially strapped school systems will have to order all new textbooks, since many present textbooks portray evolution as fact. If the law is allowed to stand concerning secular humanism defined as religion, then the tables will be turned on evolutionists; creationists will demand a stricter separation of church and state! (Then again, in light of the phenomenal growth in alternate schools, parents may well ask if such a route is worth it.) If Lytle's views prevail, there will be "Liberty schools."[30] Whether his plan ever succeeds or not is not so important as noting that there are two points in his voucher system of financing that are distinctly "American": (1) free choice, and (2) acknowledgement of the reality of a pluralistic society, a fact missing from present public education. (Others, including Milton Friedman of the University of Chicago in his book, Capitalism and Freedom, have suggested using voucher systems.) Educational vouchers, according to Lytle, are defined as "a certificate representing a sum of money issued by a public agency to parents for the education of their children."[31] Lytle notes that the only way one group of parents can have their curriculum or schedule proposals adopted is at the expense and dissatisfaction of another group of parents. In public school education, changes that deal with philosophy rather than methodology are viewed as threatening parents' rights and a struggle is inevitable. Compromise will not be found on this level.

When there was little question about value systems, there was little or no assertion of parents' rights except among such smaller groups as the Amish. Now that textbooks clearly show evidence of secular humanism and are supported by school boards and professional educators, the battle has been engaged. If alternative school systems continue to grow and flourish, there will be sufficient political thrust to demand changes in the structure of taxation. Am I being over-optimistic in this matter of alternative schools? Will they really continue to flourish? In an article in the Fall 1978 issue of the journal Adolescence entitled "Can Alternate Schools Succeed Where Benjamin Spock, Spiro Agnew and B. F. Skinner Have Failed?" Duke and Perry of Stanford University surveyed 18 alternate schools in California and concluded that discipline was rarely a problem in the alternative schools and general agreement existed among students and teachers.

In schools where there is general agreement between students and teachers, and where parents are satisfied, testified to by virtue of the fact the parents are paying for the education, the answer is, "Yes, they will succeed." And when parents find that their children may be one year ahead in reading levels compared to their counterparts in public schools, their enthusiasm turns a bit ecstatic. Let it be noted that these parents willingly and gladly defer to the professionals within their alternate school systems because on the level of philosophy/morality, there is sufficient agreement. In this kind of setting, Bort's three statements are a reality; aided by educators, parents take responsibility for the education of their children; limits as to what the school can and should do are agreed upon by parents and professionals — parents seem to have more input in the Christian school system; and the parents and professionals are working together, not blaming each other, to find solutions for the ills of society. Neither the rights of parents nor the rights of professionals are violated when there is agreement on this level. The Christian school movement is ample proof of the point.

172

Notes

[1] Harry S. Broudy, "Educational Unity in a Pluralistic Society," School Review, LXXXVI (November, 1977), 70-81.

[2] World Book, Vol. II (Chicago: Field Enterprises Educational Corp., 1966), p. 234.

[3] Elmer L. Towns. Have the Public Schools 'Had It'? (Nashville: Thomas Nelson, 1974). Towns cites R. W. Seltzer, "Public Education, Is Its Demise Near?" The Clearing House, I (no date), 6-9.

[4] William A. Bort, "Educational Chickens Come Home to the Accountability Roost," The Urban Review, X (Fall, 1978), 243-247.

[5] E. W. H. Briault, "A Distributed System of Educational Administration: An International Viewpoint," International Review of Education, XXII (1976), 429-439.

[6] Morton Hunt, "Self-Appointed Censors: New Threat to Our Schools," Reader's Digest, February, 1982, pp. 88-92, condensed from Families.

[7] National Educators Fellowship, South Pasadena, California. An organization of Christian professional educators, mostly in public schools: publishes monthly magazine called Vision.

[8] L.I.T.E., Peoria, Arizona. Citizen-parent group publishes documented newsletters on current trends in education.

[9] The Creation Research Society, Ann Arbor, Michigan. Voting members must be scientists holding at least a master's degree; publishes a quarterly journal. The Creation-Science Research Center, San Diego, California publishes the Science and Creation Series, student and teacher supplementary textbooks.

[10] James C. Hefley, Are Textbooks Harming Your Children? (Milford, Michigan: Mott Media, 1979).

[11] Ibid., pp. 16-17. [12] Ibid., p. 126. [13] Ibid., p. 129.

[14] Ibid., p. 130. [15] Ibid., p. 129. [16] Ibid., p. 138.

[17] George Hillocks, Jr., in School Review, LXXXVI (August, 1978), pp. 632-654; also see Hefley, Are Textbooks Harming, chapter 11.

[18] Hefley, _Are Textbooks Harming_, pp. 157 ff.

[19] Towns, _Have the Public Schools 'Had It'?_, p. 24.

[20] Information reported by Louis Koloze, Director of the Mid-America Region of the ASCI in a telephone conversation to this writer, 3 February 1982. This regional office is also responsible for part of Canada. The office is located in Columbus, Ohio.

[21] Alan N. Grover, _Ohio's Trojan Horse: A Warning to Christian Schools Everywhere_. (Greenville, South Carolina: Bob Jones University Press, 1977.)

[22] _Ohio v. Whisner_, 47 Ohio St. 2d 181 at 213, 214 (1976).

[23] Ibid., p. 214.

[24] Judith A. Hammond, "Opposing World Views: Secular Humanism vs. Evangelical Moralism," a paper presented at the 30th annual meeting of the Society for the Study of Social Problems, see _Sociological Abstracts_, Vol. 29 (3), S 13038, 1981, p. 71.

[25] C. T. Onions, ed., _The Shorter Oxford English Dictionary on Historical Principles_, Vol. II (Oxford, Clarendon Press, 1934), p. 1828.

[26] Paul Kurtz and Edwin H. Wilson, "Humanist Manifesto II," _Current_, ed. Grant S. McClellan, Number 156 (November 1976), pp. 29-30.

[27] Ibid., pp. 30-31.

[28] Paul A. Kienel, ed., _The Philosophy of Christian School Education_, published jointly by Association of Christian Schools International, Whittier, California; Grace Graduate School, Long Beach, California; and Christian Heritage College, El Cajon, California, pp. 7-28.

[29] Hillocks, pp. 632-664.

[30] R. J. Lytle, _Liberty Schools, A Parent's Voucher Plan: A New Way to Handle School Money_, (Farmington, Mich.: Structures Publishing Company, 1975).

[31] Lytle, _Liberty Schools_, p. 9.

TEACHERS' RIGHTS AND QUALITY EDUCATION

John R. Cryan and David Tavel

For having rights enables us to "stand up like men," to look others in the eye, and to feel in some fundamental way the equal of anyone. To think of oneself as the holder of rights is ... to have that minimal self-respect that is necessary to be worthy of the love and esteem of others. Indeed, respect for persons ... may simply be respect for their rights ....[1]

In beginning this short essay we are reminded of a controversy in the war of business advertising, as three major fast food chains sought the upper hand in the battle of the large hamburger. In an attempt to dramatize the inferiority of the competition, one hamburger maker hired three senior citizens for a TV commercial where attention is focused on a very large bun and a very small burger. The three lovable "senior" ladies seem unable to get any service. The most assertive lady raises the now classic question "Where's the beef?" Response to the commercial was overwhelming but with unexpected results. Instead of being acclaimed for its clever message, the segment was assailed for derogatory portrayal of older people. It seems that the wrong issue got the beef. Much the same appears to be the case in the debate over teachers' vs. parents' rights. There is more concern over group rights than there is over quality education.

What are rights? The common definition is "something to which one has a just claim" and "the power or privilege to which one is justly entitled." That parents have the right to "guide the education of their children" was established by the Supreme Court in 1924 and reaffirmed in 1972.[2] To act as agents for their children is a right accorded parents by the Supreme Court in 1975.[3] That parents have a right to influence curriculum content when working through school officials is assured by democratic due process. That parents are legally able, and clearly responsible, to lead and direct their children to a proper education is not debatable.

That there are rights to which the teacher is justly entitled is also a given. Originating in the First and Fourteenth Amendments of the U.S. Constitution they are stated as the rights to:

1. speak freely inside the classroom
2. speak freely outside the classroom
3. freedom of expression through personal appearance
4. a private life of little concern to the school
5. engage in civil rights activities
6. associate with friends of one's choice
7. protection from disciplinary action for exercise of constitutional rights
8. free choice of religion
9. procedural due process
10. freedom from arbitrary or discriminatory actions[4]

But, the Constitution does not refer to education and schools. It speaks to citizenship. Whereas the rights above are personal and specific to all citizens -- teachers and parents alike -- rights specific to teachers are not.

Schooling is a social institution. It is a matter under control of the states. State statutes and court decisions establish specific teacher rights of contract, pay, tenure, renewal and leave. Such statutes and rulings may not, however, restrict personal rights. Issues of citizenship within education are determined by the Constitution; issues of organization and management within education are determined by laws established by state legislatures and rules made by local school boards.

So, where's the beef? What is the controversy? Is the problem really one of "rights" or is that just a symptom of a more deeply rooted problem involving differing views of what constitutes quality education? Recognizing that dichotomizing teacher and parent rights is not useful, this paper seeks to explore the more central issue -- that of maintaining quality education. It begins with two positions. First, teachers, not parents (or administrators), are in the best position to select classroom teaching procedures most likely to lead to quality education. Second, to expand upon the preceding point, quality education is schooling by those skilled in maximizing mental NOT moral development -- schooling by those whose instructional planning is derived from specific training; schooling based upon what research is telling us about how children develop and learn; schooling which focuses on the specific and general content-process methodologies in the various disciplines.

There is a classic perception that those who can, do, and those who can't, teach. This rather common lack of respect for the teaching profession stems from general ignorance of the complexities of teaching. For years, education involved "readin, 'ritin, and 'rithmetic, taught to the tune of the hickory stick." Prior to the turn of the century the number of children graduating from school was small compared to the number required to attend. Teachers, despite the lack of adequate professional training were able to succeed with small numbers of very capable children. Children not "making it" in school were absorbed by society without penalty. Teaching was thought to be easy. Doubtless, to many it also looked easy. Who wouldn't devalue an occupation which "kept" school by "keeping" children in order for eight or nine months, which involved content with a very narrow focus, and which authorized practitioners to physically punish the young who failed to cooperate.

Today, almost nothing is the same as it was in the days of the rural one-room schoolhouse. Every facet of life has exploded into newness. Technology exceeds our ability to comprehend it. Population grows beyond the resources to manage it. The numbers of children attending school have doubled since 1900 while the percent of children graduating from school has increased four fold.[5] The amount of knowledge required to function in today's world is inconceivable when compared to that expected of the high school graduate in 1900. Does society acknowledge the difficult and complex task of the teacher? Is it recognized that any teacher must understand at least the following?

1. the evolution of thinking from conception to maturity
2. developmental stages of growth (both mind and body)
3. the assessment of growth rates and characteristics
4. the relationships between individual differences and learning
5. the specific and general content-process methodologies in all disciplines

Is it known that teachers achieve certification only after hundreds of hours of practical applications of the above knowlledge, only after close scrutiny by a seemingly endless stream of supervising professionals, and only after extensive testing (in some cases at the national level)? Is it considered easy for the teacher to help the student find the pathway to learning when even the learning itself may be obscure?

Going beyond, the teacher is expected to practice this complex expertise while interacting 4000 times daily with 20 to 40 children of mixed race and ethnic background coming from all social strata and faced with a myriad of family problems such as divorce, drug abuse, child abuse, working parents and

177

continually trying to synthesize new information. If instruction were not enough responsibility, the teacher will also conduct home visits, counsel parents, and maintain a record keeping system that would choke an Apple (computer). That untrained educators would attempt to prescribe classroom teaching methods, let alone attempt to teach, is absurd.

The role of today's teacher is to maximize the child's learning through a curriculum which originates with the informed judgment of school officials. Although there is often difference of opinion as to what curriculum should be taught, no private citizen (parent or teacher) has a constitutional right to control exposure to knowledge.[6] There is a right, however, guaranteed the teacher to teach the prescribed curriculum in whatever manner he or she sees fit. This guarantee of academic freedom (not license) is set down in the Constitution's First Amendment.[7] Teachers are obligated to use discretion in regard to methods, choosing those which best serve the demonstrated educational purpose, which are suggested by research, and which are agreed upon by the expertise of the profession.[8] In the final evaluation all teaching methods must be appropriate to the content and to the level of maturity of the pupils.

Certainly the teacher has an important position in our society. In recognizing this, the courts have held that he must not be handicapped by rigid regulation and the spectre of censure by disgruntled citizens including parents. There were days when the parent was likely to be as knowledgeable as the teacher. The more affluent parents entrusted the care and education of their children to a "master" and so began the evolution of in loco parentis - the teacher stood in place of the parent. Today there is almost no likelihood that the parent is fully knowledgeable in matters of teaching. Parents can no longer independently decide for the teacher. In the now famous Atlantic Monthly case (Keefe vs. Geanakos, 1969) the U.S. Court of Appeals held that parents' sensibilities "are not the full measure of what is proper in education."[9] In our rapidly changing society of diverse cultures and expanding technology it is a fact that parents often do not know what is educationally best for their child. Moreover, parents may often have interests and preferences which do not coincide with those of the child.[10]

There is much criticism of education and the teaching profession. The criticism centers on the "poor quality" of preparedness of today's high school graduates to function in a technological society. There are cries for extending the school day and year in hopes that more time on task will equate with more learning. There are advocates of the "back to basics" curriculum who see the emphasis on art, music, drama and debate as frills distracting from learning how to read, write and do mathematics. And there are those who would extend the "basics" downward into kindergarten thinking that "the earlier the better" is the answer. Assuring quality education is not simple.

The problem for the educators at all levels today is one which has bedeviled university level scholars for nearly a thousand years -- suspicion of those who appear to challenge established ways. Academic freedom at the collegiate level developed slowly in reaction to the maltreatment accorded some researchers whose findings disagreed with accepted truths. (Bruno and Galileo are, of course, well-known cases in point.) In the last few decades, thanks to court decisions such as mentioned elsewhere in this paper, academic freedom has been extended to secondary school teachers. However, teachers are increasingly viewed as outsiders by parents who feel alienated from mainstream America; they are increasingly teaching content which reflects the expansion in knowledge, but is foreign to the experience of many parents of school children; and their claim to decision-making authority in the classroom is challenged by those who point out that, unlike university professors, teachers are not advancing knowledge, but rather just transmitting portions of it to the young.

Assuring quality education is thus made all the more difficult because "quality" clearly means different things to different people. To some it means that education which maximizes the opportunities of the young to achieve socio-economic advancement. To others it means that which best reinforces parental beliefs and values which can briefly be described as islands of tradition in a sea of change. Clearly the teacher is caught between the varied parental expectations. As others have pointed out, groups with unique cultural outlooks are less able today to isolate themselves -- and their children -- from different ways of thinking.[11] Thus they call on the school to help perpetuate their traditions, and seek greater control over school programs and personnel to accomplish this.

Several factors have encouraged some traditionalists (often called fundamentalists) to oppose current practices and the educators they hold responsible for them. They hear of declining test scores and rising illiteracy rates. They read of violence and vandalism in increasingly costly schools. Court rulings uphold religious freedom, and this is seen as a threat to the hard-pressed old morality. Women call for equal rights, and this is viewed as a threat to the family and woman's appropriate place in it. The list of concerns is lengthy, and strongly justified. In brief, as the world moves faster and further from the old ways, these traditionalists redouble their efforts to defend that which they view as correct. Borrowing a technique from militant social groups, they demand their rights.

Where does this leave the teacher? A few decades ago this question was given one specific form -- is a teacher in a racially segregated southern community primarily responsible for upholding the values and practices of the dominant group in that community, or does a teacher's professional responsibility dictate that he give primary allegiance to over-arching ideals such as expressed in the Declaration of Independence and the Constitution. The basic issue must be treated the same way now, though some will rephrase the question to ask whose rights or which rights deserve primacy.

A paper of this nature is not the place to go into a philosophical treatise on the nature and origin of rights. It can only summarize. Rights are social in nature, the claim by some that rights are God-given notwithstanding. Rights involve relations between people. Societies establish or grant rights to the extent that it is deemed to be in a society's welfare to do so. In addition to rights that may be granted generally to all, specific rights are granted to specific groups of individuals to promote the contribution of these groups to the whole society. Thus members of particular professions are granted rights and licenses. As this country has increasingly realized the special importance of education, as the working definition of education has been expanded, and as practitioners have evinced greater training and expertise, the rights of teachers have been codified and guaranteed. To the extent that teachers are working to provide quality education, their rights to do so are being judicially protected.

Quality education in what terms? In terms of the greatest benefit to society as a whole! It has long been recognized in this country that there is a close relationship between on the one hand an educated populace, and on the other a viable democracy. (It has also been recognized that to the extent we have not had the first, we have had the latter only imperfectly.) It can be, and indeed has been demonstrated empirically that certain educational experiences are more beneficial than others in a democratic society. Those active in the movement to censor educational materials and remove specific programs from the schools tend to hold the following views: (1) truth is to be defined and upheld by authority and the law; (2) young people need the correct views, and the teacher, hired because he possessed these views, must inculcate them; (3) controversy in school must be discouraged, but if it occurs it is to be settled by recourse to authority; (4) absolutes by definition are perennial and unchanging; and (5) our public schools are dominated by the religion of secularism. This is, of course, far from a complete listing, but these points are basic to the position of the would-be censors. What has been the response of educational professionals to these views? (1) Truth cannot be defined by law, for when that happens the free flow of ideas is inhibited, and the result is not a democratic, but an authoritarian society. (2) The teacher's job is not to inculcate beliefs, but to help students develop the means for forming beliefs and actions. (3) Controversy or disagreement is a part of life. When it arises the appropriate course of action is to talk it out and if necessary compromise, not to force one view down everyone's throat in an authoritarian manner, or, as in Kanawha County, West Virginia, fight it out. (4) Some people do hold beliefs they regard as absolute and unchanging. It is necessary in a democratic society to recognize, however, that what may be absolute for me may be relative or even inappropriate from your viewpoint. (5) If our public schools are "dominated" by any religion, the best label for it would be some generalized form of Christianity. Secularism as a word, an idea, or anything else probably appears not even once in the twelve years of a child's schooling.

The point of the foregoing is that the second of these views clearly provides an education whose quality is far more consistent with the beliefs and values of a democratic society. There is no limit to the examples which can be cited to show that the education profession view is based on the use of reason, respect for differing views, and reliance on what is commonly called the democratic process. "Process" indeed is every bit as important as the end product. Those who have been unhappy with schoolbooks and the classroom behavior of some teachers have been very willing to shortcut democratic processes, and to replace reasoning with sloganeering. (Charges labeling secularism as the religion of the schools or as anti-religion exemplify a shortcutting of the reasoning process. "Secularism" is a political theory, not a religious one. It is a theory about how churches and the state should be related in society.)

The courts have recognized the role of teachers in providing quality education, and thus have upheld the right to teach in a manner dictated by the expertise and standards of the profession. The rights of teachers are justified on the grounds of specialized training and preparation, and the compatibility of the goals of the profession with those of a democratic society. Controversy between teachers, individually or as a group, and segments of society is certain to continue. Society's stake in education is certainly a significant one, and thus society as a whole has a definite role in general educational policy-making. As judicial rulings are increasingly making clear, however, where expertise is called for -- determining appropriate content, methodology, materials -- the rights of the profession are to be recognized and respected.

The courts, however, cannot enforce recognition and respect. They cannot decree an end to the considerable criticism of education and the teaching profession. This criticism centers on the "poor quality" of preparedness of today's high school graduate to function in a technological society. There are cries for extending the school day and year in hopes that more time on task will equate with more learning. There are advocates of the "back to basics" curriculum who see the emphasis on art, music, drama and debate as frills distracting from learning how to read, write and do mathematics. And there are those who would extend the "basics" downward into kindergarten thinking that "the earlier the better" is the answer. Improving and assuring quality education is not so simple. It will result from the cooperative efforts of professional teachers and informed parents who acknowledge that the complexities of teaching make it among the most demanding of professions and who acknowledge that excellence in teaching requires preparedness and a level of experience not quickly or easily reached. Just as society respects the opinion of the jurist so too must society respect the opinion of the teacher. Just as society trusts the practice of the surgeon so too must society trust the practice of the teacher. It is time to recognize that

those who can, teach
those who can't, shouldn't.

Notes

[1] Joel Feinberg, "The Nature and Value of Rights" _Journal of Value Inquiry_, IV (Winter, 1970), 252.

[2] _Pierce v. Society of Sisters_, 268 U.S. 510 (1924), and _Wisconsin v. Yoder_, 406 U.S. 205 (1972).

[3] _Wood v. Strickland_, 420 U.S. 308 (1975).

[4] Daniel J. Gatti and Richard Dev Gatti, _The Teacher and the Law_ (West Nyack, New York: Parker Publishing Co. 1972), p. 68.

[5] U.S. Bureau of the Census, _Historical Statistics of the United States, Colonial Times to 1970_, Bicentennial Edition, Part 1, (Washington: U.S. Government Printing Office, 1975). pp. 369-379.

[6] David Schimmel and Louis Fischer, _The Rights of Parents_ (Columbia, Maryland: National Committee for Citizens in Education, 1977), p. 77.

[7] David Rubin, _The Rights of Teachers_ (New York: Avon Books, 1972), p. 31.

[8] Ibid., p. 36.

[9] Ibid.

[10] Victor L. Warsfold, "A Philosophical Justification for Children's Rights" _Harvard Educational Review_, Reprint Series IX (1974), 29.

[11] David Tavel, _Church-State Issues in Education_ (Bloomington, Indiana: Phi Delta Kappa Educational Foundation, 1979), p. 6.

What is the social role performed by the American school?

Schools reflect the society in which they exist. The values which dominate society will be evident in the programs and activities of its schools. In a society as diverse as the United States we can expect that while there will be widely held general values, when translated into specific activities they will take many forms. As the nation changes through the decades, the particular expression of these values will change, too.

Some writers have contended that the social role of the school can be categorized in terms of the intended impact on society of the curriculum and teaching methods. Thus schooling which transmits without critical examination selected portions of the cultural heritage, and which teaches the skills needed to adapt to the adult world, is viewed as conservative in function. It is schooling aimed at preserving what exists. By way of contrast, a school program which limits content to the "great books," and stresses not preparation for the world of work but rather ideas as discussed in classical literature, can be labeled regressive, not in any invidious sense, but to indicate a tendency to prefer formerly existing social arrangements. A school which treats children rather than bodies of content as central to the educational program, and sees individual development rather than content mastery as the primary educational objective is seen as performing a liberalizing or progressive function.

The particular orientation may or may not be consciously selected, but the educational program shaped by it is. It is often, and erroneously, assumed that school administrators and teachers have determined that educational program. Correct is the recognition of the prevailing societal power structure as the dominant influence, a power structure that may be predominantly local, statewide, or even national. Its decisions may be narrowly self-serving or reflect a commitment to broad social goals.

Both of the following articles recognize the importance of this power structure. The first sees it as responsible for the uncertain balance which has existed between the functions of cultural transmission, preparation of future citizens, and promotion of social change. A rapidly changing future probably will result in greater stress on the school's social mission, but the role of the school will continue to be that of reflecting current and anticipated needs of society as a whole.

The companion article views all schooling activities as shaped by a definite political dimension. Even transmission of intellectual skills is imbedded in this context. The function of the school has been, and remains, determined by the culture, not of society as a whole, but of a socio-economic class freed from the necessity of labor for daily sustenance, and determined to maintain its superordinate position in America.

JUNE CANTY-LEMKE is Coordinator of Secondary Education at the University of Portland, Portland, Oregon. In addition to her administrative responsibilities she teaches in the areas of teaching methodologies and foundations of education. A former Department Chairman at Southern Utah State College, she holds the doctorate from the University of Washington.

SAM R. SNYDER is Associate Professor of Educational Theory and Social Foundations in the College of Education and Allied Professions, University of Toledo.

SURVIVING THE PRECARIOUS BALANCE: THE CHANGING SOCIAL ROLE OF SCHOOLING IN THE TWENTIETH CENTURY

June Canty-Lemke

Schools perform a variety of tasks as part of their function, including the teaching of skills like reading, writing, and calculating, and the training of young bodies. Many of the duties assigned to schools can be described as services to society, or social functions. These include the teaching of citizenship and of the values held by our culture, screening of children not yet immunized against common diseases, and providing driver's education to reduce the number of traffic fatalities. Schools can be described as reflective of society, mirroring events like de jure desegregation, and are considered to be agents of social change. The social role of schools is determined by those outside education and schools are often victims of manipulation by non-educators such as politicians and members of special interest groups.

The impact of forced changes upon the curriculum of our schools is often drastic and long range planning conducted in the best interests of students is often non-existent. Traditionally, three functions of schools (transmission of culture, preparation of future citizens, and acting as an agent of social change) have survived a precarious balance, reacting to the shifts of our society and the influence of the special interest subgroups, but the enormous upheaval of the next decades may cause such a strain on our society and the schools that they will no longer be able to survive the constant struggle to meet the demands and may be forever changed. This essay will deal with a historical view of the social role of schools in this century and with the radical changes which will be necessary to survive the tumultuous future.

When this country was founded, the role of the schools was linked to the needs of the church, to provide ministers and to enable congregations to read the Bible and hymnals. This role was changed and broadened in the nineteenth century in order to adequately serve society, and schools began to provide a myriad of services. The era of industrialization had a potent effect on schools as the new work-style etiquette was incorporated into the education process in order to meet the needs of employers. For example, skills and attitudes toward promptness were stressed and students' behavior was reinforced by the ringing of bells between class periods and at the end of breaks or recesses. The atmosphere in schools was one of increased regimentation, reflecting the environment students would encounter in the factories in which they would one day be employed. This atmosphere was diminished somewhat at the onset of the Progressive era but traces of the industrial era's atmosphere can still be found in today's schools.

The beginning of the Progressive era signaled a new social role for schools. Prominent educators and philosophers like John Dewey called for an increase in the amount of effort put forth to train the future citizens of our democratic society, demanding a change in not only the curriculum, but in the very nature of schools. The atmosphere in the progressive schools changed significantly as students were given a chance to become more involved in their own education. The virtues of democracy were stressed, teachers were not considered to be omniscient, and new courses were taught in order to educate what Dewey called the "whole child" for "complete living." While not all schools were converted to progressivism, many did feel the effects of this philosophy and were modified to some degree.

The outbreak of the second World War meant another change in the social role of schools. The War Department needed a new source of workers and, for the first time in our history, a significant number of women went to work outside their homes. There was an increased sense of nationalism throughout the country, and the economy experienced major changes. The schools, in effect, were called upon to shift back to a more conservative stance and the effects of progressivism were diminished.

The post-war years reflected a sense of conservatism. An aroused fear of communism had a strong effect on schools and students were exposed to highly patriotic materials. Textbooks were designed to give students this feeling of national pride and of the superiority of our social system. Educational films often began by showing a flag waving in the breeze. The social role of schools was again changed to meet political needs.

In 1954, the Supreme Court decision in the <u>Brown vs. Board of Education</u> (Topeka, Kansas) case began a series of major changes in the social role of schools. No longer would the practice of separate but equal schools for the races be legal. The practice would continue, but busing was to come in a decade. The schools, in recognition of their potential role as agents for social change, were logically chosen by government and court officials to serve as a forum for the new integration. The teaching of how the races could live and work cooperatively and with equal opportunity was now considered to be a major function of the schools, although this was not yet truly reflective of society. The schools were reorganized to serve as a model for society, rather than as a mirror of society.

In 1957, the schools of the United States were again asked to aid society. The launching of the Soviet spacecraft, Sputnik, caused an alarm throughout our nation as the fear of Soviet superiority was felt. The mission and curriculum of schools were altered and an increase in the emphasis on mathematics and science education was viewed as necessary to correct our position as second place holders. Educators and psychologists like Jerome Bruner were employed to design programs to educate future scientists and leaders, and programs like SCIS were developed. There was even an increase in the importance of physical education, reflecting the belief in sound bodies producing sound minds. Schools again were asked to aid in healing the ills of society.

The social unrest of the 1960's was felt throughout society and, of course, the schools were no exception. A number of special interest groups called for reform and a return to the progressivism of earlier years. Students were given increased control over their education, desegregation was continued, and courses in Black and Women's Studies began to be offered, as schools again reacted to the changes dictated by society.

The conservatism of the 1970's signaled another change for schools. We elected a more conservative administration and began to ask for more conservative schools. "Back to basics" was the motto and the reforms of the radical sixties were forgotten. Another interest group had its impact on education as Public Law 94-142 was enacted and schools were charged with the education of all handicapped Americans from birth to age twenty-one. Educators scrambled to comply with the new law and programs were quickly developed and teachers trained; even schoolbus manufacturers were alerted to the new needs of society. Terms like "mainstreaming" began to creep into our vocabulary and regular education students were asked to learn alongside new kinds of classmates as the integration of society continued.

The increasing number of non-English speaking Americans resulted in yet another change in our schools. Special interest groups were successful in getting programs such as bilingual education and English as a Second Language. Multiethnic, multi-cultural education was introduced in order to adequately prepare students for their future as citizens and workers in an increasingly international world.

The schools of the 1980's continue to reflect the demands of our ever-changing society. The future promises great changes and our schools are already beginning to feel the pangs caused by growth and shift. Trends are already beginning to surface as we move into an increasingly technological and global era. The power of special interest groups, political action committees, and the various minorities is being recognized and treated with respect by politicians and others seeking power. As the role of schools as provider of services to society continues, it is possible to predict probable emphases of education in the near future.

The politics of the eighties has caused a shift toward less federal and more state and local funding of social programs, including schools. This shift has caused an increase in the impact of regionalism on schools and will cause many changes. The quality of education in some areas will decline as financial resources become scarce due to the loss of federal funds and the inability of state and local agencies to pick up the slack. The variety of programs may change as some areas develop new programs and drop old programs in response to the demands of local groups. Schooling may no longer be the same experience for students all across the nation as the mission of schools is defined more and more by those in power at the local level.

The future has often been described as an age of information, with huge surges in the sophistication of technology and with the advent of the age of telecommunications. Futurists predict an ever-increasing number of people will be employed to work at home on computer terminals connected via telephone lines to their employers. In response to this need from employers, schools are beginning to prepare students for this age and computers are becoming more and more available for school use. Even the computer companies are arranging for programs such as matching grants in order to provide low cost computer availability for schools. Some states are beginning to require computer literacy for teacher certification and more educational software is becoming available. Computers are beginning to be used as educational tools and the fear that education would be dehumanized and all teachers replaced by computers is beginning to subside. Again, schools are changing to meet the demands of society.

Another change in society will be the increased amount of leisure time enjoyed by Americans as a result of technological advances and the changing face of our workforce. Schools will be asked to teach students how to deal with this increase in their free time. Already, state licensing agencies are beginning to require that prospective teachers take courses such as "Lifetime Health and Fitness" so that educators will be able to teach courses to their own students in the coming years. Again, as the needs of society change, so change our schools.

Another change in society that will have a major effect on our schools is the increased availability and use of day-care for children. As more households become two-working parent households due to financial necessity or the desire for personal fulfillment, as day-care becomes more readily available and socially acceptable, and the federal government continues to subsidize childcare through tax deductions, more parents will take advantage of this option for their children. The impact on schools will be felt as more children come to school as experienced students, having already attended day-care or preschool programs. These programs not only provide the social interaction that has long been considered the role of the kindergarten, but in many programs academic subjects are offered and children are exposed to such basics as reading and writing long before they attend a public elementary school. The schools will be forced to shift toward earlier emphasis on academic subjects in the primary grades in order to continue to meet the needs of these more advanced students. Another change in society that will require a change in schools is the increase in the number of single-parent homes. Schools are reacting by trying to provide more male teachers in the primary grades, an area long considered to be a female domain, in order to give students appropriate role models of both sexes to counter the absence of one of the parents.

The integration of schools by students of various races and the introduction of special education programs has already taken place, but discrimination and stereotyping continues. In response to the various minority groups' cries for equity, educational materials are being examined for various biases, including sexism and racism. Schools are trying to acquaint students with the whole spectrum of career and role choices available to them, no matter what their sex or race. In-service and pre-service teacher education programs are offering courses such as "Discrimination Awareness" to rid teachers of the tendency to project their subconscious biases to students. Schools are trying to present the kind of society students will be members of in the future, a society made up of people from many walks of life who have equal chances for success and fulfillment.

As the ability to travel and to communicate with the rest of the world increases, the earth is considered to be "shrinking." Citizenship is becoming less nationalistic and more international. Schools are being charged with the responsibility of preparing future citizens of the world, and are having to present more multi-cultural and global education programs. The transmission of our culture continues to be one of the functions of the schools, but our culture will no longer be the only one studied in depth in our classrooms. Futurists predict a return to the popularity of foreign language programs, especially Spanish and Japanese, as students prepare for careers in international business and for increased personal travel.

The final change to be discussed in this essay is the advent of an era of constant changes. As we move toward the twenty-first century, the rate of change experienced by our society will begin to increase dramatically. The social mission of schools will become more important as we struggle to prepare students for a future that we cannot adequately predict, for an environment we cannot easily describe. The future will be less like the past than in almost any age before and will make incredible demands upon society and thus upon schools. Will educators be able to survive the many pulls and tugs from all the interest groups of our society? If so, they will need to become more flexible, more able to shift easily to changing needs, and more firm so as to be able to resist the demands that will not properly or adequately meet students' needs. They will need to be able to predict the best ways to prepare students and they will need to develop short and long range goals in order to resist responding to the demands which might be trivial or fleeting. In <u>Future Shock</u>, Alvin Toffler describes many of the changes he envisions for our future. He writes,

> It is no longer sufficient for Johnny to understand the past. It is not even enough for him to understand the present, for the here-and-now environment will soon vanish. Johnny must learn to anticipate the directions and rate of change. He must, to put it technically, learn to make repeated, probabilistic, increasingly long-range assumptions about the future. And so must Johnny's teachers. [1]

The functions of schools in the future will resemble the functions of schools in the past in several important ways. Schools will continue to be charged with the task of providing academic subjects for the cognitive development of students, as well as other current functions. Schools will also continue to be charged with various services to society, or social functions, and the very survival of schools will depend on the response of educators to these challenges. As the future fast approaches, educators must ready themselves for this crucial challenge in order to continue to serve the needs and demands of society and in order to survive.

Notes

[1]Alvin Toffler, Future Shock (New York: Bantam Books, 1971), p. 403.

SOCIAL CLASS AS A DETERMINANT OF THE ROLE AND FUNCTION OF PUBLIC SCHOOLING

Sam R. Snyder

What is the role of the school as a social institution and the function of the school as an educational institution within the larger society? The first of these is a sociological question and the second a philosophical question. For purposes of this essay, however, the former question shall be addressed in an historical, rather than sociological context. This essay is an attempt to deal with the problem both descriptively, and prescriptively, i.e., how the school has functioned in our society and how it should function in the present.

Every society sets for itself the goal of initiating the young into the adult society. There are two fundamentally different orientations with respect to how this task is to be accomplished. One orientation sees educational endeavors as basically extensions of the political community. The goals, methodology, and materials of the educational establishment are directly related to the needs and aspirations of the political establishment. In this orientation, philosophy of education is a subset of political philosophy. What is valuable educationally cannot be determined except within the context of what constitutes the good society. In other words, particular political systems require particular kinds of educational systems.

The other orientation sees education as a politically neutral process. The tools of education remain essentally the same: literacy, understanding of mathematical processes, aesthetic awareness, and sensitivity to and appreciation of the human condition. Education transcends political systems, ideological conflicts, and contemporary institutional arrangements. The human condition is a constant, and education should direct its energies toward clarifying and examining the conditions of our humanity.

The American public school establishment as it has emerged in the late twentieth century is a political, economic, social and educational national institution. Furthermore, education by its very nature is a moral enterprise. Historically, education has been closely associated with organized religion. Financial and moral support for education depend upon fulfilling the needs of the community it serves, and the educational enterprise has been closely allied with the value structure of the dominant majority within that community.

The medieval tradition of parish schools emphasized the learning of Latin as preparation for clerical studies. Later, the invention of movable type and Protestantism led to the democratization of culture. We see this in colonial New England with its emphasis on literacy in English as essential for religious purposes. At the secondary and collegiate levels in Europe and the American colonies Latin was a practical subject prerequisite to vocational training for the clergy, law, and medicine.

When Harvard College was established in the seventeenth century, its avowed purpose was the education of the clergy. In a theocracy, the clergy constitute the most prestigious occupational group in the religious-political community. As New England society became increasingly secular, the goals of Harvard College expanded to include the education of gentlemen.

Formal education implies the availability of leisure time as leisure is the prerogative of those not forced to labor for their economic maintenance. In early New England formal schooling existed for the children of those who could spare the labor of their children from the domestic economy. Obviously, the younger children in working class families were those whose labor was most expendable in the domestic economy and it was the younger children who tended to be in school.

In the antebellum south the institution of slavery freed the slaveholder's family from the necessity of domestic labor. For the rural southern poor white, there was a general lack of schooling because it was generally considered unnecessary for the lower classes in an agrarian society. Teaching of the lower classes for religious purposes was carried out by the Society for the Propagation of the Gospel in Foreign Parts. Missionary work was also carried on among African slaves, but in the southern states there was a general prohibition of teaching literacy to slaves. It is significant that Jefferson's plan for education in Virginia formally excluded black children and functionally excluded the children of poor whites.

Freedom from labor and possession of leisure time are directly related to the relative amount of family income and the source of that income. The amount of income is obviously related to the ability to pay for the establishment and maintenance of educational facilities. There is abundant evidence to suggest that, by and large, schools are established by the affluent for the benefit of the affluent. Children of the poor and working class children in general tend to receive their education through direct participation in the work force or through some form of educational arrangement by which they are compensated, as in an apprenticeship or clerkship. Children of the upper classes, on the other hands, are more likely to receive their education throug formal schooling. Even in cases, such as many professions, where an apprenticeship or clerkship is required, it occurs after a lengthy period of prerequisite formal schooling, thus effectively limiting it to those of independent means. Consequently, even when formal schooling is under the auspices of a public school system, children of the affluent tend to go to school longer. Thus public education for which everyone is taxed serves to benefit the children of the affluent who tend to be fewer in number and remain in school longer.

In seventeenth century New England, for example, the Latin grammar schools were certainly not established for the benefit of the children of the lower classes, nor was Harvard College created for that purpose. At the elementary level, schools were established by the affluent to be attended by the lower classes. In New England elementary schooling was established for the socialization of young people for roles commensurate with their station in life in a commercial society. In the South during the same period, the absence of the necessity for wage labor relieved the leisure class of establishing schools for the lower classes and the landed aristocracy provided for the education of their children by private tuition.

Prior to an age of a highly developed transportation technology, social mobility was not highly correlated with geographical mobility. In New England the relative population density made formal schooling physically accessible to the majority of young people. In the south the relative sparseness of population limited access to formal schooling to a minority of youth. The rural poor of the south were limited by lack of facilities, lack of transportation, and lack of motivation.

In a young nation with seemingly unlimited wealth in the form of land, the financing of education through the sale of public lands had great appeal. Introduction of the property tax for school support enabled the affluent to provide some education for the lower classes and a great deal of education for the upper classes from public tax revenues. Literacy has been assumed as the universal goal for all social classes in American society, but the test for literacy has become progressively more rigorous over time. The concept of the literate person expanded from the ability to sign one's name to the ability to recite large portions of the Bible and to be able to spell words correctly. Basic literacy, along with a common moral code, were assumed to be prerequisites for the maintenance of the political community.

In the preceding discussion the terms "upper" and "lower" classes and "working class" were used rather loosely. However amorphous the terms may sometimes appear to be, there are a number of variables which it seems reasonable to take into consideration if one is to give the term "social class" operational meaning. Among these are (1) family income (amount and source), (2) family dwelling (location and valuation), (3) occupation of head of household, (4) social affiliations (membership in community, fraternal, and religious organizations), and (5) amount or level of education.

But do social class categories remain constant over time in the life of a community or in the life of a nation state? If social class phenomena are in fact derivative categories based upon the prevailing type of organization for economic production, then one would logically expect social class composition to change over time to reflect changes in economic organization. One would expect that social class membership would manifest itself in the political community by use of political processes to further perceived self interest.

An additional note must be made with respect to a complementary and sometimes competing social organization which has coexisted with social class and borders on being a caste system. The important attributes which identify members of the caste are ethnicity, sex, and the physically and/or mentally handicapped. True to the function of caste, educational arrangements for such persons were either categorically denied or provided for only in segregated facilities.

We are now ready to portray the five characteristics of social class and the two characteristics of social caste. Categories are general -- specificity of criteria will vary from one historical period to another and are dependent upon available data for the period. Terms such as "high," "medium," and "low" are relative only to one another. One who is "independent" is one who is freed from the necessity of labor. With respect to formal education a modicum of 3 to 6 years of instruction in literacy and morality is assumed for all social classes.

Table 1
Social Class and Caste

Social Class Orientation

	High	Medium	Low
Amount of income	High	Medium	Low
Source of income	investment	invest. + labor	labor
Occupation	independent	white collar	blue collar
Social membership	professional/ managerial	proprietor/ clerical	manual
Education	formal/apprentice	apprentice/ labor	labor

Caste Orientation

Ethnicity	white	other	black
Abnormality	none	physical	mental
Sex	male		female

With respect to caste characteristics, it should be further noted that while sex is a discrete category, physical and mental handicaps and ethnicity are not. The more obvious case is physical and mental handicaps which may be of greater or lesser severity. What is not so often recognized is that in a racist society, there is a hierarchy of ethnicity ranging from most desirable to least desirable as perceived by the dominant majority. For example, in the famous Plessy vs. Ferguson case of 1896, Plessy was declared to the "7/8 white." While in many societies that designation would be meaningless, in nineteenth century United States it meant that Plessy was a black man and had to ride in a racially segregated railroad car in the South.

It should be obvious from the table that the categories are not hard and fast and that the prototypical cases are the easiest to discern. In other words, a white male with a high income from inherited wealth is obviously at the top of the social order while a black female with little formal education doing menial labor is obviously at the bottom. The categories of white collar and blue collar are not always very helpful in themselves in identifying occupations. A low-paid clerk may remain a low-paid clerk throughout his working career or his clerkship may lead to a managerial position. On the other hand, a blue collar worker may be a casual laborer or he may be a highly-skilled craftsman such as a tool maker or machinist. Again, the mixing of class and caste categories will result in differential rewards within the system. A white woman married to a professional man will have more opportunities for social mobility than will her counterpart married to a laborer. A black attorney will have more degrees of freedom than will his black brother working as a domestic. The categories are not absolute, but represent the general boundary conditions which differentiate one group from another.

Table 2
Social Class Orientation and Education

Social Class Orientation	Value Orientation	Class Orientation	Institititutional Arrangement
Class I Maintenance	Class Security	Professional Managerial	Formal Schooling Clerkship
Class II Social Mobility	Upward Mobility	Professional Managerial	Formal Schooling Social Contact
Class II Maintenance	Class Security	Clerical Managerial	Formal Schooling Apprenticeship
Class III Social Mobility	Upward Mobility	Clerical Managerial	Formal Schooling Social Contact
Class III Maintenance	Class Security	Clerical Managerial	Formal Schooling Social Contact
Class IV Social Mobility	Upward Mobility	Skilled Labor	Formal Schooling Social Contact
Class IV Maintenance	Class Security	Casual Labor Domestic	Work Experience
Class V Caste Rejection	Rebellion	Political Strategies	Political Action
Class V Caste Acceptance	Resignation	Servitude	Work Experience

Table 2 is an attempt to represent graphically the relationship between social class orientation and education. It is recognized that while occupation is only one of the attributes of social class, it is a primary one. Because American society does not have a tradition of an "ancient regime" and it espouses a laissez faire economic ideology and a democratic political ideology, perhaps more than in any other society what one has is what one is.

It may also be noted that there is some resemblance between the schematic presented in Table 2 and the well known "Warner Scale." The following comparison can be made:

Table 3
Comparison of Social Scales

CLASS	"WARNER" SCALE
I	Upper Upper Class
IIA	Middle Upper Class
IIB	Lower Upper Class
IIIA	Upper Middle Class
IIIB	Middle Middle Class
IVA	Lower Middle Class
IVB	Upper Lower Class
VA	Middle Lower Class
VB	Lower Lower Class

While such a comparison indicates a general resemblance, there are some salient differences which should be taken into consideration. These have to do primarily with the top and bottom of the respective scales.

The top and bottom of the scale represent a greater rigidity with respect to social mobility than does the middle of the scale. In other words, for people who are born into great wealth, the probability is high that they will remain wealthy throughout their lives. Conversely, for those born into poverty the probability is high that they will live in poverty for the rest of their lives.

Interestingly, this is not the state of affairs one would expect to find among natural phenomena. If very bright adults have offspring, on the average the children will be brighter than average but not brighter than their parents. Conversely, offspring of dull parents will tend to be duller than average but not as dull as their parents. Tall parents tend to have taller than average children and short parents tend to have shorter than average children, but in both cases the tendency is toward the center.

While all natural phenomena follow measures of central tendency, social phenomena do not. Wealthy people tend to become wealthier and pass on their accumulated wealth to their offspring. Poor people tend to remain poor and to pass a heritage of poverty on to their children. This cultural transmission takes place through institutional arrangements which place power and wealth at the disposal of the powerful and wealthy and withhold them from the poverty stricken and powerless.

In the warp and woof of the social fabric the arbiter of wealth and privilege is social class membership. We assume that the members of each social class act upon their perceived self interest. However, the class that controls the means of processing and disseminating information determines the range of options available to all classes of society.

In nineteenth century America, the basic information processing skills were literary skills, the instructional medium for the acquisition of literary skills was the common school, and the dissemination of information was through the pulpit and press. After the Civil War the technological developments in transporation and communication and the mass immigrations led to the industrialization and urbanization of the United States.

As America became increasingly industrialized and urbanized, the repository of mass culture, the common school, underwent an interesting and significant transformation. In many rural and semi-rural communities, the school continued to function as it traditionally had. In many hamlets throughout the country, the school continued to be, along with the local church(es) the social and cultural center of the community until after World War II.

The period from 1890 to 1940 is the crucial era in the transformation of the school. The "old" immigrants from the British Isles, Scandinavia, and western Europe had been more or less assimilated into the general American culture. After the strong reaction to German language and culture at the time of America's entry into World War I, the issue of multiculturalism was resolved through the adoption of the "melting pot" ideology, embraced by national leaders and school spokesmen alike.

The most significant development for education on the Eastern seaboard during this half century was the arrival of the "new" immigrants. Because of changes in transportation, communication, and manufacturing technology, the cities of the Eastern seaboard had become manufacturing, trading, and commercial centers. Located to take advantage of their positions as railheads, seaports, and riverports, these cities were overwhelmed with burgeoning populations from southern and eastern Europe seeking jobs, material prosperity, freedom from political and religious persecution, and an opportunity to create a better life for their children.

The role of the school was to transform this polyglot of humanity into good Americans through exposure to the white, Anglo-Saxon Protestant institution of the public school. Through mastery of the English language, an understanding of Anglo-Saxon legal and political institutions, and acceptance of the Protestant work ethic these foreign youth could become patriotic American citizens.

Paramount in this pantheon of public virtues was the absolute necessity for the avoidance of class conflict. The public school was both the seed bed of democracy and the testing ground for the meritocracy. By providing equal opportunity for all regardless of race, religion or national origin, the public school system would not allow everyone to compete for wealth and status within the system but would assume that winners and losers alike were responsible for their own success or failure.

In the eastern United States and throughout the midwest the internal migration from the countryside to the cities increased. The capitalization of basic manufacturing and extractive industries and introduction of steam-driven machinery, the factory system, and standardized production created a great demand for unskilled and semi-skilled labor. The elimination of many skilled crafts and trades led to the curtailment of traditional apprenticeship systems and tended toward the proletarianization of the work force. Concurrently, the high rate of literacy, the widespread establishment of cheap, local newspapers as a medium for information and advertising, and the development of a low cost, efficient, interurban railway system all conspired to bring people into the city. Throughout the midwest and west the end of cheap land, fencing of the open range, mechanization of farm equipment, development of hybrid seed and improved fertilizer, and federally-financed agricultural experimentation all combined to reduce the need for unskilled farm labor and increased the need for greater capitalization of the agricultural enterprise. The national railway systems beginning to crisscross the nation from east to west not only carried manufactured goods from city to farm and farm products from farm to city, but also carried young people from lives of rural isolation and cultural deprivation to dreams of prosperity and adventure in the growing metropolises of the nation.

Stimulated by increased industrial production during World War I, the great internal migrations brought rural folk from the south to the industrial cities of the north. Share-croppers and farmhands, black and white, men and women and children with their belongings on their backs and their live-lihoods in their hands began to trek north in search of an escape from poverty and a search for job security and the dream of a better life. In particular, black people by the thousands "voted with their feet" as they searched for the opportunity for life, liberty, and the pursuit of happiness denied them anew with the end of Reconstruction in 1876.

From Plessy v. Ferguson in 1896 until Brown v. Topeka Board of Education in 1954, black Americans had no legal re-course from a caste position at the bottom of the social struc-ture. In all states whether by custom or by law, the majority of black Americans were segregated from their white counter-parts in virtually all educational facilities.

For groups other than blacks, the schools served both as a sorting device for social class membership and as a means of rationalizing and justifying the increasing rigidity of the economic corporate structure. Between the two world wars, the public school system began to function as a national school system, although it retained the formal structure of local control. There were a number of factors responsible for this development.

The enrollment of the schools increased dramatically dur-ing this period. There were a number of reasons for this. The population of the country was growing in general and in school-age children and youth in particular. With industrial-ization, urbanization, and consolidation of business enter-prises into large corporate structures, the traditional ar-rangements of small family-owned business, small-town living, and face-to-face contacts were breaking down. As these rela-tionships changed, the school, increasingly grounded in a pro-gressive ideology, emerged as the central educational agency of youth. It gradually took over many functions formerly per-formed by family, church, and community. With compulsory edu-cation laws in every state requiring school attendance, in most cases through early adolescence, not only were more children and youth than ever before attending school but they were staying in school longer.

In addition to, and partly in response to the increase in enrollment the curricula expanded with the textbook as the predominant tool of teaching methodology. With the establish-ment of normal schools and the formal training of elementary teachers, the old method of teaching reading and writing by the cathechism of look, memorize, and recite could no longer suffice. Teaching methods for each subject were developed based upon such theoretical considerations as Thorndike's Laws of Learning. Reading vocabularies were established along with dictionaries for classroom work.

High school enrollments in particular rose exponentially during the period. With more youth attending high school, curricular changes were initiated in an attempt to meet the needs of young people from diverse social backgrounds. The manual training movement was a national effort to serve high school youth who were not preparing to enter college. As the American population became more mobile, it was recognized that some degree of curriculum standardization was desirable, and the vehicle for that movement was the standardized textbook. In addition to increased enrollments, the use of standardized textbooks, and the increasing standardization of curricula, the testing movement was gaining strength after the national experience with I.Q. tests during World War I.

The rationale behind the I.Q. as a sorting device is disarmingly simple. In every society there are a few people who are leaders and many people who are followers. It follows that the leaders have some special qualities or characteristics that the followers do not have or have in lesser quantity. Whatever these qualities are, it seems obvious, at least to the leaders, that they are in short supply. These elusive qualities or abilities, or leadership potential, are named intelligence. Some people are obviously more intelligent than others. If there were just some way to identify the more intelligent from those less intelligent, society could train the former for leadership positions. Behold the Intelligence Quotient!

It was found that a test, or a series of tests, could be devised which yield a score or Intelligence Quotient (I.Q.). People with a high I.Q. score relative to their chronological age were more intelligent than people with low I.Q. scores.

When the affluent, white, Anglo-Saxon Protestant males who devised the I.Q. tests began to test various populations within the United States, they found that the people who tended to do well on the I.Q. tests were affluent, white, Anglo-Saxon males. This group was also over-represented in positions of leadership among professions, business, industry, and politics. As a group they were the most successful in terms of affluence, prestigious occupations, and positions of economic power and social prestige.

Every society struggles to maintain itself and the ruling class in any society attempts to replicate the social structure which maintains and perpetuates the power and status of the ruling elite. After World War Two, the secondary school became increasingly what one author has referred to as a "sorting machine" designed to fulfill the manpower needs of the American military-industrial complex. This was done through the use of a system of "social persuaders" such as vocational guidance, tracking, and ability grouping.

Within the past thirty years, two simultaneous and somewhat contradictory developments have occurred which may profoundly change the character of public schooling in the United States. The first is that the public school system is no longer the primary educational and cultural force on the lives of the young. The second is that because of both demographic and political factors the school rigidifies class lines to a greater extent than it has in the past.

The public school as we know it is essentially a nineteenth century institution rooted in the technology of the printed word. The replication of the social structure through the school was possible because the school was the repository of language and literature -- the school represented adult literate society. The school, the church, and the family-based community represented civilization, morality, and social structure, and each reinforced the other. At the bottom of the social scale, depending upon time and place, was the black, the immigrant Catholic, or the non-Christian. At the top of the social scale was the white, Anglo-Saxon Protestant. The well-ordered family, like the well-ordered community, had at its head the benevolent father, just as the universe itself had its Heavenly Father.

The one experience common to virtually all able-bodied nineteenth century American youth, rich or poor, black or white, rural or urban, male or female, was to a greater or lesser extent the common school experience. One of the reasons for the great success of the common school movement was its relatively high failure rate. The common school population could be represented by the shape of a pyramid with many students enrolled at the base in the lower grades and a few emerging at the apex. What the student learned through the schooling process was the shape of the social structure and his or her place in it.

With the enactment of compulsory education laws around the turn of the century, the secondary school became a logical extension of the common school movement. Elementary school education through the eighth grade became the norm for the great majority of American youth. The sorting-out process was then moved up into the high school. In medium-sized and larger cities the district high school became common in the early twentieth century. Two kinds of sorting, extramural and intramural, occurred at the secondary level.

When city school systems first created high school districts, the high schools were placed in those areas which had the greatest number of children going on to secondary school. Not coincidentally, these districts tended to be those populated by the more affluent professional and managerial class. Reciprocally, after the establishment of district high schools, the presence of a secondary school in the district became an incentive for those who were upwardly mobile to secure a secondary education for their children. In addition, social mobility has been closely associated with geographical mobility. In the rapidly growing cities of late nineteenth and early twentieth century America, as the more affluent moved out from the center of the city, the less well-off economically took their places in the pattern known as the "trickle down" theory.

Intramurally, sorting by social class was accomplished through the medium of curriculum differentiation. "Tracking" systems early led students in the district high schools into programs oriented toward college preparation, general education, business and commercial training, or manual training. Social class was closely associated with occupational groups, and the comprehensive high school provided vocational training for the lower classes and pre-vocational training for the upper classes.

By the mid-twentieth century the process of suburbanization was beginning to occur in the metropolitan areas of the country. As increasingly large numbers of affluent people left the city for residence in surrounding semi-rural settings, the initial reaction on the part of the cities was to extend the corporation limits to include the burgeoning new areas. However, the new suburbanites soon recognized that it was to their financial advantage to incorporate their bedroom communities into autonomous political entities and provide for their own police and fire protection, utilities, municipal governance, and schooling. Through a national program of subsidization for private transportation and suburban housing, the suburbanites had access to the cultural, commercial, and recreational facilities of the city but did not have to accept responsibility for their maintenance.

The relatively affluent suburban public school systems soon began to compete with the older central city school systems. With a strong financial base in a more affluent, more highly educated, status-conscious clientele, these systems could provide new buildings, the latest curriculum materials, higher salary schedules, and a homogeneous student population oriented toward education as a means of upward social mobility. As suburban populations proliferated, industry followed the educated work force into suburbia and over a period of several decades predominant transportation patterns shifted from urban/suburban to inter-suburban leaving the central city increasingly isolated, segregated and abandoned.

By the end of the Vietnam War the aging of the population, lowered birth rate, and a stagnating economy all led to a divisiveness between city and suburban dweller, rich and poor, white and black, well-educated and unskilled. The geographical and social differences have been intensified and reinforced by the public school structure.

To what extent is it reasonable to predict that the future of public education will be an extension of the present? The public school system in general, and the comprehensive high school in particular, worked relatively well in avoiding class conflict and in perpetuating the social structure of American society in the past. This was true because, with the exception of caste considerations, public education was a near universal experience for all classes of American youth.

If current trends continue, one may expect to find large scale abandonment of public education in favor of private educational ventures subsidized by public funds much in the same way that public transportation systems were abandoned in favor of subsidized private modes of transportation.

To avoid increasing dichotomization of society, some other means of replicating the social structure will have to be found. This may take the form of conscription of youth for service to the state (analogous to universal military training), a greater reliance upon electronic media controlled by the industrial military complex for cultural conditioning, or the use of community-based behavior control centers for infants.

Whatever the response, social control through the incarceration of large numbers of children and youth for social indoctrination will appear increasingly expensive, cumbersome, and inefficient.

PART NINE -- PRIVATE SCHOOLS FOR BLACKS

Are existing private schools a viable educational alternative for blacks?

The twentieth century has seen a significant movement of blacks to the industrialized north, especially in the decades following World War Two. In some cities the increase in the number of blacks has been accompanied by the effective exercise of political power, as evidenced by the election of black mayors in cities such as Chicago, Cleveland, Detroit, and Gary. Partly for reasons examined in studies by Coleman and Jencks, public schools in some of these communities have failed to satisfy the educational aspirations of blacks who consider a white dominated power structure insensitive to their wishes. Private schools, selective in their admissions, college preparatory in their program, and aided with public moneys, have sought to make themselves an attractive alternative. But are they?

The first article takes the position that thus far neither public nor private schools have met the needs of minority students, nor is there evidence that either is prepared to make the commitment necessary to address effectively the educational problems of minorities. For academically oriented minority youth, however, the non-public school may provide some opportunities that today's hard-pressed public school cannot equal.

Any educational system likely to assist blacks in their struggle for equality will probably have to be under the control of blacks, claims the second article. Many existing private schools, far from being acceptable to blacks, tend to mirror the shortcomings which exist in American society, perhaps in an even more unfavorable way than the public schools.

LEON CARTER is Director of Minority Affairs at the University of Toledo. Formerly he was Director of the university's Upward Bound program. His academic specialization is in educational sociology, the field in which he is completing the doctorate.

HERBERT DOUGLAS is Professor and Chairman of the Department of Law and Justice Studies at Glassboro Sate College, New Jersey. He also teaches and writes in the area of sociology of education, and holds the doctorate from the University of Toledo.

MINORITIES AND MERITOCRACY

Leon J. Carter III

Ironically, the most persistent and staunchest allies of the American educational system have come from among the minority citizenry. Traditionally, Hispanic America, Indian America, Asian America and especially Black America have viewed education as the major lifeline to economic independence and social respectability. Education has always been a value of the highest magnitude. Second only to the mystique of religion, the struggle for quality education has occupied a unique and singular attention in the consciousness of minority America. Almost achieving deification, education has been held sacred. The vision kindled and protected has withstood the death grip of segregation, Jim Crowism, and the "separate but equal" ideology of mainstream America. The dream has survived the Ku Klux Klan; Little Rock, Arkansas; and the discrimination of the industrialized north. Hazards such as "genetic inferiority," white flight, and most recently Reaganomics have appeared and threatened that hope. The dream has survived, however, indicative of the almost unquestioned faith that minority America has continued to place in the power of schooling to show the way out of poverty.

Unlike white America, the minority communities have had few routes to economic power other than education. When the economy was primarily agrarian, survival in the dominant culture was dictated by the ability to scratch out a marginal livelihood. The onset of industrialization necessitated the acquisition of entirely new sets of skills. Systematically, industrialization required a progression of higher order skills, which demanded an academic background that could not be acquired by on-the-job training. With the gradual -- and not so gradual -- transformation of the American economy, a greater variety and complexity of skills was called for, and the nation's schools increasingly were expected to respond to this call. Thus it is no coincidence that the educational system began to reform itself in the same manner as the industrial system. Now in the post-industrial era the schools continue to be pressured to comply with the demands of the economy.

The effort to fulfill the personnel requirements of business and industry has led, in part, to schools performing the "social-sorter" function. Thus we see the variety of twentieth century tools developed to accomplish this screening: I. Q. tests, entrance examinations, attitude inventories, and a wide range of other instruments and procedures useful in labeling students. Once labeled, students could then be "sorted out," directed into terminal programs euphemistically labeled vocational. In practice this has often led to minorities being given little access to the educational system at the very time a rapidly changing national society has been escalating its educational demands.

In still other ways, ethnic and racial minorities have been discouraged from participating in the supposedly meritocratic system. The financing of schooling from the local property tax has resulted in extreme disparities between schools and school systems. Statewide funding arrangements have yet to close the gap; proposals for fiscal equity have usually died or been severely distorted in legislative chambers. Judicial efforts often accomplished little more, for while the courts have mandated bussing, the educational results have been at best mixed. Majoritarian America may have accepted, perhaps begrudgingly, the admission of minority students into "white" schools, but clearly it has not accepted the bussing of whites to "minority" schools.

The pace at which the barriers preventing full educational participation were reduced has been haphazard and slow. Integration has been delayed and thwarted by communities seeking to keep the benefits of the educational experience in the domain of the wealthier and more privileged segments of American society. The view of the schools as "social sorters" has held center stage for many decades. Use of this concept has continually reaffirmed the acceptance by the majority of an educational system whereby the "talented" are chosen and moved ahead on the basis of their achievement. As a result, the educational enterprise has contributed systematically, methodologically, and voluntarily to the perpetuation of inequality. Democracy and meritocracy have enjoyed the status of strange bedfellows in the body politic of American education.

Under the guise of equality and opportunity for all, the educational system, in reality, has supported academic genocide. Literally millions of America's poor and racially identifiable minorities have been systematically excluded from the higher levels of the educational process, forced out by the hostile atmosphere of the schools, their faculties, administrators, students, and the community at large. Minority America has fought back with the only resources available to it -- violence and litigation. The violence, while providing an immediate emotional outlet, solved nothing. Hostile reactions became more pronounced and retaliation was often swift and brutal.

Litigation efforts regarding the legitimate concerns of minority America were scarcely addressed by the courts until the historic decision in Brown v. Board of Education in 1954. Since then there have been several judicial decisions in favor of minority America's access to the educational system. Notable federal legislative efforts were the 1964 Civil Rights Act and the 1965 Higher Education Act which included among other items the provision that students should not be denied access to college because they are non-white or because their families are poor. The point, however, is that educational institutions -- elementary, secondary and higher education -- have had three centuries of existence in America, but only in the last twenty-eight years has there been a national attempt to provide equal educational access and equal quality education for America's minority communities. In effect formal education in this country has remained a closed system. The progress promised by successful litigation has been more myth than reality. This is as true in education as elsewhere.

During the civil rights movement of the 1960s and early 1970s there was uneven progress toward greater educational opportunity for minority Americans. The major emphasis during this time was on access to all levels of education, but more specifically to higher education. Factors were operating against equality, however. As a reaction to the Brown decision and succeeding court rulings, white America retrenched in what has become popularly known as "white flight." This phenomenon precipitated three primary events which had a significant impact on the educational opportunities of the minority population.

The first event was the establishment of economically segregated schools in suburbia. Many of these academic retreats were private, and as such required tuition fees which effectively excluded students from poor families. Minority communities, over-represented in the work force at the lower wage scale indices, could not afford to send offspring to the suburban schools even if access were granted. The second event occurred simultaneously: the erosion of the tax base in the metropolitan city proper. As the affluent residents of the city fled to outlying areas, the tax base, which supported the city schools, was siphoned off. The city experienced a very real decline in the financial resources at its disposal to operate the multitude of services required by city inhabitants. As in most cases of fiscal anxiety and tax shortfalls, the areas which are reduced first are the areas that provide

213

educational and social services. As the number of minority students, especially in the central or inner city schools, appeared to increase, there were less resources available to provide a commensurate delivery of educational services. While the fiscal restraints of the central city were tight, the attitudes of the predominantly white teaching staffs were beginning to shift.

As central city schools became predominantly minority in nature, the long-standing white prejudice toward minorities and especially blacks began to resurface. The myths of the "genetic inferiority" of blacks students, that black Americans have a "limited intellectual range," that blacks are more prone to commit crimes and are lazy and unclean, constituted a central thesis. In conjunction with the decline in the economic prosperity of the city, these attitudes fueled the third event: teacher flight to suburban schools or from the profession. The exercise of either of these choices did little to enhance the capability of an embattled public school system to provide quality education for all students. More importantly, this shift in the pattern of education at the primary and secondary levels had a negative impact on the participation and successful matriculation rates of minority individuals in higher educational institutions. Minority populations, over-represented on the high school non-completion curve, constituted a significant portion of the population which did not gain access to post-secondary educational activities. The "social-sorter" function of the school had become the dominant fact of life for the minority student.

Teacher attitudes toward the minority student often have been characterized by apathy and indifference. The benign, and sometimes malignant neglect of the minority student adversely influenced educational expectations -- what schools could teach, what students could learn. It appears that these attitudes have submerged and resurfaced in American schools -- public and private -- often enough to leave many minority members questioning the faith earlier generations placed in schooling. The door seemingly leading out of the poverty cycle was not conventional but revolving. The harsh reality of the unfulfilled promise of education has fostered disillusionment with the idea of an American meritocracy.

Meanwhile, the United States has been transformed into a credentialed society. The high school diploma has given way to the bachelor's degree which, in turn, is giving way to the master's or specialist degree. Entry level criteria for the work force have continuously expanded. Significant and profound change has been introduced by the maturation of the electronics age. The impact of the computer has rivaled the impact of the printing press. Computer literacy has become the "foreign language" of the future. A new age has arrived, and with it a new conceptualization of the universe and our relationship with that universe is in the process of unfolding. If minority students are restricted from full participation in the richness of the new dimensions, they will be systematically precluded from the emancipation offered by the infusion of high technology into the urban classroom. The proceeds from this "new" frontier may have a trickle down effect, but the minority community would still be denied full partnership. What option, then, for minority Americans?

During the years of affluence following World War Two expansion of non-public schooling occurred, especially in heavily Roman Catholic areas. A variety of circumstances -- Catholic parents deserting the parochial schools at the very time the church and religious orders were building new ones, and the schools themselves seeking public funding -- raised the possibility of these schools providing the services sought by the minorities. There was a potential clientele hoping that the private school would operate differently in its acceptance of, instructional methodology for, and attitudes toward the minority student. There were private schools seeking academic respectability, and getting it with considerable help from Congress and several state legislatures.

Private schools could claim to have several potential advantages over public schools. They could be selective in admissions, and if they guessed wrong they could expel an undesirable student. They would not have to provide a variety of programs, and seek to meet a variety of post-secondary level goals. The possibility for pursuit of academic excellence appeared good. The emphasis -- the sole emphasis -- could be college preparation, which for minorities was an essential ingredient of educational opportunity.

Many private schools have other attractions. They are likely to be geographically and culturally removed from the minority neighborhood, thereby giving the minority student additional experience in the wider environment. The more complete break with one's social and educational background could mean an excellent opportunity to peer beyond familiar horizons and participate in a diversified cultural setting. Finally, if a minority youngster has to make an adjustment to the majoritarian society, perhaps the culture shock should come during one's formative years rather than when one is trying to find a place in the economic world.

215

There is another side to the discussion, however. Increasingly private schools involve faculty, students, and parents from the same general population groups that provide the faculty, students, and parents for public schools. The same ethnocentric baggage which is carried by one is also carried by the other. The racial and cultural polarity found in the public sector rears its head in the private one. The outside world shapes the private school as much as it does the public one, albeit often in different ways, as when parents seek admittance for their youngsters to a school which is trying to be forward-looking but which is, in the parental eyes, a place with good old-fashioned discipline and hard work.

Private schools reflect the limitations of public schools in other ways. In search of certification status and public funding, they ape the public institutions in an effort to get full approval from state education departments and accrediting bodies. Like their public counterparts, private schools do poorly in anticipating and recognizing the needs of their minority constituency as distinct and separate from those of the majority of students. The history, traditions, and cultural contributions and experience of minority groups are largely ignored. The social and organizational skills necessary for the student to make a smooth transition between cultures are assumed to be operational. Little attempt is made to help the minority youngster adjust to new academic and environmental challenges.

What then are some generalizations which can be drawn from a comparison of the public and private systems? Despite similarities in structure and faculty attitudes, the private school could represent a more viable option for minority students, especially the academically talented minority student. The private school profile exhibits some characteristics that separate it from the public school system. First, private schools find it easier to set high academic standards -- standards which are the same for anyone matriculating. Academic perseverance, discipline, and excellence are expected of all. Quality academic performance is the rule rather than the exception. Starting with its selective admissions criteria, the private school can more easily establish and maintain an atmosphere of disciplined academic, moral, and social behavior. Teachers will demand more, and it is a reasonable hypothesis that academic performance -- by individuals of any group -- will be influenced by standards established by the teachers.

One characteristic of some significance may be the cost factor. While this may on the surface seem to be a negative

216

comment about private schools, it really can be a plus. Education is an investment, in many cases a substantial one, especially for lower income minority families. For such a family to opt for a private school education indicates a belief in the value of sacrificing for a quality educational preparation. This belief can represent a great incentive for the minority student to succeed in his school work. There may be a similar impact on the parents, who, having made this extra educational investment, take greater interest and get involved in the work of the private school. Family background and attitude toward schooling are probably the most important factors in influencing student academic achievement. It is reasonable to hypothesize that the minority family whose priorities incline it to pay private school tuition will set higher expectations both for its youngsters enrolled and the school itself.

Reference has already been made to the culture shock a minority youngster will experience in the private school. Like tuition, this too is not a totally negative factor. Minorities are at some point going to have to make an adjustment to the majoritarian culture if they are to live and function in a broader world. If, in the private school, the student can withstand the cultural pressures, the rigorous academic regimen, and the feeling of isolation, then the acquisition of enhanced academic and survival skills and the development of a wider cultural perspective are bench marks of potential success. The student may emerge a more academically competent and confident person, better able to profit from the college environment which increases his access to the meritocratic society.

One of the repetitive parallels between America at the turn of the nineteenth century and America today is the diversity of "others" that the cities and their educational institutions are asked to assimilate. Thus faced with a duality of missions, academic preparation versus social sorting, public and private schools historically have paid more attention to the social sorting role. This duality has increased the dysfunctionalism of the city's urban school. Private schools, although heavily imprinted with the prevailing social and political moods, nonetheless have opted to emphasize academic preparation. True pedagogical reform has been at an impasse in public education because the basic hierarchical structure of the bureaucracy of education has been remarkably resistant to change. Private schools are not generally encumbered by the traditional infrastructure of public education. While graduation requirements may be dictated by the state legislature, the private school can be more flexible in its methodology, choice of educational materials and academic instruction. Given this relative degree of autonomy, the private school should be able to react more rapidly to environmental and technological changes. This ability may have a profound impact on private education's ability to deliver, qualitatively and quantitatively, more diverse, hence more appropriate, educational preparation.

It is my contention that given the traditionally conservative context of schooling for all students, and especially minority students, neither the private nor public sectors have adequately delivered the promised skills and motivation that minority students particularly require to be academically and economically successful. There is little substantive indication that either system is totally committed to implementing the solutions needed to address the deep-seated problems that have encompassed minority education in the United States. The revolving door is still the revolving door.

Educational systems, reflecting the dominant thematic concepts of mainstream America will continue to be powerless to change or adapt readily to a rapidly changing universe. The lag time between educational theory and practice is already enormous, and considering the complexity and range of cultural and racial interrelationships, there are no simple answers. Given this broad generalization, it is easy to understand why the commitment to improve the quality of minority education is in a state of erosion. The immediate future is a bleak one, for there are few alternatives which might serve to reduce the problem to a more manageable level. As a result, minority access to full partnership in the American meritocratic process is significantly barred.

Private schools, in many respects, are in a position similar to that of public schools in regard to serving minority populations. The same external social, political, economic and demographic pressures which impact on one are significantly felt by the other. However, for the academically talented minority youth the private educational enterprise might become a more viable alternative than public education. Nevertheless, as presently configured, both private and public education cannot fulfill the mythical promise of full meritocratic equity in mainstream America. The dual realities of equal access and equal educational opportunity remain rhetorical in nature and elusive in substance.

BLACKS AND PRIVATE SCHOOLS: A CRITICAL ASSESSMENT

Herbert Douglas

The 1981 Coleman report, along with the reports of research by Greeley and others, have renewed the debate over the educational advantages offered by non-public schools. These recent findings suggest that private school attendance increases the achievement levels of Black students. The notion is advanced that private schools possess certain intrinsic qualities which generate such results. Yet the question of whether private schools represent a viable educational alternative for Black youth remains. And it is doubtful whether this question can be given an affirmative response.

W.E.B. DuBois, the Father of Black Studies, made the following observation in an address delivered in 1930:

> How are we going to place the Black American on a sure foundation in the modern state? The modern state is primarily business and industry. Its industrial problems must be settled before its cultural problems can really and successfully be attacked.... The Negro has not found a solid foundation in that state as yet. He is mainly the unskilled laborer; the casual employee, the man hired last and fired first; the man who must subsist upon the lowest wage and consequently share an undue burden of poverty, crime, insanity, and ignorance.[1]

This commentary is quite revealing of the status of Blacks in America at the time. Yet, one wonders how much change has occurred in the half century which has elapsed since DuBois offered those remarks.

To be sure, there is empirical evidence to support the notion that some Black advancement has occurred in the ensuing years. There have been increases in Black enrollments at virtually every level of schooling from pre-school institutions to colleges and universities. The Black Bourgeoisie, those Blacks who have achieved middle class status, has also expanded. This change reflects the greater diversity which is seen in the types of vocational and professional responsibilities Black men and women have been able to acquire.[2] Yet, major economic and educational problems persist, and concern and disenchantment over the persistence of such debilitating issues continue to dominate the consciousness of many Black

Americans. Much of that concern has been focused upon Black youth.

Recently, bourgeois publications such as _Time_ and _Newsweek_ have produced issues featuring such themes as "Youth Crime" and "Black Youth: A Lost Generation." The focus of many of the articles contained in these publications is of major concern to Blacks, for it reminds us of the continuing problems of underdevelopment, dependency and lack of adequate participation of Black youth in the significant institutional life of this nation -- except for penal institutions, the military, and the public welfare system.

The problem of poverty is endemic within Black America. Current government data indicate that more than one-sixth of all Black workers in the U.S. are unemployed, as are more than fifty percent of all Black teenagers. In addition to these realities we must face the fact that the income gap between Black and White families in the nation is widening. While the number of White children living in poverty declined in the latter part of the 1970's, the number of poor Black children increased.[3] Despite the fact that 1979 was designated as the International Year of the Child, the prospects for improving the condition of Black children, the most vital element of the Black community, remain indeed grim. With racism and conservatism so prominent in the debate over public issues and policy concerns of the day, the social and economic conditions faced by all sectors of Black society, especially youth, may continue to deteriorate. These are some of the essential aspects of the American political economy which confront Blacks in their struggle to survive and progress in the United States.

One successful effort during the civil rights movement was the 1954 Supreme Court ruling in _Brown vs. Board of Education_. The Court found racially separate schools to be unconstitutional. Those who had fought to bring this development to fruition viewed it as both a culminating effort in the struggle against segregation within society and an opportunity for a new beginning in the effort to create an open, non-racist society. Since _Brown_, there has been much disillusionment over school integration. Many Blacks find the "one-way integration" which has dominated the process to be distasteful due to the racist implications which it harbors. Blacks are also disillusioned over the pace of desegregation and the large number of students who are still attending schools which are essentially segregated.[4] Acklyn Lynch has captured another significant concern among Blacks, when he states that "integration as defined by White America meant the acceptance of the dominant ethic along with acquiescence to the authority and power of the existing social and political institutions."[5] Thus the relevance of current educational programs available to Black youth, the value of proposed educational reforms for Black liberation, and the search for viable alternatives for educating Black youth are significant elements of the continuing debate within the Black community.

It is against this background that the question of Blacks and formal education must be addressed. It appears to this writer that the view that private schools, generally speaking, are properly characterized as a "symptom of democracy's failure," rather than a viable educational alternative for Black youth is on target. Black people are concerned about the values and hegemonic notions to which our youth are exposed as a part of their schooling -- ideas which are viewed as inimical to the success of any liberation struggle. Black youth attending private non-sectarian institutions may receive an even greater dose of these bourgeois notions than their counterparts within the existing public school system. Liberation schools run by Black nationalist or similar types of Black organizations could provide an effective antidote to the inculcation of such notions which promote false consciousness among Black youth.

Other problems attend any consideration of private schools as a viable educational alternative for Black youth. Evidence to support the notion that private schools have overcome the self-fulfilling prophecy as a destructive force impacting upon the efforts to enhance the educational achievement of Black youth is sparse at best. Do the class and racial biases which often inform teachers' expectations of lower class and minority youth automatically disappear when such youth enter private schools?

The alleged greater receptivity of private schools to enroll more minority youth can have a deleterious impact upon the educational development of those left behind in the public schools. It is quite plausible to suggest that the private schools will siphon off the gifted and more highly motivated Black youth, Dubois' "talented tenth," leaving behind what they would consider the dross of the race.[6] The public schools would then be left with the task of providing meaningful education for these problem-ridden youth without the benefits and stimulation of their more able peers. Such a development could have a chilling effect upon efforts to increase the educational achievement of Black students.

Black people continue to manifest concern over who will ultimately control the minds of Black children, and thus the lack of accountability of the educational institutions attended by Black youth is viewed as a major problem. Montgomery has suggested that the demand of Blacks for community control of the school means "not only physical control, but ... the control of information and learning for the liberation of the human spirit."[7] And Boggs has argued that Blacks must achieve community control of the schools in order to provide an educational program which can overcome an "individualist, opportunist orientation of American education [which] has been ruinous to the American community, [and] most obviously ... to the Black community."[8] What is the potential of private secular schools to respond positively to such concerns of Blacks?

Those who support the voucher system as a viable educational alternative for Black youth argue that the mechanism of the market place offers an adequate response to accountability concerns. Foster has offered the following arguments in support of the voucher system as an alternative for financing private schools which could provide viable educational opportunities for Black youth:

> Individuals would have greater freedom within the public education system because they would not be required to accept standardized programs offered in assigned public schools. Middle income and poor parents would have much the same freedom to choose schools that wealth parents can exercise....

> A range of choices in the schools would become available. Small new schools of all types could come into operation -- African Free School, Community School Workshop, Montessori, Summerhill, open classroom, and traditional style schools, among others....

> A form of accountability to parents would be introduced since parents would be free to withdraw their children from the school if it did not perform in accordance with their desires.[9]

This writer would simply observe that Foster's comments represent outcomes that he and other supporters of voucher systems and other alternative financing proposals hope to stimulate. Yet, there is nothing inherent in any of these plans which guarantees such results. And it is important to note that a critique and analysis of the free market system would be an important dimension of any educational program de-

222

vised for Black youth. Such a treatment would not be based upon the assumption that the capitalist economic system represents the solution to the class and color contradictions which are the sources of the oppression of Black Americans.

As mentioned earlier in this paper, both Coleman and Greeley have reported the results of research efforts which supposedly demonstrate the superiority of private schools for the academic achievement of Black and other minority students. The recent Coleman report has received a positive response from some commentators. Ravitch hails the report for demonstrating "statistically that absenteeism and class-cutting contribute to lower achievement levels (when family background is held constant)." [10] She goes on to observe:

> The new Coleman report also gives educators,
> public and private, a considerable body of evidence
> demonstrating that school policy affects student
> achievement and student behavior. Most important,
> the report means that school officials and education
> policymakers must reexamine their curricula, their
> programs, and their policies.... The new Coleman report
> reminds us that those who teach and administer schools
> have an important and difficult job, with the power
> to change the lives of their students. It is now up
> to the adults responsible for the schools to establish
> the standards, expectations, and values that make up
> the kind of stable, purposeful environment in which
> all students can learn and work productively. [11]

It is doubtful that the kind of reassessment and the reforms which it generates will adequately respond to the concerns of Blacks.

However, the findings of Coleman's study Public and Private Schools have generated new controversy. Erickson has noted that "Coleman's evidence suggested that private schools made an independent contribution (independent of the influence of students' home backgrounds, that is) to their students' superior academic achievement." [12] Yet, as Erickson was quick to observe: "There is no way that Coleman's evidence could demonstrate, rather than suggest, the academic superiority of the private schools." [13] He contends that Coleman is comparing unequal groups in the data presented. Thus he argues: "We can never conclusively prove that any part of the academic superiority of the private school group over the public school group is attributable to the schools attended rather than the homes lived in." [14]

223

There are important issues concerning the education of Black youth which the above discussion does not touch upon. The available data suggest that only about eleven percent of the total pupil population in the country is currently enrolled in private schools. Given this fact, it seems reasonable for one to conclude that, at least for the foreseeable future, the majority of Black youth are going to have to seek educational opportunities within the public school system, especially the urban schools. So, the most important educational issue facing the Black community today is how to improve the quality of the education which is available within these problem-ridden institutions. Private educational institutions offer no antidote for this set of problems. As suggested earlier in this paper, they might even contribute to a further weakening of public education in the United States -- a devastating prospect for Blacks and the poor.

There is also a need to consider some of the concerns which have been voiced by Blacks about the content of the educational programs to which Black youth are exposed. DuBois and others have spoken to the need for a Black education which challenges certain assumptions about the nature and content of the American experience and other historical and contemporary concerns. It does not appear to this writer that the private schools, with the possible exception of those operated by Blacks themselves, are up to this revisionist task.

Robert Staples has captured a number of additional concerns of Blacks with the existing educational opportunities available to the youth of the race. He observes:

> Education for Black youth has never been a high priority among the colonial rulers in the United States. Blacks have and continue to receive an inferior education at every level. And, it is partially this substandard education that maintains their colonial status. Moreover, within the educational institutions, the goals, values, and attitudes of the colonizer are the only ones that are accorded any legitimacy. The educational system selects those values and attitudes favored by the colonizer and conveys them to Black youth as universal truths. Schools remain one of the major institutions for socializing colonial youth into the oppressive system of the colonizer. In fact, Afro-American youth is taught that the only legitimate social system is the same one that is oppressing them.

Although Whites are marshalling a violent fight against desegregation of their schools, the benefits of school integration are also beginning to be questioned by many Afro-Americans. In many predominantly White schools, Blacks find a kind of educational apartheid. Extensive use of a tracking system often consigns a majority of Black students to the educationally slow classrooms. Even within the same classroom, the Black student will discover that his White teacher expects little of him and subsequently he begins to expect little of himself....

Many of these Black students will find it hard to secure employment in the labor force if they cannot read well enough to fill out a job application form....[15]

This writer has yet to see the evidence that these problems are substantially alleviated in private schools, especially those operated by dominant group members. In fact, such institutions may well exacerbate some of the problems which have been identified here.

There is an increasing awareness of other changes needed in educational programs available to Black youth. As Hare has pointed out, Black youth need exposure to instructors who "reject the value-free" approach of White scholarship.[16] Such teachers must help these students to acquire the appropriate norms and values, and identify alternative institutional arrangements and a new ideology which are conducive to the success of the struggle against racism, colonialism and class oppression.

There are a growing number of Blacks in the United States who see the need for politicizing Black education. We have maintained that such a thrust for Black education is necessary if Black youth are to receive the insights necessary to successfully struggle against the racial and class oppression which Blacks suffer in this society. And this argument is supported by Washington who observes:

Deliberately politicizing children appears to be a much more powerful mechanism for effecting change than any of the previously mentioned institutions. Politicizing children means that children can be taught systematically and factually about themselves and the institutions that currently affect their lives.[17]

Most private schools have little to offer to this effort. In fact, it appears reasonable to conclude that such an educational orientation would be inimical to the maintenance of the status quo orientation of such institutions and the values, norms and institutional arrangements which they promote.

Black youth are being asked to bear a major burden of the capitalist crisis of American society. As Staples has pointed out, this fact is reflected in the disproportionate representation of Black youth in the reserve army of labor, high rates of underemployment and unemployment, increasing involvement in violence and crime, and mainifestations of alienation which are reflected in rebelliousness, distorted "machoism," drug addiction, and suicide.[18] It is no accident that Black youth are grossly overrepresented within the populations of our penal institutions, and disproportionately represented within the military, especially at the lower ranks of that establishment. If the situation continues as is, all hopes for a brighter future for these youth, and therefore for the race as a whole, will evaporate.

The defense and progress of Black youth continue as top priorities within the Black community. This paper has discussed a number of challenges confronting that effort. Given those concerns, there seems to be little in the way of an antidote available in the private institutions which currently exist. And there is little to suggest that we are at the dawning of a major breakthrough in private education which will serve to alleviate the persistent problems which are discussed here.

Are there many schools, public or private, which are prepared to provide students with something other than hegemonic values and a pro-capitalist viewpoint? How many private schools are preparing their students to effectively challenge the values and institutional order which dominate their lives and from which are derived the contradictions which are reflected within the legacy of oppression experienced by Afro-Americans? It is doubtful that major initiatives will be undertaken on a significant basis in either public or private schools. Yet, the fact remains that the public schools of urban America will continue to be the only educational resource available to most Black youth. Given this fact, Blacks must continue to strive to strengthen those institutions so that they can provide a more meaningful education for their youth. And at the same time, Blacks must find ways to provide truly viable alternatives where they can take charge of the educational process and make it more meaningful and beneficial to Black people.

Educators need to be reminded that the central theme of the Black experience in the United States is the quest for freedom -- freedom from the racial and class oppressions which have confronted the lives of Blacks from slavery until the present. The education of Black youth must arm them with the skills and insights necessary to wage that struggle with increasing success. If the schools which propose to provide educational opportunities for Black youth fail to adequately meet these challenges, then the survival and progress of the Afro-American is placed in even greater jeopardy.

Notes

[1]Herbert Aptheker, ed., Dubois, The Education of Black People (Amherst: University of Massachusetts Press, 1973), p. 73.

[2]For further discussion see The State of Black America 1979 (New York: National Urban League, 1979), p. 1, and The State of Black America 1980 (New York: National Urban League, 1980), p. 1.

[3]For further discussion see Marian Wright Edelman, Portrait of Inequality: Black and White Children in America (Washington, D.C.: 1980).

[4]For further discussion see U.S. Commission of Civil Rights, Desegregation of the Nation (Washington, D.C.: 1979).

[5]Acklyn Lynch, "Resource Papers; Education," African Congress, ed. Imamu Amiri Baraka (New York: William Morrow and Company, 1972), p. 287.

[6]Dennis A. Williams, et al., "The Bright Flight," Newsweek. April 20, 1981.

[7]H. Lee Montgomery, "The Education of Black Children," What Black Educators Are Saying, ed. Nathan Wright, Jr., (San Francisco: Leswing Press, 1970).

[8]Grace Lee Boggs, "Education: The Great Obsession," Education to Govern, (Detroit: The All African Peoples Union, 1972), p. 22.

[9]Benjamin Foster, Jr., "Financing Education: The Case for Vouchers," The Black Scholar, IV (May-June, 1973), 12.

[10] Diane Ravitch, "The Meaning of the New Coleman Report," _Phi Delta Kappan_ LXII (June, 1981), 720.

[11] Ibid.

[12] Donald A. Erickson, "The Superior Climate of Private Schools," _Momentum_, (October, 1981), p. 5.

[13] Ibid. [14] Ibid.

[15] Robert Staples, "To Be Young, Black and Oppressed," _The Black Scholar_, VII (December, 1975), 4-5.

[16] Nathan Hare, "The Challenge of a Black Scholar," _The Black Scholar_, I (December, 1969), 5.

[17] Ernest D. Washington, "Politicizing Black Children," _The Black Scholar_, IV (May-June, 1973), 6.

[18] For further elaboration see Staples, "To Be Young," pp. 2-9 and Robert Staples, "Black Manhood in the 1970's: A Critical Look Back," _The Black Scholar_, XII (May-June, 1981), 2-9.

PART TEN -- BILINGUAL PROGRAMS

Are specially funded bilingual education programs a desirable feature of American schooling?

The teaching of languages other than English in American schools has a long history. Many church-related schools of the late nineteenth century were established primarily to preserve the language and culture of the "old country." Starting in 1960 the federal government became actively involved in bilingual education with programs aimed at children who, because of minimal proficiency in English, experienced limited success in school. Today funding for bilingual programs is one of the largest items in the Department of Education budget. Federal directives, especially since 1970, and the Supreme Court's <u>Lau</u> decision in 1974 have prompted many states to offer some form of bilingual education. Most such programs are basically transitional in nature, but some seek to insure the continuation of the parents' primary language.

The issue of bilingual education has unmistakable social overtones. Indeed, controversy may stem from the recognition that this is less an educational issue than a political one. Do we wish to increase educational opportunity? If so, bilingual programs may be an appropriate means. Do we wish to promote social mobility among minority groups? If so, bilingual education may be a contributory factor. Do we wish to promote cultural pluralism? If so, bilingual programs may serve a useful purpose. As educational goals, however, these are not universally accepted. There is disagreement not only over explicit goals of bilingual education, but also over the nature of the programs and which youngsters should be involved in them. Even where supporters and opponents agree on a likely outcome, an example would be preserving the parents' non-English language, they disagree over its desirability as a goal of the educational program.

The first of the two articles in this section dispels the common American notion of monolingualism as the usual language pattern, and cites research findings which conclude that bilingualism can promote children's learning. Appropriate bilingual programs can result in benefits to both the individual and society.

The second article views the basic purposes of public education as ill-served by programs which have the effect of promoting not a sense of community, but a sense of being different. Advancing private purposes may be desirable, but it is not a public goal of sufficient merit to justify special programs such as bilingual education.

SAMIR ABU-ABSI is Associate Professor of English and Director of the Linguistics Program at the University of Toledo. His doctorate in Linguistics is from Indiana University. PEGGY WILLIAMS is a graduate student at the University of Toledo, specializing in English as a second language.

DAVID TAVEL is Professor and Director of the Division of Educational Foundations at the University of Toledo.

A CASE FOR BILINGUAL EDUCATION

Samir Abu-Absi and Peggy Williams

Background

For over one billion people in the world, who speak more than one language fluently, bilingualism is a way of life. This phenomenon is not the product of modern times since, historically, monolingualism has been the exception rather than the rule. Even in the United States, which shows a high degree of linguistic homogeneity, about 13% of the population, or 23 million people, come from a non-English language background. Of these, some 10.6 million are native speakers of Spanish, making the U.S. the fifth largest country in the world in Hispanic population. Contrary to popular belief, the majority of non-native English speakers, 67% or 18.5 million, are not recent immigrants, but were born in the United States. An estimated 5 million school-age children have limited English proficiency which prevents them from succeeding in schools where English is the sole medium of instruction.[1]

The United States is a multilingual, multicultural society which has received immigrants in large numbers and continues to do so. And although English has the unofficial status of being the national language, there exist circumstances which favor the bilingual provision of educational and social services. While individual states have their own policy with respect to bilingual education, federal policy exists in the form of legislation and precedents set by the courts. Through Title VI of the Civil Rights Act of 1964, the federal government has intervened to prevent discrimination, in any program receiving federal financial assistance, against any person on the grounds of race, color, or national origin. Additionally, the Bilingual Education Act of 1968 (Title VII of the Elementary and Secondary Education Act of 1965) offered financial assistance to projects aimed at meeting the educational needs of children whose dominant language was not English. Thus the federal government has supplemented a legal mandate for bilingual education with financial inducements.

It should not be assumed, however, that bilingual education in the United States is an innovation of the sixties. Before the turn of the century, there was no concentrated effort to make English the sole language in communities which were settled by non-English speaking

Europeans. Thus bilingual schools, both private and public, flourished in the nineteenth century and schooling was done in languages such as French, German, and Dutch, with English being introduced as a second language. In New Mexico Spanish had an equal status with English as an official state language.[2] European languages and cultures, however, came to be viewed with suspicion following World War I. Consequently, most Americans who grew up speaking a language other than English were forced through legislation or social pressure to give up their native tongues. The "melting pot" concept has thus contributed to obscuring the complex and interesting ethnic history of this nation.

Bilingualism and Intelligence

Most studies done before 1960 concluded that bilingualism had a detrimental effect on the cognitive development of children as reflected in lower I.Q. scores and decreased verbal ability. Moreover, bilingualism was said to have negative consequences socially, in promoting ethnocentrism, and economically, in the form of low productivity. The conclusion that was generally accepted was that bilingualism is a disadvantage which must be dealt with. A critical evaluation, however, suggests that these early studies were poorly designed, based on too small a sample to be statistically valid, and often ignored important sociolinguistic variables.

A more recent study which has received wide publicity was carried out by the American Institute of Research with the aim of evaluating Title VII-funded programs. Even this report, which has generally been uncritically accepted, contained a number of flaws which were summarized by one critic as follows:

Only five and a half months were allowed between the pre-test and the post-test, which is not considered enough time to provide a valid measure of growth. The comparability of control students used in the study was questionable, since students in the bilingual program were more likely to be there because they had lower academic standing and English competence to begin with. Further, teacher assessment of language dominance was used with no check on its accuracy. And despite great variation in program design and outcomes, all programs were combined for reporting purposes.[3]

There are a number of well constructed studies, done in the U.S.A. and abroad, which refute the notion that bilingualism constitutes a disadvantage in the cognitive domain. A landmark study was carried out in Canada in 1962 with a group of French-English bilinguals and a closely matched monolingual control group. The aim of the study was to pinpoint the components of the deficit that bilingual children were supposed to have in order to develop strategies to overcome such a disadvantage. The following statement by one of the researchers sums up the unexpected results which were revealed by this study.

> What surprised us, though, was that French-English bilingual children in the Montreal setting scored significantly ahead of carefully matched monolinguals on both verbal and nonverbal measures of intelligence. Furthermore, the patterns of test results suggested that bilinguals had a more diversified structure of intelligence, as measured, and more flexibility in thought.[4]

Later studies from around the world using a variety of research techniques confirmed the above conclusions and discovered other cognitive benefits which can be associated with bilingualism. For instance, bilingual children were found to perform better than their monolingual counterparts on concept formation tasks.[5] Bilinguals, even at the first grade level, were reported to have an advantage over their monolingual peers on a task of rule discovery.[6] Also, bilingual children were discovered to excel in verbal originality and divergent thinking, which is a special type of cognitive flexibility.[7] Still, other research demonstrated that bilingualism can enhance a person's analytical skills[8] Moreover, bilingualism has been linked to the early occurrence of an important stage of language development: the ability to recognize the arbitrary relationship between form and meaning.[9]

In sum, all recent research which has attempted to control sociolinguistic and socioeconomic factors has concluded that, far from being a disadvantage, bilingualism can enhance the cognitive development of children.

Bilingualism in a Social Setting

As demonstrated by an abundance of research, bilingualism is a complex phenomenon which occurs in various degrees and which depends on age, attitude, and a number of other sociological factors. It is, therefore, of utmost importance to recognize and encourage bilingual situations which have positive effects and, conversely, to avoid those situations which have detrimental consequences. A significant factor affecting the consequences of bilingualism is the relationship between the bilingual's two languages and two cultures. A desirable situation, referred to as additive bilingualism, is characterized as "the acquisition of two socially useful and prestigious languages which are mutually viable."[10]Subtractive bilingualism, on the other hand, refers to a situation where one language threatens to replace, or at least dominate, the other.

Examples of subtractive bilingualism from around the world have been described and analyzed. One such case concerns Finnish-Swedish bilingual children who migrated to Sweden at the age of seven or eight and whose linguistic skills declined to the extent that they became "semilingual" in both their languages. This group of children exhibited a significantly lower level of cognitive skills than those children who migrated when they were ten years of age or older. This situation can be explained by the fact that the younger immigrant group had to shift to a second language before their first language skills were completely developed. In contrast, the children who made the switch to Swedish at a later age had reached a level of competence in Finnish which allowed them to function with native-like competence in both languages.[11]

A similar situation was found in the United States with Mexican-American children who had started their schooling in English as contrasted with Mexican immigrants who came to the United States after finishing the sixth grade in Mexico. Students in the latter group were observed to acquire English quickly and outperform their peers in the first group. This implies that interrupting the development of first language skills before they are fully developed at the age of ten or eleven can have a negative effect linguistically and cognitively.[12]

Instances of subtractive bilingualism are typical of minority groups whose ethnic languages are replaced by a more useful and prestigious national language. Social pressures are often so great that minority children are made to feel inferior and ashamed of their linguistic and cultural heritage. Thus, minority children have been known to reject or hide knowledge of their native language. Such is the case among Spanish-speaking students who were observed adopting "anglicized mispronunciations" of Spanish in order to disclaim their heritage and thus avoid being stigmatized by the majority group.[13]

Additive bilingualism results when the first language is fully developed and is in no danger of being replaced, or when the first language has a socially prominent status and can thus be reinforced outside the school. The first situation applies, for instance, in the case of the older Mexican and Finnish immigrants who experienced no difficulties with either of their two languages. The second situation, where the first language is in no danger of being lost, can be exemplified by the St. Lambert experiment in Canada. Here, children from the dominant English-Canadian population were educated exclusively in French throughout their primary grades. Their secondary schooling was subsequently done in both English and French. These students had no difficulty reconciling their two languages and developed the same competence in English as their peers who went to regular English schools.[14]

One criticism of bilingualism stems from the notion that it leads to biculturalism, a state which, some suggest, is detrimental to a person's sense of identity. There have been suggestions that biculturalism results in a feeling of anomie, marginality, or schizophrenia. This identity problem is supposed to arise from the existence in the bilingual's mind of two irreconcilable world views.[15] In dealing with this issue, Lambert distinguishes between subtractive and additive biculturalism and cites three studies, summarized below, by way of illustration.[16]

Research done with French-American communities in New England and Louisiana shows that individuals coped with their dual heritage in different ways. Some oriented themselves toward one background (i.e. either French or American) to the exclusion of the other, while others tried not to think of themselves in ethnic terms. This is an example of subtractive biculturalism which is characterized by a person giving up one aspect of a dual heritage. Nevertheless, there was still another group which managed to identify positively with both cultures and thus became more competent in both French and English -- an example of additive biculturalism.

A study of adolescent children of English-French mixed marriages in Canada showed that they were less biased than a homogenous group of either French or English Canadians. These children were familiar with the behavioral characteristics of both cultures and managed to develop a dual allegiance which permitted them to identify with both parents. Another study conducted in Canada, the St. Lambert experiment referred to above as an example of additive bilingualism, can be used to illustrate additive biculturalism. The children who participated in this project felt at ease in both settings and identified with both groups. They also reflected an improved attitude toward French-Canadians and the French way of life. These students became bilingual and bicultural without having to lose or suppress their native language or their identity.

Bilingual Education Options

Various types of bilingual education programs can be developed to fit the needs of a particular country or a particular community. These programs range from being strictly transitional, with the ultimate goal of effecting a shift to the new language, to being full bilingual programs aimed at producing balanced bilinguals capable of manipulating all language skills in both languages.[17] Needless to say, there can be other types of programs which can be aimed at maintaining certain skills in the native language, for instance: speaking, while developing literacy as well as oral fluency in the second language. In any event, it is obvious that there is no one model which is suitable for all situations, since every community has its own goals, needs, and values.

One issue which is often raised in communities within the United States relates to the choice between bilingual education and teaching English as a second language (ESL). But rather than thinking of bilingual education and ESL as being alternative options, they can be seen as complementary components of one comprehensive program. As such, ESL becomes an important and effective component of bilingual education, assuming that care is taken in avoiding the creation of a subtractive relationship between English and the student's mother tongue. Experiments, such as the one carried out at the Rock Point community school on the Navajo reservation, clearly illustrate the superiority of bilingual education with an ESL component over an ESL only program. A comparison of students in these two programs reveals that those in the bilingual program were above grade level in English reading at the end of their sixth year while the ESL only students were over a year below grade level.[18] The significance of these results lies in demonstrating the importance of maintaining the native language through the sixth grade level in order for the benefits of bilingual education to be realized. Unfortunately, most programs in the United States have tended to be transitional in nature and to terminate sometime before the end of the third year of schooling.

The controversy over bilingual education has not always remained within the realm of the objective and the rational. Opponents of bilingual education have often attacked it on political and emotional grounds, and without much consideration of the complexities of the issue. One of the more interesting contradictions of American attitudes toward foreign language education is described by one scholar as follows.

> The most obvious anomaly -- or absurdity -- of our educational policy regarding foreign-language learning is the fact that we spend perhaps a billion dollars a year to teach the languages -- in the schools, the colleges and universities, the Foreign Service Institute, the Department of Defense, AID, USIA, CIA, etc. (and to a large extent to adults who are too old ever to master a new tongue) -- yet virtually no part of the effort goes to maintain and to develop the competence of American children who speak the same languages natively. [19]

Tragically, the problem does not stop with the lack of support for natively spoken languages in America, but extends to an effort to suppress the development of these languages and to discourage their use. This attitude is present among many well-meaning Americans, including teachers, administrators, and politicians, who have taken a precious national resource -- the bilingual skills of American children -- and turned it into a liability and a handicap.

While some bilingual education programs can be criticized for not achieving the desired goals, the concept of bilingual education itself cannot be attacked on the grounds of any scientific evidence. In fact, the research has clearly demonstrated that bilingual education, if properly provided, will result in a variety of personal and societal benefits. But besides having the proper design for a program which would suit the needs of a certain community, it is important that the community at large approach the issue with understanding and a lack of prejudice.

Notes

[1]Francois Grosjean, Life with Two Languages: An Introduction to Bilingualism (Cambridge, Mass.: Harvard University Press, 1982), and Educational Testing Service, Bilingual Education (Princeton, N.J.: E.T.S., 1976).

[2]See Vera P. John and Vivian M. Horner, Early Childhood Bilingual Education (New York: Modern Language Association, 1971), pp. xv-xvi; and E. Glyn Lewis, Bilingualism and Bilingual Education: A Comparative Study (Albuquerque, N.M.: Pergamon Press, 1981), p. 336.

[3]Rudolph C. Troike, "Synthesis of Research on Bilingual Education," Educational Leadership, (March, 1981), p. 449.

[4]Wallace E. Lambert, "The Effects of Bilingualism on the Individual: Cognitive and Sociocultural Consequences" in Bilingualism: Psychological, Social, and Educational Implications, ed., Peter A. Hornby, (New York: Academic Press, 1977), p. 16.

[5]W. W. Liedke and L. D. Nelson, "Concept Formation and Bilingualism," Alberta Journal of Educational Research, XIV (1968), 225-232.

[6]B. C. Bain, "Toward an Integration of Piaget and Vygotsky: Bilingual Considerations," Linguistics, CLX (1975), 5-20.

[7]Merrill Swain and James Cummins, "Bilingualism, Cognitive Functioning and Education," Language Teaching and Linguistics: Abstracts (New York: Cambridge University Press, 1979), pp. 4-18.

[8]James Cummins and R. Mullcahy, "Orientation to Language in Ukrainian-English Bilingual Children," Child Development, XLIX (1978), 1239-1242.

[9]James Cummins, "Bilingualism and the Development of Metalinguistic Awareness," Journal of Cross-cultural Psychology, XXIX (June, 1978) 131-149.

[10]Fred Genesee, "Summary and Discussion," in Hornby, ed., Bilingualism, p. 153.

[11]Tove Skutnabb-Kangas and Pertii Toukomaa, Teaching Migrant Children's Mother Tongue and Learning the Language of the Host Country in the Context of the Socio-cultural Situation

of the Migrant Family (Tampere, Finland: Tutkimuksia Research Reports, 1976).

[12]Troike, "Synthesis of Research," pp. 498-504.

[13]Ibid.

[14]Wallace E. Lambert and G. Richard Tucker, Bilingual Education of Children: The St. Lambert Experiment (Rowley, Mass.: Newbury House, 1972).

[15]A brief summary of such views is given in Fred Genesee, "Summary and Discussion" in Hornby, Bilingualism.

[16]Lambert, "Effects of Bilingualism," pp. 15-27.

[17]For a description of various types of programs, see Joshua A. Fishman and John Lovas, "Bilingual Education in a Sociolinguistic Perspective" in The Language Education of Minority Children, ed., Bernard Spolsky (Rowley, Mass.: Newbury House, 1972).

[18]See Troike, "Synthesis of Research," pp. 498-504, for a summary. For more detail, refer to L. Vorih and P. Rosier, "Rocky Point Community School: An Example of a Navajo-English Bilingual Elementary School Program," TESOL Quarterly, XII (September, 1978), 263-271.

[19]A. Bruce Gaarder, "Bilingualism and Education," in Spolsky, Language Education, p. 57.

BILINGUAL EDUCATION AND AMERICAN GOALS AND VALUES

David Tavel

In 1968 Congress passed a Bilingual Education Act whose stated major purpose was to assist local school districts in meeting the needs of children with limited facility in use of the English language. Now sixteen years and approximately a billion dollars of federal expenditure later, the advisability of such legislation needs to be examined, not from the perspective of whether it is good politics, but to determine its consistency with and contribution to the fulfillment of the ideals, values, and goals of Americans. Certainly passage of the bill as Title VII of the Elementary and Secondary Education Act was as politically inspired as the original E.S.E.A. three years earlier. The views expressed in this brief paper, however, are based not on the presumed ulterior motives of legislators with an eye toward re-election campaigns, but rather on the historic role of the American school and the experience of immigrants and national minorities. The aim of this paper is admittedly to present a case against continuation of federally or state sponsored bilingual education programs.

Being against new programs or federal expenditure for an ostensible educational purpose is commonly regarded in the teaching profession today as tantamount to heresy. With an acquisitiveness that would have delighted our late nineteenth century industrial robber barons, educators have taken full advantage of the door to the public largesse being opened by the 1958 National Defense Education Act and the above mentioned E.S.E.A. first in 1965. Advocates of bilingual and bilingual-bicultural education, like proponents of other causes such as the new math, the new social studies, and Head Start, have successfully lobbied for funds to institute what are generally categorized as either transitional or maintenance programs.

Transitional programs, the more easily justified type, aim to help youngsters master basic subjects during the first few years of school by receiving instruction in the "native" language. As the individual develops greater proficiency in English, the "native" language is phased out. In this manner youngsters with limited mastery of English will not be handicapped linguistically during their early school experiences. The transition is expected to take three or four years, after which instruction is to be in the dominant English language.

Maintenance programs derive from the belief that the "native" language should be actively preserved by the school program. They are in the tradition of efforts by such nineteenth century immigrants as those Germans who sought to enroll their children in schools which would teach that language in addition to the national tongue. A maintenance program is designed to provide continual in-school experiences which involve not only the language, but also the culture of the ethnic group from which the children have come. In contrast to transitional programs, maintenance ones are not intended to end after a few years, but to continue through the full extent of a youngster's schooling.

Before looking directly at these programs we need to consider whether the American public school is an appropriate place for bilingual education. Stated another way, even if efforts to preserve and emphasize linguistic and ethnic differences are held desirable, should public resources be used to that end? A sketch of some aspects of the growth of public education is necessary at this point.

The Puritan concern with education in colonial Massachusetts is too well known to require any detailed discussion. The development of publicly supported schooling was an expression of their conviction that education was too important a matter to be left in the hands of parents, for the welfare of the body public took precedence over the interests of the family group. Thus there began the American practice of government requiring teachers and schools, and authorizing taxation for the support of both. The colonists did not bring with them from Europe any tradition of public responsibility for education, but quickly in the American environment they learned that individual survival depended upon community survival.

As pioneers from a variety of backgrounds moved westward, the frontier consisting of villages and smaller settlements was marked by localism and regionalism which were a far cry from the community solidarity of colonial New England. Public education came into existence when and where a sense of community developed. In the century which witnessed the American Revolution, a sense of communal or public purpose declined. The Revolution did not immediately change that because it did not result in a radical restructuring of American society. It was a political revolution establishing a republican political system, and its impact on many citizens, especially those in the rural areas relatively far removed from effective government, was minimal.

242

In the absence of a sense of public purpose private schools flourished. Their dominance was to be short-lived, however, as ideas underlying the American Revolution began to take concrete form and manifest themselves in political acts. One such idea was that the people were to exercise political power through representatives answerable to them. This was not advocacy of anarchy, for the liberty envisioned was not that of the individual to do whatsoever he liked; it was the liberty of "the people" collectively. When education was discussed it was in terms of teaching "the people" to exercise their freedoms -- speech, press, and assembly, to name but three. Education came to be viewed as essential for a people who were free to collectively govern themselves.

As truly public schools -- known as common schools -- developed during the middle third of the nineteenth century, their underlying rationale was essentially the same as that of the Puritan schools. The welfare of the community, in this case the national community, justified public expenditures for schooling. The public school was to provide an avenue along which young people of all social, economic, and cultural backgrounds could travel. This was consistent with the belief in equality of opportunity, and whether the ideal was or was not fully realized, that public school was viewed as for everyone. Only because it was for everyone was it entitled to public support. Eventually, starting with Massachusetts in 1852, the states began to require school attendance. In the face of increasing immigration and stresses brought on by industrialization and urbanization, schooling as necessary for the common good was re-emphasized. The promotion of both education and that common good once again became a major responsibility of government.

In the continually expanding and ever more heterogeneous cities of the mid and late nineteenth century the sense of community which had been so essential to the seventeenth century New England colonists appeared under attack. The need to Americanize immigrants was universally evident. The nation was being transformed; schooling had to be transformed. The disappearance of district schools absorbed into city systems and the passage of compulsory attendance laws became major features of this educational transformation. The national motto was "E Pluribus Unum," and the American school was expected to play a major role in creating One Out of Many.

Although constantly subject to the influence of "privatist" forces stressing the divergent aspects of American society, the American school and its teachers continued to struggle to build a sense of community. In this effort they were supported overwhelmingly by the American people. Legislatures mandated increased financial support, required school attendance, and even dictated that youngsters study their nation's history, government, and geography. At the same time, the country's individualistic tradition resulted in room for dissenters; not everyone was required to attend the public school. Even though the state legislatures legally controlled the school systems, cities and towns largely had a free rein to make their schools reflect dominant local values.

The courts, too, reflected this constant tension between the private and the public realms. The nation's highest tribunal in 1923 overturned a Nebraska statute banning the teaching of German, and two years later ruled unconstitutional an Oregon law which had been based on the reasoning that if the state was responsible for seeing to it that all children receive an appropriate education, it was equally appropriate for the state to provide that education and require attendance at public schools. The most consistent theme running through the Supreme Court's rulings was protection of the private rights of parents. It is noteworthy, however, that in dissenting from the majority's ruling in the Nebraska decision Justice Oliver Wendell Holmes, one of the nation's most distinguished jurists, noted that there might be appropriate circumstances which would justify the state exercising its right to take appropriate measures to promote the common welfare through education.

The American school today may temporarily have ceased to be regarded by many as a repository of national morality and cohesiveness. Even voices from the scholarly professions can be heard in criticism, although it is important to note that, as Gallup polls continually reveal, the views of educators are not necessarily representative of those of the public at large, and the latter seem to have more faith in the public schools. Nevertheless, our educational systems are not closing down, much of the public continues to take great pride in them, and many parents still see them as a positive force in promoting the skills needed in a democratic society. The main "privatist" schools, largely under religious domination, receive considerable publicity from the communications media when they open their doors, but many enroll infinitesimally small numbers of students and have a history of tenuous and brief existence. Even persons under threat of theological penalties for not using religious schools show, by sending their children to the American public school, that they have shed the ghetto mentality insofar as wanting their children in the mainstream of American society.

In addition to building a sense of community, the public school has also been responsible for meeting the nation's need for a populace able to fulfill political obligations and actively participate in the economy. To these ends educational opportunity constantly expanded through the decades of the twentieth century. By the end of World War One nearly every American child of appropriate age was attending elementary school. By the 1970s the same could be said for the high school. Today over fifty percent of the population takes advantage of post-secondary education. The literacy rate for the American people is estimated at 98 percent. These figures compare favorably with those of any other nation. They provide a picture of the country as a whole, however, and to the extent they are averages there are people who are not beneficiaries of our educational opportunities.

As America has become a more affluent nation, disparities between the "haves" and the "have-nots" not only have grown, but have become increasingly viewed as necessitating corrective social action. On the political side many people feel in effect disenfranchised by the absence of basic policy differences among the candidates and by an electoral college system which guarantees the continued domination of national politics by the two major parties. On the economic side, this country experiences the greatest disparity between the wealthy and the rest to be found among western industrialized nations. These conditions have led to a vocal demand for equality, often expressed in terms of rights. Most significant were the years of the 1960s, although the Civil Rights decades can be said to have begun with the Supreme Court decision in 1954 holding that segregated schools were unconstitutional. Sweden's long-time observer of the American scene, Cunnar Myrdal, noted in his classic <u>An American Dilemma</u> that Americans who had long proclaimed their belief in equality did not necessarily practice it, that the very same people who vocally accepted equality as a general tenet of faith could treat their fellow Americans unequally. Black Americans have been the best known victims of unequal treatment. As the nation's largest minority, and favored with prominent leadership, they came to occupy the limelight in the civil rights struggle.

Another significant minority in the United States consists of the Hispanic population, twelve to fourteen million persons possessing in varying degrees a common ancestry. Far from being a single cultural group, they have different backgrounds and speak different dialects. Approximately seven million are Mexican Americans, two million Puerto Ricans, three quarters of a million Cubans, a million from other

American countries, and roughly a million and a half with other Spanish backgrounds. Some have ancestors who lived in what are today the United States before the arrival of the settlers at Jamestown or the Pilgrims at Plymouth. Others are among our most recent arrivals, those emigrating from Cuba during the past three decades and those constantly crossing the border, legally and otherwise, from Mexico.

Because the Hispanics were almost all located in the southwest, and because that was the last contiguous area from which states emerged, contact between Anglo-Americans and Hispanics has been briefer than white-black contact, and social interaction has been primarily regional rather than national. Developing political awareness by the Hispanics of the southwest is being reinforced by constantly increasing numbers nationally due to immigration. An additional factor has been the urbanization of the Hispanic population as part of the urbanization of American society. Thus for example, the nearly one million Puerto Ricans who have emigrated from that island during the past four decades have settled in east coast cities, most notably New York City. New York has become one of the three states, California and Texas being the other two, where nearly three out of every four Hispanic Americans reside. Once urbanized, Hispanics have found their situation as a cultural minority influenced by complicating factors which have left many of them with poorly paying jobs, less than the best of educational opportunities, and residential segregation.

The battle for improved opportunity for Hispanics has been waged on several educational fronts. In light of the Court ruling in Brown v. Board of Education of Topeka, which held separate educational facilities as inherently unequal, some Hispanics have gone to court seeking to end de facto segregation which isolates their children in schools separated from the dominant Anglo-American population. Others have challenged the system of financing schools which relies heavily on the property tax. Such a system works a hardship on a poorer school district which, even though residents may tax themselves at a higher rate, lacks funding necessary to provide its young with as good an education as is available in wealthier districts. A third front, consisting of efforts to improve the place of Hispanic language and culture in the schools, has been led by educators with a clear vocational stake in the preservation of the Spanish inheritance.

One element common to the above approaches is a quest for equality. The widespread acceptance of an ideal of equality has already been noted. Attempts at practical application,

246

however, reveal discrepancies between conceptions of equality. The view that equality lies in the absence of legal barriers which would limit an individual's opportunities, such as the opportunity to get an education comparable to that available to others, has a long history in this country. We have in recent decades gone beyond this position as we have admitted that some persons are handicapped by inequitable economic and social conditions. Advocates of bilingual education programs, for example, would point out that neither de facto segregation, uneven tax resources, nor English language dominated education exist because of discriminatory legislation. Equality of opportunity is not simply a legal matter. Beginning with the Civil Rights Act of 1964, more Americans have expected the government to protect a person from discrimination based on sex, race, cultural background, economic condition, and social status.

Even the more positive governmental role has been considered inadequate by some critics, who see the right to equality as meaningful only in a context where material means have been provided equally to all. Affirmative action and reverse discrimination programs are desired. In effect, it is not equality of opportunity which is sought, but rather equality of result or outcome. It is not expected that everyone will experience the same education, acquire the same knowledge, earn the same income, and have the same material status. Advocates of this view of equality do, however, seek to end what they see as extreme differences between people which cannot be attributed to ability, effort, and contribution to society.

Whether both types of equality can or should exist in an open or free society is beyond the scope of this paper. Concern here is with what the schools can do, or more specifically, what bilingual education programs can do to promote equality. The remainder of this paper thus addresses the question "To what extent are transitional and maintenance bilingual programs likely to contribute to promotion of (1) a sense of national community and (2) equality of opportunity and of condition?"

A community rightly understood is an aggregate of persons who hold common interests, common values, and common goals. It is not synonymous with a state or a nation because the latter require political organization. A political unit can be imposed on people, but a sense of community comes from each individual member. Although community cannot be imposed, the state can take measures to generate common experiences which may contribute to building a sense of community. Indeed, a democratic state has this obligation for, as John Dewey has pointed out, democracy exists in and through community. "It is the idea of community life itself." Do bilingual programs contribute to a sense of community? Since this discussion concerns federal and state funding of such programs, the question can be reworded to indicate a sense of national or state community.

Transitional bilingual programs wherein the intent is to facilitate learning the language of the majority group may appear to have the potential to make such a contribution. When, however, we recall the alacrity with which most youngsters pick up the language of their environment, there is good cause to wonder if the tax expenditures aren't doing what otherwise would happen naturally. Other than asking whether the results justify the cost, there is probably little to say about the impact of transitional plans on building a sense of community. It is when we turn to maintenance programs designed to strengthen ethnicity that we find a stronger case against tax supported bilingual education.

As with many governmental programs, the scope of the Bilingual Education Act has been expanded over the years, and since 1974 a major feature has been efforts to preserve minority language and culture. This, of course, is completely different from providing resources to assist youngsters to whom English is a foreign language. It is difficult if not impossible to justify use of public funds to assist any group in promoting its private culture. Proponents of maintenance bilingualism, using such nice phrases as "cultural pluralism" and "democracy," actually do want to sidetrack tax moneys for their own provincial purposes. Such a role for the government was never envisioned by the founders of the republic, nor endorsed by the Constitution. Paradoxically, public funding of maintenance programs may not only inhibit the growth of national community, but also have a divisive impact on the cultural minority receiving the funds. Is there a black position on "black English"? Is there one Spanish dialect to be preferred (through financing production of instructional materials) to the others? The newspapers dutifully reported on the conflict in Chicago's Greek community in 1973. It had been brought on by the introduction of a federally sponsored bilingual program -- a program which displeased parents of Greek ancestry who saw their children being singled out for less of an American education and more of a Greek one.

The clash among Chicago's Greeks exemplifies another serious problem. The desirability of getting an ethnic group to conform to the culture features of its ethnicity appears to be part of the gospel of faith among bilingual proponents. They assume that all parents give their first allegiance to the ethnic group, that the worth of programs reinforcing the minority cultural heritage is self-evident. In an American environment which encourages each man to set out on his own road and become whatever he wills, there is being promoted a fundamental inconsistency, for at one and the same time individuals are being advised to adhere to their ethnic background and also to free themselves from the ghetto mentality in order to become the cosmopolitan American.

An elementary school youngster is in no position to say "no" to his school program. Why deny the possibility that he and his parents favor school attendance as the means to acquire the tools that will enable him to enter mainstream America? Why deny the possibility that forcing him into a bilingual program, of either the transitional or maintenance type, will mean tying him to the ethnic background his family is trying to leave. Studies by Thernstrom and others clearly reveal how greatly immigrants of the past century have relied on the public schools to lead their children into an American community. It is not unreasonable to conclude that bilingual programs assume that linguistic, ethnic, and religious minorities prefer membership in a much smaller group than an American community. In the absence of supportive evidence, such presumptuousness should not be rewarded with public funds.

It is easy to view schooling as designed to reinforce the culture and value systems of the parents. Those who accept this "privatist" orientation tend to look favorably on the non-public schools. There is no basis for universal taxation to support public (or any) schooling if preserving private values is its purpose. Not only universal taxation but also compulsory schooling would be unjustified. Reinforcing parental values is not the major purpose of schooling in our society, however. The American school system developed in an environment marked by pluralism. Its major purpose was to develop a sense of community among the disparate elements which made up the young nation. It is no coincidence that the major efforts at making schooling compulsory coincided with the major periods of immigration. It is understandable that parents would not want the school to undermine the beliefs and values they seek to instill in their youngsters. The school, however, exists not primarily to serve parental purposes but to serve public purposes.

It has long been recognized as in the public interest that educational opportunity should be maximized in order to contribute to the development of adults who will make political, social, and economic contributions appropriate to a democratic society. Promoting educational opportunity is a public purpose. Much of the argumentation supporting the view that bilingual programs promote such opportunity for the individual is hypothetical, based more on hope than on fact. Complicating the matter is the recognition that seeming accomplishment in school does not necessarily carry over. Some observers of the American scene contend that our society is racist, sexist, undemocratic, and hypocritical, and the school which teaches a youngster that success will follow honesty, hard work, thrift, and perseverance is preparing him for unreality. The school which bends over backwards to assist someone with a physiological or cultural handicap may be preparing that person for a rude awakening in "the cruel world."

If we look, for example, at the requirements to implement a bilingual program, we note the need for (1) new teachers sufficiently bilingual and bicultural themselves to be able to implement transitional and maintenance programs, (2) in-service programs for current teachers, (3) funding for new college programs to prepare future and present teachers, and (4) new instructional materials. Expenditures for these and related necessities may merely delude youngsters in such programs and their parents into believing that the economic world they will some day enter will be bilingual. Still another example derives from the evidence that for several possible reasons schools have given pupils grades, credits, and diplomas that have not been earned. Pupils are promoted without having evinced mastery of normal intellectual skills. They graduate, and find no one will hire them. In an Anglo-speaking world, whatever encourages youngsters to believe they will get their fair share of the pie with their non-English language, is misleading; the education they receive is dysfunctional. This message may not have hit home yet in the United States, but it is widely known elsewhere. French Canada is an outstanding example.

Whose educational opportunities are supposed to be expanded by bilingual programs? Federal legislation designates five groups. First can be mentioned recent arrivals from places such as Cuba, Mexico, and southeast Asia. They have all come to this country voluntarily, and while assisting them may be highly laudable, it is questionable whether major outlays of tax moneys for full-scale programs on their behalf are justified when millions of hardpressed Americans need new opportunities. Secondly are children from non-English speaking homes who have had only minimal exposure to English. It would appear that more would be done to improve their opportunities by concentrating solely on the language they will need in the economic and political world. The same could be said of two other groups, children who speak English and another language equally well (or poorly), and children who themselves use English but have another language in the home which they may understand but do not normally use. Finally we have children with minimal accomplishment in any area, and who are likely to have problems in learning anything.

One basic flaw in the view that bilingual programs contribute to educational opportunity is the belief that language problems are the major explanation for limited school success. There has been a failure to recognize that the very social and economic factors which hinder learning English are likely to inhibit learning other subjects, including one's native tongue. Even if this judgment were to be in error, and the only effective obstacle to equalizing educational opportunity were the linguistic barrier, this does not call for federal or state organization and sponsoring of bilingual programs. The way to learn English is to use English.

Maintenance bilingual programs contribute nothing to the educational opportunities of the youngster hoping to find a place for himself in the world of work. Transitional programs may be compatible with the goal of equalizing opportunity, but evidence of their superiority to immersing the youngster totally in English is at best quite inconclusive. Furthermore, it is highly questionable whether the bureaucracy of government is the appropriate place to determine the methods and materials which will be used in such highly individualized activities as teaching and learning.

Whether a bilingual or bilingual-bicultural program would contribute to equality of result or outcome is really irrelevant because it is doubtful that this has ever been accepted as a desired goal in American society. Even those features of a welfare state which have been enacted into law cannot be construed as leading down the road to equalizing the condition of all Americans. Neither those responsible for bringing this country into being, nor those who came later and were responsible for creating public school systems thought in terms of equality of outcome. The common school was not expected to turn out persons who would become equally rich. It was to provide opportunity for schooling from which people would certainly emerge unequal, and because of which they would have the tools and attitudes a democratic society required. Schooling would not make the worker as wealthy as his employer, but by contributing to his becoming an effective worker it would help him avoid poverty. Schooling would not make each man a likely presidential candidate, but it would enable each to exercise the franchise intelligently.

Assessing the contribution of bilingual education programs to the public goals of American society has been the intent of this paper. It has been made a difficult task by the fact that there are clearly different types of such programs and some have decidedly different objectives. Furthermore, it is easy to argue for bilingual programs. Who could be against expanding educational opportunity, exposing English-speaking youngsters to a second language, promoting understanding between different ethnic groups, and lessening prejudices which have their basis in ignorance of other cultures? Compounding the difficulty is the willingness of the educational establishment to take on additional responsibilities if federal funds accompany them.

Several additional questions should be raised, and while evidence where needed may be insufficient to provide definitive answers, the questions themselves generate serious doubts about the efficacy of governmentally financed bilingual programs.

Can children lacking in proficiency in the English language be helped by our schools without passing laws and implementing programs of several years duration, the cost of which is likely to outweigh the benefits?

What evidence is there that fourteen years of federally financed bilingualism have made a difference in student achievement and in promoting the goals of public education?

What evidence is there that any federally financed educational program has achieved its stated goals and justified its cost?

Since schooling, especially at the lower grade levels, does not have to be based on competition, is it really an argument that we need bilingual programs to help some children compete?

Might not such programs actually end up segregating children, at first temporarily, then permanently, as some move through school at a rate different from those in the usual program?

As for efforts through the Act to maintain native languages and cultures, is it not likely that, to the extent proficiency in English is increased, the youngster's family language will fall into disuse and there will be greater loss of his non-English culture?

Are not ethnic linguistic emphases likely to contribute to the growing division among Americans?

Is promoting the attachment of the young to particular linguistic and cultural ties a proper function of government?

What justification is there in the expansion from the original linguistic concern of the bilingual legislation to the point where just about anything and anyone not in the WASP tradition may be served by the program?

Is it not strange that though for three decades most of the world has been rushing to teach its young English, we are embarking on programs which are likely to take time away from mastery of English so that it can be spent preserving a minority language?

Are ethnic and cultural minorities really behind bilingual programs, or are they really in effect part of the silent majority for whom self-appointed experts develop plans which legislators enact without any meaningful public consultation?

How much of the Hispanic bilingual movement is simply a "me too" response upon seeing money allocated to improve education for blacks?

Are intergroup relations really improved when the federal government uses tax moneys of one group to promote the ethnicity of another?

Finally, do we really develop a sense of national community by stressing differences among people?

In conclusion, with regard to maintenance bilingual programs, to the extent they use tax moneys and take up school time which might be spent promoting proficiency in English and a sense of community, they are counterproductive and not in the public interest. As for transitional programs whose purpose is the promotion of English language skills, in the ab-

253

sence of substantial evidence showing that these programs are better than what takes place without them in adequately supported schools, it is reasonable to conclude that what we need are not bilingual programs, but just more time better spent teaching English.

What recognition should schools give to black English or other dialects?

Bilingual programs have tended to concentrate on recognized languages of a particular national origin. Thus persons of Hispanic background have been recipients of considerable attention, and the Supreme Court's decision in <u>Lau vs. Nichols</u> upheld the civil rights claim of Chinese speaking youngsters. Are students who speak various English dialects entitled to the same services and protections? As discussed in the first article in this section, a federal court, while rejecting the constitutional challenge brought by parents of black students, ruled that the school system had to recognize the particular problems of youngsters who spoke black English, and take appropriate measures to overcome language deficiencies. The decision did not call for a specific program or course, but it raises the question of the amount and kind of attention which should be given to the various dialects spoken by school children.

Is there a place for black English in the school program comparable, for example, to what is allocated for ethnic studies? The first of these articles answers in the affirmative, concluding that black English is linguistically legitimate and teachers must be trained to deal with language problems resulting from its use by students.

The second article approaches the question indirectly by examining the role language plays in learning. It concludes that neither the replacement of standard English with black English (or any other dialect), nor the simultaneous use of two languages contributes to learning. To the extent that a place is found for black English in the curriculum we are likely to increase rather than mitigate learning difficulties.

LANGSTON BANNISTER teaches educational sociology and history of education courses at the University of Toledo. He is a former English teacher and school counselor in secondary schools of San Francisco and Oakland, California. He also has directed the University of Toledo's Teacher Corps program. His doctorate is from the University of Massachusetts.

ROBERT WILHOYTE is Chairman, Department of Educational Theory and Social Foundations, College of Education and Allied Professions, University of Toledo. A former mathematics teacher in Bloomington, Indiana High School, he now teaches

courses in the area of educational philosophy. His
doctorate is from Indiana University.

PERSPECTIVES ON BLACK ENGLISH

Langston Bannister

The issue of Black English is one among many cyclical and polemic issues symptomatic of unresolved black-white relations in this country. The use of Black English in the classroom is often cited as a chief cause for the lack of achievement of minority youth. On occasion the perennial debates and discussions point out that schools fail to meet the diverse needs of our pluralistic society. In light of these discussions and the crucial role of the teacher in the teaching-learning process it is evident that our teacher training institutions have been remiss in fulfilling their obligations to adequately prepare teachers who are capable and willing to meet the challenges of diverse classrooms. In spite of innovative programs these institutions do not equip prospective teachers with the necessary skills and knowledge to sensitize them to meet the needs of all students, especially the culturally different.

The purpose of this paper is to briefly examine the origin of Black English as a field of inquiry. Also, the paper will delineate the ongoing debates between linguists and educators. Additionally involved in the controversy over the use of Black English is the gap between school policies and practices and the expectations of minority communities. The paper will review the practices of middle class teachers, black and white, toward minority youth. Finally the paper will review the relatively recent Ann Arbor King decision regarding the teacher's responsibility in the classroom for youngsters coming from different cultural backgrounds. More specifically, it will focus on the implications of the King decision and the need to take into account the language of the students while teaching reading.

Historical Background of Black English

The lack of clarity and the paucity of definitive statements about Black English is the result of the number of disciplines which had to give their sanction to its legitimacy. These disciplines include anthropology, education, linguistics, psychology and sociology. Before the sixties, very little serious thought of scholarly work had been done in the field of Black English or sociolinguistics. Most researchers and linguists felt that since Black English was only another variation of standard English it was not worthy of serious investigation or study. At the same time educators operated with the myth that Black English was simply a dialect which represented bad language usage and was the result of low intelligence. These myths and false assumptions which grew out of ignorance and ethnocentric biases served to perpetuate prejudices against those who were different from the middle class. It was not until the late sixties that sufficient federal funds were allocated to motivate and encourage writers and researchers to examine the issue of Black English more thoroughly and systematically.

Research, postulating a Creole base for Black English, emerged in the mid sixties. It suggested that Black English was more than just a dialect or an inferior variation of middle class English. This research produced a definitive statement which differed from those of the purists who had long maintained that Black English was simply the result of inferior people with lazy tongues. Also, during this time the first authoritative work in sociolingustics was published and became the standard text for graduate study.

Within a decade, there was a consensus among linguists that Black English was a systematic, rule-governed language which was the result of the struggle of black Americans to combine the cultures of Africa and America. Also, linguists agreed that Black English consisted of unique lexical (vocabulary), phonological (pronunciation) and grammatical (syntax) features which were distinguishable from middle class English.

By the late 1970's, an inextricable link was established between language, culture and experiences which produced Black English. The statement, "It bees dat way sometime" uses the word bees to indicate a recurring event rather than a one-time occurrence. Further, from a cultural standpoint, this statement also connotes a way of looking at life and its harsh realities and injustices with the recognition that one must still go "right on." This briefly illustrates that when a child learns a language, he unknowingly accepts a view of the world that is inherent in the particular structure of the language. Thus, when teachers spend most of their time on the structure of a child's language they are distorting the child's view of himself and his world. In addition, they are also ignoring the more important aspects of a child's learning process, i.e., the extent of his comprehension of the intended meaning.

In spite of the unique language style of most black Americans, there are examples of blacks and whites from a particular geographical area or in a particular economic bracket speaking the same language. Regional and economic variations occur in middle class English as well. Although Black English is recognized as a valid and viable means of communication, it is important to acknowledge that not all black Americans speak Black English. Just as there are differences between Black English and middle class English, there are also differences within Black English. There are blacks in higher economic, educational, occupational and social brackets who almost never speak Black English. Similarly, there are middle class blacks who use what is referred to as "media" English, i.e., it has the approval and respect of the general population and educational institutions. Also, there are differences between the speech patterns of urban, central city and rural blacks. Many middle class blacks are bi-dialectal, using a casual or more informal speech in their intraracial interactions and using the "media" English for the occupational and interracial social interactions. This capacity to switch between Black English and media English corresponds to the same phenomenon which is characteristic of other groups that switch between formal and informal or casual English. Sometimes the decision when to switch is made on a subconscious level and is determined by the nature of the occasion, the audience and the intended effect of the message.

Historically, Negro dialect was the term used to describe the way black folks talked when they wanted to cloak the meaning of their words in a different form of language. Negro dialect was an effective way for blacks to state their version of reality without offending whites. Thus, one of the unique features of Black language has always been the necessity to speak without letting whites know either the context or the more subtle meanings of the communication. This was a carry-over from the slave experience when it was necessary to say what one thought whites wanted to hear and to say it in a manner which pleased whites. During the sixties black dialect became a euphemism for Negro dialect and it still had connotations of nonstandard English. Even when many blacks use standard English they use a different intonation, resonance and vocal quality. There is still an ethnic flavor. Langston Hughes used Black slang and jive talk in much of his poetry just as Phyllis Wheatley and Paul Lawrence Dunbar had used Negro dialect much earlier. It was the slaves' desire for privacy which led to the development of Black slang and Negro dialect.

During the sixties, Stokely Carmichael and H. Rap Brown used the term "Black Power" to symbolize that blacks were no longer content to allow whites to define the parameters of their language. (It has to be recognized that language is more than just speech. Language includes experience.) It was imperative that blacks define their own perception of reality and in terms which express their true inner feelings. The process of actions by the dominant culture and reaction by the minority group continues to produce changes in language and speech patterns. This process accounts for the change in the use of Black rather than Negro. It was felt that the word Negro denied the existence of African ancestry and that the term Black facilitates making this vital connection and simultaneously connotes a sense of uniqueness and strength. The term Negro designated what those of African descent were in the eyes of the dominant culture and the term Black designated who they were according to their own terminology and on their own terms.

Deficit vs. Difference Models

Most of the compensatory programs developed for the "disadvantaged" and the "culturally deprived" were shaped by the deficit theorists who saw the differences in language as deficits or shortcomings. They asserted that Black English was not only different but that it was also inferior, illogical and solely expressive in function. Such views were used as justification for sending language arts teachers to summer workshops to find instructional approaches which would repair these shortcomings and bring minority students up to standard. Even with the best of intentions, teachers were unaware that remediation and drilling were not the most appropriate remedies to improve reading skills. Instead, such practices confirmed for the learner his lack of readiness and in some instances, his lack of ability. The deficit model concerned itself primarily with cognitive skills related to the meaning of language. Remediation efforts were geared to the structure of language rather than the meaning of language; thus, teachers never really heard what children meant or how well they may have comprehended particular concepts since they were corrected before having an opportunity to finish. The teacher's false assumption was that meaning was conveyed by the structure rather than the language used by the students.

From an historical perspective, the educational programs designed for use during the sixties were a repeat of those programs used "on" the immigrants at the turn of the century. The underlying classicist and racist assumption compelled the do-gooders to rescue the children from their homes and bring them into the schools to learn manners and obedience, including how to speak properly. Thus, the preschool programs for the immigrants at the turn of the century became Headstart,

Follow Through and Upward Bound for the minorities during the sixties. Once again, the schools went through the laborious task of trying to stamp out diversity and give all groups the same outlook on life. The classicist assumptions became more racist in tone as Anglo educators sought to determine the appropriate programs for the minorities who had refused to blend in the melting pot. The schools had been designated as the institution most likely to maintain the status quo with the benign cooperation of the groups they were allegedly trying to help enter America's mainstream. Integration meant the standardization and uniformity rather than the coexistence of diverse cultural groups. Schools sought to negate ethnic and cultural plurality.

During the late sixties linguists attempted to correct this thinking by introducing a difference model which asserted that Black English was as much of a language system as standard English. No variation of language was either superior or inferior to any other variation. Linguists analyzed the language patterns of street gangs in New York and helped to corroborate the intricacies of language and culture. Others conducted similar field studies of the speech patterns of blacks in Detroit with similar results. Also, the Southwest Regional Laboratory for Educational Research and Development conducted extensive research into Black speech patterns in Los Angeles.

The major difference between the deficit and difference theorists was their attitudes toward black children and their language. The deficit theorists concluded that the black children, because of their cognitive deficits, were unable to form concepts, think logically or use full sentences. Thus, they felt justified in attempting to eradicate Black speech patterns and replace them with middle class English. Inherent in the deficit model was the assumption that Black English was inferior; therefore, the children who used it were "bad." Of course, with their perceptive survival skills minority youth recognized that there was something about their language (themselves) that their teachers disliked. This was attested to by the number of times they were misunderstood and corrected. Teachers did not realize that as a corrective measure, the repetitive drills on structure and pronunciation undermined the students' search for meaning in their reading. A resulting loss of self-esteem caused the students to adopt a defensive posture of silence or minimal communication which teachers interpreted as an inability to communicate. The cycle was completed. The teachers' negative attitudes created in their students negative attitudes towards their language (themselves) and undermined their self-confidence which in turn resulted in minimal effort.

Linguists or difference theorists favored a second-language approach using the techniques developed for teaching English as a second language. The bidialectal or biloquial theory holds that a person has a right to speak the dialect of his home and community but that the person should also learn standard English for occupational, social and economic reasons. Teachers using this instructional approach need knowledge and skill in switching styles, and understanding and appreciation of cultural differences while still motivating students to perform academically. In this bidialectal approach the child's primary language is not condemned; instead, the child is taught to use it more efficiently through a "compare and contrast" method which involves learning the rules of both language systems. Some linguists promoted the idea of using both the child's original language and middle class English in the classroom. Such a process would help bilingual teachers to understand the importance of student attitudes and goals when trying to teach children a second language and at the same time promote fluency in the first language. This thinking parallels the research used in the Ann Arbor King court decision which will be discussed in more detail later in the paper.

The controversy over the legitimacy of Black English began with arguments and counter arguments between linguists and educators. Also at issue was what to do about the use of Black English in the classroom. Some educators responded to the use of repetition drills by charging the difference theorists with using bi-dialectalism as one more expensive scheme for keeping things as they were in the classroom. He pointed out that the proposed enforced bi-dialectalism was built on the assumption that since the prejudices of the middle class could or would not change it was the minorities who would have to change their speech patterns.

Part of the rationale for convincing minorities to change their speech patterns lay in occupational and economic potential gains. Shuy stated that the obligatory bi-dialectalism for minorities as a unilateral condition for employment was another form of exploitation and another way of making blacks behave as whites would like them to. Instead, the need was to improve the teaching of standard English. He proposed that the schools teach the majority to understand the lifestyle and language of the minority. If the majorities could be cured of their prejudices and the minorities could get an equal-quality education, then the differences between dialects would be unlikely to hurt anyone very much. But the school's failure to acknowledge the validity of Black English was another way of perpetuating middle class values and simultaneously putting minority youth at a disadvantage.

Gulf Between School and Community

It should be pointed out that the critics and supporters of Black English as a viable language system which could be used in the classroom did not fall along racial lines. There was much confusion in the black community as residents tried to hold onto their faith in the schools but were faced with the reality of their children's lack of success. Initially black parents and black teachers, though for different reasons, felt that Black English should not be used in the classroom. Teachers generally felt that this language grew out of the slave experience and reprsented a past era. The black parents wanted the program most likely to help their children learn to read. They realized more acutely than anyone else that the school was the last hope for their children to read if they were to succeed. They feared that if Black English were legitimized their children would not be motivated to learn middle class or mainstream English. However, any casual conversation with black students will reveal their willingness and eagerness to learn middle class English or learn how to talk properly if it will improve their chances for "making it."

Parents send their children to school in part to be taught how to read; however, many teachers are dismayed to discover that the children do not already know how to read when they reach school. During a typical parent-teacher conference in a central city school the black parent usually inquires about the child's behavior in the classroom. The teacher's response, not always to the question, is that the child is experiencing difficulty learning to read. Implicit in this brief exchange is the perennial question of whose responsibility is it to teach the child to read. The parent, by virtue of the initial question, has fulfilled the home's responsibility by insuring that the child is present, neatly dressed and well behaved. From the parent's perspective, it is clearly the teacher's responsibility to teach the child to read. However, since the teacher's other experiences indicate that most of the children already know how to read when they come to school this is a new requirement and someone has to accept responsibility for it. So, the school and the community blame each other for the child's failure. The gap between the two continues to widen because the antithetical lifestyles preclude any attempt to communicate in a productive and mutually beneficial manner. This ever-widening gap is characterized by charges and countercharges. Blacks charge that the schools are engaged in a conspiracy to deliberately keep their children from learning. School personnel charge that they have been given an impossible task, or at least one that the larger society has not dealt with adequately.

To complicate the issue of Black English during the sixties, community militants stressed the need for a common and distinct language which would help to promote unity among black people. They perceived the use of Black English as a necessary and sufficient condition for black unity. This represented a different kind of split between the community and the home. Militants stressed that language was as important for togetherness and at-homeness as it was for making it on the job. These mixed messages were often sent to the school with the result that the latter, by default, could choose to ignore the problems of language and reading and continue to teach as if all pupils were the same in their learning styles.

Hostility existed among teachers, administrators, and community leaders which caused linguists to censor their data for fear that the dialect differences might be interpreted by the school as indicative of cultural deprivation or mental inferiority or seized upon by black racists as evidence of some sort of mythical soul. Thus, they were cautious in releasing their findings without placing them in historical, social and linguistic contexts which served to explain why Black English came into existence and survived efforts to deny it validity.

Middle Class Teachers and Minority Youth

Those middle class teachers who unwittingly adopted an eradicationist point of view failed to remember that among the reasons for their own school success had been the presence and insistence of teachers and parents who believed that they could learn what was expected and required to them. They failed to see that a large part of the reason why minority children don't learn to read is that very little is either expected or required of them. The concept of the self-fulfilling prophecy was proposed to explain teacher attitudes and expectations as causes for achievement and success in school. There was considerable evidence which suggested that a child's speech is a crucial cue which influences the teacher's response for developing expectations. Some researchers postulated that a basic reason so many minority youth fail in school is that they are not being taught either efficiently or fairly.

Complicating communication between middle class teachers and minority youth is the number of teachers who come from the lower middle class. These teachers prefer not to have constant reminders of their recent past in the form of "improper" English in the classroom. They become insecure when they hear speech patterns which they thought they had left behind. They become very rigid in their responses and oftentimes mistake this rigidity for the firmness necessary when dealing with youth who expect adults to exercise the authority of their positions. At the same time, there are lower middle class teachers secure in themselves and thus able to use their switching abilities to the advantage of their students, i.e., they use standard English for instruction and in turn demand this from their students. They then can switch to Black English when entering into social interactions with their students. These teachers provide excellent role models for students who are able to observe and learn the rules for switching styles by observing teachers. This is not a technique which can easily be learned or used in an expedient manner for some children may quickly perceive the condescension involved.

Ironically, many of the arguments of black parents and lower middle class teachers support eradicationists who feel that only middle class English should be spoken in the classroom. Eradicationists agree with the conclusion of the purists that there is only one correct language. This same logic was used with the immigrants who went through their respective Americanization processes.

Black English in Court

Almost five years passed with very little activity in terms of research, articles or funded projects in the area of Black English as the era of Civil Rights and the Great Society programs gradually came to a halt. Then in mid-1977 a suit was filed on behalf of eleven black children from a housing project in Ann Arbor, Michigan. These students constituted thirteen percent of the enrollment in that city's Martin Luther King Elementary School. The question at issue was "whether or not the children have a language barrier and whether that barrier impedes their participation in the instructional program offered.... [I]f the defendant Board has not taken 'appropriate action' this failure denies equal educational opportunity to plaintiffs 'on account of race.'"

On 12 July 1979 came the ruling in Martin Luther King Junior Elementary School Children v. Ann Arbor School District

<u>Board</u>. Judge Joiner held that "The instruction in standard
English of children who use 'Black English' at home by insensitive teachers who treat the children's language system
as inferior can cause a barrier to learning to read and use
standard English." He added:

> The evidence clearly suggests that no matter
> how well-intentioned the teachers are, they are not
> likely to be successful in overcoming the language
> barrier caused by their failure to take into account
> the home language system when they are helped ...
> to recognize the existence of the language system
> used by the children in their home community and to
> use that knowledge as a way of helping the children
> to learn to read standard English.

The judge ordered the school board to present an acceptable
program to acquaint all teachers with the principles of Black
English and with concepts of teaching that take into account
a student's home language. He suggested that teachers need
to have a general understanding of how language is learned and
recognize that all dialects are legitimate. This did not
imply that teachers had to become thoroughly familiar with
the structure of Black English or any of the other number of
dialects; they did however need to know enough to be able to
distinguish between a dialectal difference and an actual mistake.

Implications for Schools

Research by this writer has produced evidence that three
major variables seriously hamper productive student-teacher
relationships in central city classrooms. They are (1) differences in teachers' and students' perceptions of the use of
exercising authority, (2) differences in regard to notions and
use of time, and (3) differences in the use of language. Most
of the difficulties encountered by minority youth are directly
related to their language patterns and the fact that these
patterns differ from the school's language. Research has
shown that teachers' negative attitudes toward minority youth
who speak Black English do affect their teaching techniques in
ways which cause students to concentrate more on pronunciation
and structure and less on meaning comprehension. In the King
case there were forty different allegations. The major issue
was language differences. Teacher failure to recognize the
validity of Black English as a viable system of communication
is one of the major reasons for the lack of success among minority youth. Of even more crucial importance is the effect

of negative attitudes by middle class teachers toward youngsters who speak Black English.

Effective communication is of ultimate importance for teachers and students since their chief means of interaction is language. Thus, the mismatch makes for an impasse as students continue to use language for functional purposes and teachers continue to insist upon correct structure with less regard for meaning or comprehension. It is very difficult for teachers to interact verbally with students who fail to give clear signals that they have heard and understood. Similarly, it is difficult for students to feel competent when their responses are constantly corrected or misunderstood. The children quickly learn the importance of nonverbal behavior, and at the same time teachers learn to expect less from the children.

It is this writer's contention that teachers have the responsibility to initiate interactions and bring students to the point where they are more likely to interact spontaneously. Teachers need to find ways to insure that their interactions take place in a context of mutual trust and respect. Such qualities will help to motivate pupils to communicate more readily and competently. For too long teachers have concentrated their attention and efforts toward changing the structure and the pronunciation of the student's language and have actually ended up inhibiting the use of language.

The myth that minority youth are nonverbal and noncommunicative is the result of teachers' tendency to equate verbal quantity with proficiency. However, there is overwhelming evidence that language is important for minority youth in school, home and community interactions. There are countless words in their daily vocabulary used to describe the various forms of verbal communication -- rapping, running it down, shucking, gripping, copping a plea, jiving and signifying. Each of these verbal types serves a particular function as the speaker attempts to blend style to achieve verbal power. Further, each interchange is characterized by a high degree of personal style and oftentimes is regarded more as a performance than a verbal exchange. In this connection it should be pointed out that Black English consists of both language and style. Language refers to sounds and grammatical structure together to communicate meaning in a larger context. In other words, language is the words and style is what you do with the words. Yet, the teacher's perception is that the minority student doesn't care about language. Implicit in the teacher's ethnocentric bias is the hidden agenda -- the children's language must be polite, mannerly and proper.

Also, it is further evidence of the teacher's preoccupation with form and structure at the expense of function.

It is the school's function to help children learn how to use and expand their linguistic repertoires appropriately rather than to leave the child in a no-win situation when he is told either to use middle class language or not to speak at all in the classroom. This means that teachers need to increase their knowledge of children's language and create a more diversified instructional approach especially when teaching reading. Schools already offer an array of reading programs utilizing various teaching strategies which can be adapted to different learning styles. Some of those teaching strategies identified as individualized instruction can be adapted to the various learning styles of minority youth. It is incumbent upon school personnel to make the necessary adjustments in areas of curriculum, teaching styles, student-teacher interactions, and flexible scheduling, all of which would be helpful to classroom teachers in their work with the several learning styles of minority youth.

Summary

Black English continues to be a challenging and complex issue. Consensus is difficult because of the sociopolitical, racial, class and educational implications. No one discipline is able to give a sufficiently comprehensive picture of the totality of language of which Black English is one dimension. The Ann Arbor court decision helped to clarify the legitimacy and validity of Black English as a viable means of communication. In light of the general confusion regarding the recommendations it is important to reiterate that the judge did not require that Black English be taught in schools or that teachers must learn to speak Black English and develop appropriate materials. However, the necessary but insufficient decision did stress the need for teachers to become knowledgeable about the structure and the history of Black English and Black culture to the extent necessary to become sensitive to the unique needs of culturally different students. Teachers must be able to distinguish between an actual mistake, lack of comprehension, and simply different pronunciation.

In light of the potentially adverse impact of negative teacher attitudes on the education of minority youth, it is incumbent upon teacher training institutions to give prospective teachers a more realistic picture of the demanding challenges of heterogeneous classrooms. They must also provide teachers with more knowledge of linguistics and language differences. This means that educators, researchers and practitioners must coordinate their efforts to make research findings available more quickly and in a manner which will be of greater usefulness to teachers. Similarly, teachers of minority youth need enlightened administrators who will give them the support needed to depart from traditional but ineffective curriculum and methodology.

IS EDUCATIONAL DEVELOPMENT FACILITATED OR RETARDED BY THE TEACHING OF BLACK ENGLISH?

Robert Wilhoyte

> It is terrible to see how a single unclear
> idea, a single formula without meaning, will
> act like an obstruction of inert matter in
> an artery, hindering the nutrition of the
> brain and condemning its victim to pine away
> in the fullness of his intellectual vigor
> and in the midst of intellectual plenty.
>
> Charles Sanders Peirce

The topic of Black English and the question of whether it should be used as a vehicle for instruction in public education have been examined in some detail for several years, but especially since a 1979 Ann Arbor, Michigan court ruling on behalf of black students. In addition to the wide coverage given by the media, and perhaps because of it, many papers examining this topic have been written and published. As in all cases of complex issues involving language and/or education, the many aspects of the many issues are multifacted. It is not the intent here to even attempt a summary -- to say nothing of a synthesis -- of the two principal sides of the issue, that is, "Yes, we should teach Black English," vs. "No, we should not teach Black English." Rather, an attempt will be made to present a brief overview of the function of language in the process of cognitive growth. To the extent that this attempt is successful, a judgment can then be made about the efficacy of introducing any alternative to standard English.

Stated another way, what gets publicity is the issue of equalizing educational opportunity. "Black English" in the schools is seen by some as the answer to the problem resulting from students using at home a dialect which differs significantly from standard English. In the absence of an intensive examination of the role language plays in learning, the advocacy of an alleged panacea has to be treated as a tragic simplification of highly complex concerns. No one is opposed to promoting educational opportunity, but neither court decisions calling for special attention to problems of minorities nor expenditure of tax moneys for programs approved by the federal bureaucracy is likely to have much positive impact on such opportunity. Few issues so clearly reveal the importance of turning to educators whose expertise lies in the fields of linguistics (the study of the structure and development of language) and semantics (the branch of linguistics concerned with meaning).

In the following paragraphs the primary linguistic focus will be on nouns and verbs; the primary educational focus will be on concepts; and the primary semantic focus will be on meaning and reference. The overall intent is to present an explanation of how both active and passive learning occurs. Clearly this is a necessary condition which must be met before any attempt can be made to ascertain how the learning process can be either facilitated or retarded.

We all know[1] that children arrive at school in the first grade after having learned certain predictable concepts. For example, if on the first day of school, we ask a child if he has a kitten at home, we would expect to get either affirmative or negative responses. We would not expect anyone to say, either verbally or behaviorally, "What are you talking about teacher?" On the other hand, if we said to the same youngster, "Do you find that protractors are hard to use?" we would expect to get nothing but a confused, puzzled look. First grade children have learned the concept for which the word "kitten" is the placeholder in language. But they have not learned the concept for which "protractor" is the linguistic placeholder. Given a list of words, preferably nouns, teachers could separate them into three categories: (1) those which are the placeholders for concepts which children have formed by age six, (2) those which are the placeholders for concepts which children have not formed by age six, and (3) those which are the placeholders for which children may or may not have formed the concepts by age six.

Are there any nouns which have to be excluded from the above sorting? Clearly proper nouns, which have reference but no meaning, do not qualify. That is, if a word is not meaningful, then it is obvious that that word cannot be a placeholder in language for a concept. If, however, a word does qualify as a placeholder in language for a concept, how do children manage to learn the concept? Although this may come as a suprise to many (maybe most) secondary and college teachers, this is not accomplished by memorizing a definition. Actually research has pretty well documented how this happens. In the language of the classical conditioning theorist or behaviorist, the child can be said to have learned the concept when he responds to the conditioned stimulus (word) in the same manner as he did to the unconditioned stimulus (thing). For example, the child may be said to have learned the meaning of "ghost" if he emits the same response(s) to a sentence containing the word ghost as he does to a white visual stimulus coming toward him with the proper background audio and visual effects. The child screams, runs, has an elevated heart rate, pale skin color, and so on. This means of verifying that a child has acquired a concept, however, can and does become restricting. It is most applicable in the psychomotor domain where skills are the educational objective in primary focus. In the cognitive domain a treatment of behavioral verification as both necessary and sufficient evidence that a child has learned a concept reduces meaning to reference, and concepts to skills. For example, all children in a first grade class might respond "bow wow" to the stimulus "dog," but this should not be treated as sufficient evidence that the children understand the concept in question. In order to further clarify this point, suppose that all physical object dogs were alike -- identical. [2] If this were the case, then "dog" would be a proper noun. Dogness could be quantified numerically as "few," "many," and "all." Dogness could also be qualified with such terms as "well trained," "lazy," and so forth. But there would be no way to make meaningful assertions about collies, hounds, etc.

The word "Dog" would thus be treated as any proper name. And just as we could treat "pointing to" as sufficient evidence that Clara knows which boy is called "Joe," in a similar manner we would treat behavioral verification as sufficient evidence that children know which animal is called "Dog." He would be both misusing language and making a claim about education that reduces all of education to training.

What then is a necessary condition for concept learning? Meaning. This does not mean that if this condition is met that concept learning will occur. It merely means that if it is not met, concept learning cannot occur. Clearly there are other conditions that also must be met. And what is a necessary condition for meaning? Differentiation. That is, the elements in a set must be similar to each other, yet different. [3] In the language of education, the instances of a concept must be similar to each other yet different. And in the vocabulary of the methods course, it is the responsibility of the teacher (the one who facilitates the learning of concepts) to order, arrange and orchestrate the presentation of the instances of a concept in such a way that maximum learning occurs in minimum time.

Of course it is not the case that concepts are learned in isolation from each other (spatially) or that one concept is learned completely and then another is begun (temporarily).

Rather there is much interaction. The learning curve is exponential. There is a snowball effect. Learning one concept facilitates the learning of another. This same phenomenon is manifested in a more complicated, albeit a more familiar, setting when we are able to ascertain the meaning of an unfamiliar word by the way that it is used in a given context.

The teacher's responsibility in the case of concept learning in general and in the case of learning concepts for which certain words in language are the placeholders in particular is clearly evident. Seldom if ever, however, has there been direct focus on language per se as content. That is, the focus is always on subject matter areas: mathematics, science, social studies, etc. To the extent that there is a focus, it is on syntax (grammar) rather than on semantics, and, for this reason, it (grammar) is treated as a thing-in-itself rather than in an educational setting.

As already pointed out, learning concepts that correspond to the common norms in language often results in a reduction, which must be understood in several contexts. One aspect is the reduction of meaning to reference. This occurs most readily when referents are evident, i.e., in the case of nouns in language and physical objects as things. In this case the error is reductionism: the belief that words have no meaning apart from the objects to which they refer. In cases where reference is covert rather than overt, the teacher has even a greater challenge. Again the teacher must facilitate the learning of concepts. But how does the teacher control for "level of difficulty" in presenting instances of a concept such as anxiety, or even solubility? All too often "teachers" short circuit the entire learning process by having their students memorize definitions. This practice is damnable, the fact that so many people do it notwithstanding.

Consider briefly such relatively simple educatonal questions as when and how to use the word "many" rather than "much," when and how to use the word "constant" rather than "continuous," and when and how to use the word "any" rather than "all." Examine for instance the following statement: "I believe that any of my fourth grade students can multiply any two digit numbers by any two digit number and get the correct product." Could the word "any" be replaced with the word "all" in every instance without changing the meaning? Would the meaning be more affected in one case than in another? If not, why not? If so, why?

Consider the following story. The content is appropriate for the fifth or sixth grade, but the method of presentation here makes it appropriate for teachers of fifth or sixth graders. The scene is the office of Mr. Ed, a methods teacher at Elders College. John Larn is a student in Mr. Ed's class.

John Larn: Good morning sir. Do you have a moment?

Mr. Ed.:   Well John, I do have to finish reading the galleys on my new book. What's your problem?

J.L.:   It has to do with what you said in class this morning.

Mr. E: What specifically?

J.L.:   Do you remember your comment about how to teach division using single digit divisors so that 4th graders realize that all problems are one of two kinds: either there is a remainder or there is not?

Mr. E.:   Yes, of course I remember that. If a number goes into another number an even number of times, then there is no remainder. If not, there is a remainder.

J.L.:   Suppose I said that I wanted to divide 16 by 5 evenly, what would you say?

Mr. E: I would say, "Don't be silly." Every 4th grader should know that 5 goes into 16 3 times with a remainder of 1.

J.L.:   Apparently there is at last one 4th grader who is confused about this, sir. As you know, I am doing my pre-student teaching field work at Elm Elementary School. Well today, a fourth grade boy told me this story. He said that once upon a time 5 men went fishing out on Lake Erie. They only expected to be gone for 2 or 3 hours, so they did not take any food. However, after about an hour and a half, their outboard motor quit working. The water was calm, and they just had to wait until someone discovered them. One person, a pizza lover, did happen to bring along a pizza – a large pizza – 16 inches around the outside (in circumference). He of course wanted to share his pizza with his friends, so he took out his tape measure, which he always carried, and asked his friend, Moe, to compare the size of each man's

275

piece. When Moe was a boy in the 4th grade, he always got A's in arithmetic. Moe said, "5 goes into 16 3 times. So he cut each of us a 3 inch piece." "Wait," Joe said, "5 does not go into 16 evenly. There will be a remainder of 1. Who gets that?" Moe looked at the others hoping that someone would tell him what to say and do. Finally, Doe said, "Moe should have it, because, after all, it is his pizza." Doe, who had been quiet until now, then said, "I think we should also divide the 1 inch piece into 5 equal parts." Each of the other men looked at Doe in amazement. Was Doe serious? Didn't he know that 1 is smaller than 5? Roe remembered how many times his 4th grade teacher told him that division is a short cut for subtraction. To divide one by 5 is the same as subtracting 1 five times. But how can anyone subtrace 5 from 1? By now each man had received and eaten his 3 inch piece of pizza, and Joe who didn't want to embarras Doe, quickly threw the 1 inch piece into the water, where it was devoured by a large carp.

Mr. E.:   Is that the end of the story, John?

J.L.:   Yes, sir. I remember that you often say in class that some problems in life are so complicated that they cannot be solved. Is this one of them?

Mr. E.:   It can't be solved in the 4th grade. Advanced 5th graders could solve it. They would merely have to change the improper fraction 16/5 to the mixed number 3 1/5.

J.L.:   That's all?

Mr. E.:   Sure.

J.L.:   I never was very good at math, sir. I think I will look for a job teaching kindergarten children.

Mr. E.:   Everyone should do what he does best, John.

This story should function in a way similar to pictures where the observer is challenged to find a large number of some particular design or figure. How many critical and relevant comments could a perceptive teacher make after reading this story? How many levels are represented? The fourth

276

grade, the methods student, the methods teacher, are there others? Either implicit or explicit? Are the levels sometimes confused? Could anyone read this story and learn anything about the concepts for which "many" and "much" are the placeholders in language. Could this story function as "an instance" of the concepts many and much? Suppose teacher A said, "How much pizza should each man get?" and suppose teacher B replies, "No, the appropriate question is 'How many pieces should each person get?'" Who is right? How do we know? Does it matter? Are they both right? Is one misusing language? Are they both misusing language? How do we know?

What is the purpose of all the foregoing? First, to render explicit the differentiation implicit between language, on the one hand, and the external world, on the other; and second to focus on the necessary conditions which the teacher must treat as the "raw material" of a lesson plan if cognitive growth is to be facilitated. If the teacher "meets" this challenge by lecturing, in general, and by introducing definitions, in particular, then he is successful only in demonstrating an instance of educational fraud.

In order to put "the problem" into clearer focus, suppose that a learner is presented with only one instance of a concept. For the sake of simplicity, consider the concept for which "cup" is the placeholder in language. If a learner is given the opportunity to examine only one cup, and is then asked to translate the properties of the cup into language, he does not have any choice except to equate cupness with any and all of the particular properties that the observed cup just happens to possess. If the learner is then asked to select a cup from a set of objects, some of which are cups of varying sizes, shapes, and colors, then clearly, as a consequence of this learning experience and only this learning experience, the learner would seek a cup identical to the one which was used when the "concept was taught." At this stage in the learning process, the word "cup" functions only as a proper noun. Meaning is reduced to reference, and the degree of cognitive growth that has occurred is appropriate if and only if cups-in-the-world are extended but not differentiated, that is, there are many cups, but they are all identical. Concept learning could not have occurred. The learner would be forced to try and remember the properties of the cup.

In a similar manner, when a definition is given, the definition is substituted for the description, and the thinking of the learner replaces the sensations (seeing and feeing the cup), but otherwise there is no difference; the learner

277

must memorize a series of linked words in both cases. For example, examine the following definition:

triangle = closed, three sided polygon in two dimensional space

When a learner memorizes (is able to make a noise that corresponds to each of the words in the definition, with the proper pauses for pronunciation) the definitions and then uses the word to be defined and the definition interchangeably, the reductio-ad-absurdum is complete (i.e., education is totally reduced to lexicography) if and when students have memorized a definition for each word in the language. And, superimposed on this, would be a meta-language consisting of a definition for each word and/or rule of grammar.[4]

The argument would perhaps be clearer if attention is focused on the all-to-familiar instances in mathematics where the argument is applicable. Definitions are replaced with formulas. The student "memorizes" the formula. The student is then given a homework assignment or a test in which he is expected to "solve a problem" using the formula. There are no educational differences between this example and that of the student who is expected to demonstrate a mastery of the concept of "cup" after having been exposed to only one instance. This example is merely more complicated. The underlying negative educational similarities are the same.

What then can be concluded regarding the addition, or the substitution, of another system of syntax in the formal educational system? Before this question can be answered it is necessary to summarize clearly and succinctly the brief explication set forth above. Most people, to some extent, have experienced and learned about the way in which mathematics is taught in the formal setting of education. A reduction, identical to that of meaning to reference where the common nouns are the placeholders in language for concepts, occurs. But relational words in language, in general, and in mathematical operations, in particular, are the placeholders for concepts. The educational reduction in both cases is _from_ understanding, as a possibility, _to_ the product of memory, as an actuality. If the _whole_ of language were taught as a discipline such as mathematics is now taught, then, presumably, the criticisms directed at mathematics education would be directed to all of education. There should be little doubt about the appropriateness of such criticism.

Given this brief representation of the manner in which language now functions in the educational system, would the

278

introduction of an alternative system of syntax (word groups and sentence structure) be likely to facilitate or retard education as cognitive growth? A response to this question is easier if the same question is asked in a simpler context: Would the process of quantification be facilitated or retarded by the introduction and simultaneous use of another system of quantification? One example would be the substitution of the metric system of weights and measures. Another example would be the introduction of a number system with a base other than 10. It must be emphasized that the issue here is not that of replacing one system with another, in which case the evaluation would focus on the adequacy and scope of the alternative systems. Rather the proposal is that of the introduction and simultaneous use of two alternative systems. It should be clear that this would be analogous to playing two games of chess on one board. The only way to avoid confusion would be to isolate the use of the two systems. That is, "simultaneous use of" would become "cotemporal use of."

In the particular instance of the proposal to use Black English as a vehicle for instruction in formal education, assuming that Black English, as a system of syntax, is comparable to the system now in use [5] it should be clear that confusion could and would only be avoided by the increasing isolation of the two systems in practice.

Historically this lesson has already been learned. Integregation in the schools was looked upon as merely a problem of blending people according to their respective skin color, as statisticians treat blending black and white beads in a barrel, as it were. After "success" was attained, i.e., after some school system was blended some place (by definition the ratio of blacks and whites in a particular school was the same as the ratio of blacks and whites in the community in which the school is located), those responsible for bringing about this "monumental" bit of social engineering looked at each other and said how self-satisfied they were. But their satisfaction was short lived. They soon realized that they had not even begun to solve the real problem, and they had to substitute the term 'defacto segregation' for the term 'integration' in their language.

It is lamentable that the schools should have to endure yet another social experiment in order to learn that something will not work when even minimal reflection on the issue should establish beyond anyone's reasonable doubt that it will not. But then again it must be remembered that research in education for 30 years has been such that when someone stated that he was going to write a proposal to get public funds to sup-

279

port a study that would determine whether there are more rooms than buildings in the world, we had to pause and think before we realized that he was joking.

Notes

[1] Contrary to what often, unfortunately, happens in ordinary language! The words "know" and "understand" are not being used interchangeably here. To "know" is to be aware, to be able to discriminate between objects. It is the result of training and/or the product of memory. To "understand," on the other hand, is to be able to explain; cf., Benjamin S. Bloom, ed., Taxonomy of Educational Objectives: Handbook I, Cognitive Domain. (New York: David McKay, 1956).

[2] This is the same basic problem as that of looking at two identical twins and saying which is Joan and which is Jane. Adding individuals does not change the nature of the problem. Only one word or description is necessary (e.g., The Smith Twins) and there is only reference - no meaning.

[3] It is unfortunate that this simple point is often misunderstood and distorted even by so-called "educators." When confronted with the reality of a differentiated set, and the lack of correspondence between words and objects (i.e., meaning has not emerged but is not reduced to reference) they express their despair by uttering such claims as knowledge and truth are relative, values are relative, beauty is in the eye of the beholder, etc.

[4] The fact that the back to basics movement speeds up this reduction to absurdity should not be a consolation to anyone.

[5] An example of this point is whether divisibility by 10 renders the metric system of linear measure superior to the British system commonly used in the United States.

PART TWELVE -- PROGRAMS FOR THE GIFTED

Should our schools have special programs for gifted and talented students?

The emphasis in the American creed on the equality of all persons has had an adverse impact on the idea of singling out any group for special treatment. Programs, such as discussed in other parts of this book, which do designate particular students to be recipients of selectively administered aid, usually are justified as contributing to equalization. Efforts on behalf of gifted and talented students can only with great difficulty be aided by such a claim. It has taken a sometimes painful awareness that we are not as a nation best and first in everything to generate support for programs which run counter to our heritage of Jacksonian egalitarianism. Thus, for example, it took the successful flight of the Soviet Union's Sputnik to spur activity here on behalf of mathematics and science programs and special attention to the education of our most gifted young people.

The two articles in this section depart somewhat from the partisan approach to educational controversies taken by the other writers. Both contributors here consider the strengths and limitations, the problems and concerns, of programs for the gifted. In a sense the articles supplement one another, but they part company where they examine programs in a broader context.

The first article supports special programs for gifted and talented youngsters, but notes that they suffer from the vacciliation of American society in making a commitment to these students. Furthermore, the reliance on local initiative encouraged by the Reagan administration means a greater dependence on that public opinion whose ambivalence may lead to a decline in programs already operating.

The second article expresses the concern with elitism, and takes the position that gifted children are unlikely to provide society with benefits beyond those generated by the "average" student. It sees special programs as evidence of the failure of our schools to respond to student diversity, and thus on both social and education grounds rejects the concept of such programs for the gifted and talented.

VIRGINIA SCHAEFER is Director of Gifted Programs for the Toledo, Ohio Public Schools. She has taught language arts, social studies, mathematics and art at the junior high level, has served as an assistant principal, and has experience as principal of two elementary schools and a junior high school.

JAMES R. GRESS is Associate Professor and Chairman, Department of Elementary and Early Childhood Education, University of Toledo. His research and publications have been in the areas of school curriculum, school effectiveness, and teacher education. His doctorate is from Northwestern University.

EDUCATION FOR THE GIFTED

Virginia Schaefer

> We must dream of an aristocracy of achievement
> arising out of a democracy of opportunity.
>
> Thomas Jefferson

It is perhaps significant that gifted education still qualifies as one of the areas which is most often included in any discussion of modern educational controversies. Although only a relatively few educators might openly quarrel with the conclusions of the 1971 Marland Report that "These (gifted and talented) are children who require differentiated educational programs and/or services beyond those normally provided by the regular school programs in order to realize their contribution to self and society," gifted education has continued to suffer from the constant to and fro movement with which America approaches and then retreats from its deepest concerns.[1]

With the launching of Sputnik in 1957, there was a sudden widespread interest in the gifted. Public education was made the scapegoat for having failed to identify its gifted and produce sufficient high-level manpower to meet the threat of its ideological adversary. Universities and school systems researched the relative efficacy of special curricular and administrative procedures, the possible causes and cures of academic underachievement, and the problems of identification and prediction. Programs for the gifted proliferated primarily in the fields of science and technology. From 1956 to 1959 there were more articles in professional literature concerning gifted education than in the previous thirty years.

However, by the early 1960's, the national attention was beginning its retreat from a concern for gifted education and moving toward the concerns of the civil rights movement. What appeared was democracy's perennial dilemma over championing excellence and equality simultaneously, this in spite of the repeated distinctions educators make between equality and sameness of educational opportunity. Pressures to serve the handicapped, the disadvantaged, and the average population increased in an era of rising educational costs. As a result, gifted programs and the extra funds to support them decreased.

The 1970's brought an unmistakable revival of interest in the gifted. This resulted primarily from the 1970 Congressional mandate that added "Provisions Related to Gifted and

Talented Children" to the Elementary and Secondary Amendments of 1969 (Public Law 91-230). The Marland Report was a response to this mandate and set the stage for doing something significant about the deteriorating condition of programs for the gifted.

It becomes obvious that historically the field of gifted education has been a sociopolitical pawn dependent upon national crises and a recognized need for leadership to generate sporadic attention to the social value of gifted students and subsequently to create support for funding special educational programs.[2] The current upswing in support for gifted education has its roots in the acute problems facing this nation. However, severe reductions in federal fiscal support and the shift from federal to local control through block grants may result again in the abandonment of significant programming for the gifted.

In addition to financial considerations, there are attitudinal factors which affect the commitment to gifted education which may merit comment. These concerns are generally expressed through one or more of the following questions or comments:

> Isn't what is good for the gifted good for all children? We don't have proper tests for identification. The gifted have all the advantages already. Won't gifted program support elitism? Special planning for this group is undemocratic. The gifted can make it on their own.[3]

If a program is of the proper level or calibre for the gifted, it would be inappropriate for others. We are able to identify giftedness, as numerous studies have shown, if we make an effort to do so. Special programs for gifted students are not undemocratic but only recognize a commitment to providing an education for each child in keeping with his potential. A. Harry Passow writing in the December, 1955, Teachers College Record stated:

> We cannot leave the talented child to his own devices, for the evidence is mounting that, while some individuals do emerge despite lack of education and guidance, some do not. Nor should there be raised a false conflict between education for all children and special provisions for education of the talented. The Education Policies Commission recently (1955) wrote, "To educate the gifted at the expense of educating the vast majority of children would deny

American principles. Nevertheless, to neglect the gifted would equally deny American principles and also endanger national welfare by a wastage of talent."

Assuming then that the issue is not the "whether" of gifted education, we can address the issues of who are the gifted, how can we identify them, and what constitutes an adequate and appropriate curriculum.

Who Are the Gifted?

Historically, educators have sought to define giftedness in a way that would ensure that outstanding academic potential in children was recognized and encouraged. Most conceptual definitions of giftedness include some reference to intelligence without attempting to define the term. Renzulli noted that definitions of <u>gifted</u> differ in terms of the number of performance areas that are specified and/or in the degree of excellence that must be exhibited.[4] Terman sought students who scored in the top one percent on the 1916 version of the Stanford-Binet Intelligence Scale. DeHaan and Havighurst indicated that the top 16 percent of any class or school population should be regarded as gifted or talented.[5] Several much broader definitions have been proposed, such as that the gifted and talented child is "one who shows consistently remarkable performance in any worthwhile line of endeavor."[6]

Definitions also differ on whether or not evidence of potential alone is a sufficient condition for giftedness. According to some definitions, a child who exhibited potential but was performing poorly in school or on achievement tests still could be considered gifted. Flieger and Bish define gifted students as those who possess a superior intellectual potential and functional ability to achieve academically in the top 15 to 20 percent of the school population.[7] Such definitions require the demonstration of high level skills or knowledge in addition to potential.

A new perspective on the definition of giftedness was introduced as a result of the Study of Mathematically Precocious Youth (SMPY) initiated by Julian C. Stanley at The Johns Hopkins University in 1971. Students were identified who were talented in specific academic areas. A student might be identified as academically gifted in one or more specific areas without necessarily exhibiting general intellectual superiority overall.

Although academically talented and gifted are often used interchangeably, Renzulli argued that giftedness should be defined in terms of the interaction of three clusters of traits: above-average general ability, high levels of task commitment, and high levels of creativity. Accordingly, "gifted and talented children are those possessing or capable of developing this composite set of traits and applying them to any potentially valuable area of human performance." [8] A further differentiation between "gifted" and "talented" sometimes refers to "talented" as those students who have high potential or demonstrated achievement in a single academic or performing area as opposed to "giftedness" across the spectrum of intellectual ability.

Prior to 1971, only four states had laws or regulations in which giftedness was defined. As a result of the Marland Report in 1971, for the first time a definition of gifted and talented children was proposed at the national level. It is this definition, found in Public Law 91-230, which is most widely accepted today.

Gifted children are those identified by professionally qualified persons who, by virtue of outstanding abilities, are capable of high performance. These are children who require differentiated educational programs and/or services beyond those normally provided by the regular school programs in order to realize their contribution to self and society.

Children capable of high performance include those with demonstrative achievement and/or potential ability in any of the following areas, singly or in combinations: (1) general intellectual ability, (2) specific academic aptitude, (3) creative or productive thinking, (4) leadership ability, (5) visual and performing arts, (6) psychomotor ability.

Subsequent federal legislation dropped the category of psychomotor ability. By 1979, 46 states either had developed definitions for giftedness or had formulated working guidelines along the lines of the federal definition.

Identification of Gifted and Talented Students

Assuming a relatively general acceptance of the federal definition of giftedness, the problem of an operational definition for the identification of gifted students remains. Most identification of gifted students continues to be of general intellectual ability as reflected by IQ. Some states make a specific requirement for eligibility for state-funded programs. These requirements may take the form of indicating scores of a specific number of standard deviations above the mean on individual or group tests of intelligence or, less specifically, some upper range (2 - 10%) on measures of ability.

Experts typically recommend the use of individual tests of intelligence such as the Wechsler Intelligence Scale for Children - Revised (WISC-R) or the Stanford-Binet. Control by the test administrator is far greater, and thus, the results more reliable. However, most school systems use group administered tests. This is not surprising in view of the high cost in time and money of administering individual tests. Ohio is recognizing these restraints by currently considering permitting, as an alternative to individual tests, the use of two standardized group tests administered within 12 months prior to placement.

The second area of giftedness addressed in the federal definition is specific academic aptitude. It is important to note that many systems use measures of general intellectual and specific academic abilities interchangeably. The local program objectives should determine the measure of academic aptitude to be used. For example, a program such as the SMPY, referred to earlier, is intended for the mathematically gifted. Since mathematical giftedness is a specific aptitude, it should not be equated with a high intelligence quotient as measured by a general abilities test. An individual's IQ is composed of many factors of which mathematical aptitude is only one. A person with a high IQ _may_ have high mathematical aptitude and relatively low verbal aptitude; another person with the same high IQ score may have low mathematical aptitude and extremely high verbal aptitude. Screening for programs intended for students with specific academic aptitudes must contain separate aptitude sections related to those areas.

General abilities tests do not usually include a sufficient number of items in a specific academic area to yield a valid and definitive score. Programs such as SMPY have used in-grade measures of academic aptitude as a first stage in the identification process. After the first stage is complete, a pool of highly able talent has been identified. A second screening is then done intended to separate the mathematically gifted students from those who are merely very able in mathematics. The second screening in this kind of identification process must be difficult enough to spread out these able students from the upper few percent on the first screening measure over a wider range of scores on the second screening measure. Measures that are ideal for this purpose are those that are designed for students in higher grade levels.

Where systems include the demonstration of a high level of achievement of skills or knowledge in addition to potential as one of the criteria for determining giftedness, a number of group-administered assessment instruments are used. Commonly used in-grade nationally normed measures are the California Achievement Tests, California Basic Skills Tests, Iowa Tests of Basic Skills, and the Metropolitan Achievement Test. Classroom performance as indicated by grades and cumulative record data is also widely used. Grades assigned by the classroom teacher are a more subjective measure than achievement tests. The range between letter grades is generally not so well defined as a more precisely calibrated test score and, of course, the element of teacher judgment is a part of the grading process. Nevertheless, grades are strong indicators of potential success. Students identified through this process have performed well in the past and in most cases will continue to do so.

Identification of students gifted in the areas of creative or productive thinking and leadership has depended to a great extent upon informal/subjective means. This can to some degree be attributed to the relatively vague and intangible nature of the categories and to a greater difficulty with regard to qualification/standardization. Guilford was the first to point out that some types of thinking involved in creative problem solving are not assessed by typical achievement and aptitude tests.[9] Torrance suggested that some children who score only moderately high on intelligence tests score high on creativity tests and are capable of high levels of achievement.[10] Components of particular importance to creativity are sensitivity to problems, word fluency, ideational fluency, association fluency, and originality. In examining tests of creativity, the feature which is immediately noted is that the tests are divergent in nature. There is no one right answer. The student's own creative response to an item is rewarded as opposed to the IQ or achievement test where there is only one right answer.

Creativity tests are available, notably Torrance Tests of Creative Thinking - Verbal and Figural, and Guilford's Tests of Creativity - Verbal, Figural. Here again, the costs in terms of time, money and necessary training for administering and scoring these tests have prohibited their use in many systems.

To a great extent, creativity and leadership abilities are assessed on the basis of teacher checklists. These take a number of forms which are designed to obtain teacher estimates of a student's behavioral characteristics. Widely used is some adaptation of the Renzulli-Hartman Scale for Rating Behavioral Characteristics of Superior Students. Such checklists are based on those characteristics which may be observed more often or to a greater degree in gifted students than in other children. The dimensions and characteristics generally included in such checklists are:

Learning:

      Advanced vocabulary, fluency
      Large storehouse of information
      Quick mastery/recall of facts
      Insight/observant
      Reads frequently at a high level
      Logical

Creativity:

      Curious
      Many and unusual ideas/solutions
      Uninhibited
      Risk taker
      Keen sense of humor
      Emotional and aesthetic sensitivity
      Nonconforming
      Critical

Leadership:

      Responsible
      Self-confident and well-liked
      Cooperative and sociable
      Verbal facility
      Flexible
      Tends to direct or dominate

Motivation:

      Persistent
      Becomes absorbed in chosen tasks
      Self-assertive in beliefs
      Self-critical/strives toward perfection
      Moral concern/judgmental
      Organized

Identification in these areas also frequently takes the form of peer, parent, or self-nominations. Nominations also are a primary means of identifying giftedness in the category of visual and performing arts in addition to auditions and experts' evaluations or products submitted for review. The key issue in formulating an identification procedure for gifted and talented students is whether a specifically defined program exists or whether a school system is attempting to formulate a program to serve the needs of all gifted and talented students. The methods should be molded into a selection process which will maximize attempts to identify students who would benefit from the present or anticipated program.

Identification of Culturally Different or Disadvantaged Students

Procedures used to locate gifted individuals are even more problematic in identifying the gifted among the disadvantaged and culturally different than among the general population. In educational terms, Newland defines "disadvantaged" as "to denote those segments of our society whose style of life is discernibly less nurturant to conventional learning than the average of the total society."[11] Because of factors related to their environment, it may be exceedingly difficult to identify disadvantaged gifted students especially in the later grades. Innate ability may well have been severely depressed by a combination of peer group pressures, a lack of nurturing environment, and other environmentally related socioeconomic handicaps.

Strong reliance on standardized group tests of mental ability to identify giftedness within disadvantaged or culturally different populations may be unwise. While they may constitute a part of the identification procedure, they should not be the sole or even major criterion for identification. It may be appropriate to use only selected subscales of intelligence tests -- usually the nonverbal or performance ones. An abbreviated Binet for the Disadvantaged (ABDA) was devised in 1971 by Bruch for disadvantaged black children, and the System of Multicultural Pluralistic Assessment (SOMPA) was produced seven years later by Mercer and Lewis to adjust test scores in relation to a child's socio-cultural group.[12] Many studies have indicated that disadvantaged and culturally different youth tend to perform much better on tests of creativity in relation to their middle-class peers than they do on standardized aptitude and achievements tests. Torrance has adopted the position that tests of creativity should be the primary component of identification with disadvantaged populations.

Evaluation of Identification Procedures

A national survey of identification practices in the field of gifted and talented education was conducted by the Educational Improvement Center-South, Sewell, New Jersey, under the auspices of the U.S. Office of Gifted and Talented. A contract was awarded in 1981 to survey, compile, and assess current identification instruments and procedures. Members of the gifted education community throughout the United States were surveyed for their perceptions and judgments of what represents the most frequently and effectively used tests, instruments, and techniques in the identification of gifted and talented students. They were asked to respond in relation to the federally defined categories of giftedness.

The results of this survey were published in 1982 as the National Report on Identification: Assessment and Recommendations for Comprehensive Identification of Gifted and Talented Youth. Its findings are both significant and disturbing. The survey indicates a widespread use of indefensible practices that violate equity, the federal definition, and many psychometric standards. There continues to be a significant gap between what leaders in the field of gifted education stress in terms of the critical factors in identification and what is actively applied.

The federal definition of giftedness is stated in terms of educational need not privilege. However, an emerging pattern of identification practices most often screens out those who most need the programs: the underachieving, the handicapped, the disadvantaged, the bilingual, and those gifted in the categories of creativity, leadership, or visual and performing arts. Survey information further indicates that it is common practice to use tests and instruments in ways which are inappropriate or which do not conform to what is intended and described in the published test manuals.

The disturbing fact is that the decade since the Marland Report has not seen significant progress in correcting problems of identification cited in that report. The two most prevalent problems in identification continue to be the inappropriate use or misuse of certain instruments and the inadequacy of existing measures to identify certain subpopulations. It may be hoped that the Richert study will provide the information necessary for overcoming these problems.

Placement Procedures

Final decisions for student placements in gifted programs are generally made on the basis of a composite profile analysis of scores on the various tests/techniques employed. The Baldwin Identification Matrix is a systematic approach for pulling together assessment techniques into a workable, practical, non-discriminatory format incorporating a weighting of test scores and results of other assessment items included in the identification process. The total scores thus arrived at can be used in a variety of ways to:

(1) Rank order students

   and select a predetermined number from the top of the ranked list, or

   survey the range and decide how many students the program should include, or

   determine which students should be included based on a percentage of the ranked list.

(2) Select students with strengths in specific areas for specialized programs.

(3) Discover specific information to be used in the program planning phase.

Organizational Strategies and Curriculum

Perhaps one of the biggest problems facing gifted education today is the problem of curriculum legitimacy. The issue appears to be not whether gifted students <u>need</u> differentiated programs and services but rather what constitutes an appropriately differentiated program and differentiated services.

The myth persists that some semblance of a program for the gifted is better than no program at all, and students, once in a gifted program, tend to respond favorably to it regardless of either its structure or focus. Consequently, it is sometimes difficult to show that the <u>nature</u> of a particular program has made a difference as opposed to the mere fact that some program occurred. Even positive evaluations may be more of a manifestation of Hawthorne effect than "significant difference."

Differentiated education is essentially a curriculum problem -- a problem of the design and arrangement of educational experiences. Program objectives and specific content components to be addressed should largely determine the most appropriate organizational pattern.

Enrichment of education implies that subject matter is presented in greater depth for the gifted than for other students. It is intended to be broader in scope and requires more advanced skills. Material is added to the standard course, but the grade or course placement is not advanced. The most common forms of educational enrichment are general academic enrichment, cultural enrichment, and specific academic enrichment. Enrichment programs are often used in the elementary grades and may take the form of pull-out programs where identified students are grouped for some portion of the day or week.

General academic enrichment may not provide the type of advanced stimulation that students gifted in a specific area need. It often consists of offering such subject matter as a special high-level social studies course for all high IQ students, or perhaps something essentially non-academic like chess or creative thinking (process-oriented). Cultural enrichment involves providing special cultural experiences beyond those offered in the usual school curriculum. Classes in music appreciation, the performing arts, or foreign languages may be offered to all identified gifted. There is nothing wrong with these programs, but they do not meet the needs of students gifted in specific areas such as mathematics. That form of educational enrichment termed specific academic enrichment generally provides for special programming in a specific academic area of the curriculum. Julian C. Stanley, Director of SMPY, states, "The more relevant and excellent the enrichment, the more it calls for acceleration of subject matter or grade placement."[13] When these conditions are met, what is taking place is educational acceleration.

Accelerated education is based on the concept of individual differences and connotes the idea of a person's moving through one or more subject areas more quickly than in the standard program. This may take a number of forms. That used most often at the elementary level is advancing the student one or more years above the standard age-grade. Early kindergarten entrance is a further example. Ungraded classrooms also offer the opportunity at the elementary level for a student to advance more easily through material that would normally not be available due to the limiting structure of grade level pacing.

293

Acceleration may be provided also within the standard grade level placement. One of these strategies offers increasingly difficult or compacted content within a curriculum without actually advancing in grade level. This approach is commonly used at junior and senior high school levels. Honors courses may provide acceleration in the sense of offering content much broader in scope and requiring work involving the development of more advanced skills.

The Advanced Placement Program administered by the College Board is a cooperative educational endeavor by high schools and colleges which permits qualified students to complete college-level courses while they are still in secondary school. In some cases, students may actually enroll in on-campus classes for credit. The various modes of acceleration have the advantage for school systems of being able to provide opportunities for gifted students within the already existing grade structure.

Whatever technique of acceleration is utilized, one primary concern exists. The work presented to the student must not encompass curriculum content which he will likely be required to repeat later in his academic studies. For example, if a fifth grade student is offered advanced work in mathematics only to be later confronted with the same content as a seventh grader, the school has accomplished little more than postponing the frustrations of not being challenged by the school curriculum.

It may be appropriate to note the concern often voiced by those opposed to educational acceleration that the social-emotional growth and creative development of these students are hindered. There are numerous cases of students who have made extremely good social adjustments. Children at any age level are clearly diverse in the areas of social, emotional, and physical development. Gifted children generally develop faster than their age peers in these areas as well so that the social and emotional environment in higher grade levels may, in fact, be more mature and therefore more congenial.

As we become more knowledgeable about identifying giftedness at early ages, we must plan for program intervention more carefully and consistently. Talent can perhaps be most economically developed through an accelerative mode. We know we can teach content and that schools are organized to handle gifted children best within content areas (especially at grades 7-12). Consequently, building a foundational program for gifted students within the basic content areas seems essential.

There is little richness to a curriculum that does not have a strong content base or focus. In reality, it is far easier to identify aptitude that corresponds to a content area such as mathematics and the verbal arts than it is to conceptualize programming in another fashion. Specific content areas provide the match for specific aptitudes. Good content acceleration allows for faster pacing of well-organized, compressed, and appropriate learning materials for the gifted.

A misconception concerning the use of content area with the gifted is that there are more important areas of learning for them to explore for purposes of developing their potential creativity. As Julian Stanley noted, creativity without subject matter competency has no meaning. Creative mathematicians in real life must be proficient in mathematics before they can apply math principles and concepts in new and diverse ways.

Conclusion

There is little doubt that education of the gifted remains an area of educational controversy. The content of current writing on gifted education differs little from that of a decade ago. In fact, considerable portions of many publications directed toward gifted education are devoted to reprints of previous articles. This probably does not indicate general agreement on who are the gifted and what is appropriate programming for them. It seems, rather, to indicate that in spite of a great deal of research and study we are still struggling with the same problems because in the field of education for the gifted there are no easy, clear-cut solutions.

Although few educators may quarrel with the conclusion of the 1971 Marland Report that "These (gifted and talented) are children who require differentiated educational programs...,"[14] there is still relatively little agreement in the two areas of greatest concern:

> How can we identify persons who have the highest potential for superior performance?

> What types of learning experiences should we provide to develop this potential?[15]

Until we can provide satisfactory answers to these questions, programs which are developed to serve superior students will continue to be extremely vulnerable to their critics.

Notes

[1] See discussion in A. J. Tannenbaum, "A Backward and Forward Glance at the Gifted," The National Elementary Principal, LI (February, 1972), 14-23.

[2] For a detailed discussion see T. G. Newland, The Gifted in Socio-Educational Perspective (Englewood Cliffs, N.J.: Prentice-Hall, 1976).

[3] R. A. Martinson, "The Gifted and Talented - Whose Responsibility," The National Elementary Principal, LI (February, 1972), 46.

[4] J. S. Renzulli, "What Makes Giftedness? Reexamining a Definition," Phi Delta Kappan, LX (November, 1978), 180-184, 261.

[5] For a detailed discussion see R. F. DeHaan and R. J. Havighurst, Educating Gifted Children (Chicago: University of Chicago Press, 1957).

[6] Paul Witty, "Who Are the Gifted?" Education for the Gifted, Fifty-seventh Yearbook of the National Society for the Study of Education, Part II (Chicago: University of Chicago Press, 1958), p. 62.

[7] L. A. Flieger and C. E. Bish, "The Gifted and Talented," Review of Educational Research, XXIX (December, 1959), 409.

[8] Renzulli, "What Makes Giftedness?" p. 261.

[9] Lynn H. Fox, "Identification of the Academically Gifted," American Psychologist, XXXVI (October, 1981), 1107-1108.

[10] For a thorough discussion see E. P. Torrance, Gifted Child in the Classroom (New York: Macmillan, 1965).

[11] Newland, The Gifted in Socio-Educational Perspective, p. 47.

[12] T. B. Mercer and J. G. Lewis, "Using the System of Multicultural Assessment (SOMPA) to Identify the Gifted Minority Child," in Educational Planning for the Gifted (Reston, Va.: Council for Exceptional Children, 1978).

[13] J. C. Stanley, "Identifying and Nurturing the Intellectually Gifted," Phi Delta Kappan, LVIII (November, 1976), 234-237.

[14] Quoted in Renzulli, "What Makes Giftedness?" p. 181. The government report is S. P. Marland, Education of the Gifted and Talented, Report to the Congress of the United States by the U.S. Commissioner of Education (Washington: U.S. Government Printing Office, 1972).

[15] These issues are explored in J. S. Renzulli, S. M. Reis, and L. H. Smith, The Revolving Door Identification Model (Mansfield Center, Conn.: Creative Learning Press, 1981).

PROGRAMS FOR THE GIFTED AND TALENTED
AND THE CHALLENGE OF THE COMMON SCHOOL

James R. Gress

Like other movements in American public schooling, special programs for the gifted or, more recently, programs for the gifted and talented (PG/T) have roots in western culture and history. Plato realized the significance of special education for the gifted. Programs have been documented in European schools as early as the sixteenth century. Given only slight attention until the twentieth century, PG/T emerged in American schools little more than sixty years ago. Much of the growth and development of special programs has been associated with behaviorist advances in the measurement of psychological phenomena and the assessment of individual differences. Special attention to the gifted also has been associated with the child study movement and a humanistic psychology which values individual differences. In many ways, the evolution of special programs in American schools corresponds to an ebb and flow of the uniquely American tension between equality and excellence.

Programs for the gifted have evolved through three periods of development in American schools. In each period, a renewed initiative was made to enhance excellence in schooling, at least for the most gifted or talented students. At the same time, the American public schools have been a locus of broader social initiatives to insure equality of opportunity. In the 1920's and '30's, Lewis Terman's work in the genetic studies of genius, the initiation of his longitudinal study of approximately 1500 children with high IQ's, and the work of Leta Stetler Hollingworth led to introduction of special school groupings, program acceleration and other forms of "enrichment" for gifted students. During the same period, opportunity for free public schooling was being extended to a variety of European immigrants and to the offspring of the unschooled living at the nation's rural fringes.

Relative neglect of domestic concerns during World War II was followed by renewed interest in schools in the 1950's and early 60's. The National Defense Education Act, initiatives by the Ford and Carnegie foundations, the National Education Association's Project on Academically Talented Students led by Harvard President James B. Conant, and the work of Paul Witty prompted and reflected a resurgence of interest in special and sometimes separate schooling for the gifted. A renewed push for excellence was being made. The 1960's and '70's were a time of extending equal school opportunities to American minorities, primarily blacks. The period also witnessed use of school facilities to provide affirmative action for minorities, women and the handicapped.

Commissioner of Education Sidney P. Marland's 1971 response[1] to congressional inquiry into the Elementary and Secondary Education Amendments of 1969 addressed the status of education for gifted students. The commissioner's landmark statement was followed by further growth and development of special programs. Public Law 93-380 established the Office of Gifted and Talented in a period of unprecedented federal funding for public education. Supported by Paul Torrance's work on creativity,[2] this culminated in Public Law 95-561, "The Gifted and Talented Act of 1978." During the 1970's the PG/T movement was also served by the synthesis of thinking carried out by Joseph Renzulli,[3] among others. Following the dismantling of the Gifted and Talented Office, the elimination of categorical federal support for programs for the gifted, and an inflating economy, the current status of special programs is unclear.

Today, education for the gifted is without federal leadership, and seems subject to a variety of differing state and local initiatives. Programs are administered by the special education establishment in twenty-eight states and by a variety of state school bureaucracies in the other twenty-two. Perhaps a resurgence of the momentum for excellence in our schools, sparked by the current storm of school criticism, such as A Nation at Risk, will result in a revival of programs for the gifted. Perhaps direction for the future will be found in the developmental perspective advocated by educators like Barbara Clark.[4] For now two issues are central to the examination of special programs: (1) the identification of gifted and talented students, and (2) the design of curriculum options.

Who Are the Gifted and Talented?

The growth and development of programs for the gifted has been paralleled by an expanding definition of gifted and, ultimately, gifted and talented. Early PG/T advocates focused on intellectual ability alone. In 1926, Terman identified gifted as the "top one percent in general intellectual ability."[5] Terman's definition ignored other basic human functions --sensation, feeling and intuition as well as social sensitivity--and created a hierarchy which prized academic learning more than any other. In 1940, Paul Witty defined giftedness

300

somewhat more broadly as "performance [which] is consistently remarkable in any potentially valuable area."[6] However, the postwar movement of the '50's again underscored the pre-eminence of intellectual ability in school success. Gifted students were the "most educable." According to Conant, gifted students were those "who have the ability to study effectively and rewardingly ... [the school's] tough courses"[7] in mathematics and the natural sciences.

A broadening of definition occurred again in Sidney Marland's landmark report and the subsequent federal legislation it spawned. The gifted and talented were those with "demonstrated achievement or potential ability in any of the following categories: (1) general intellectual ability, (2) specific academic aptitude, (3) creative or productive thinking, (4) leadership ability, (5) visual and performing arts or (6) psychomotor ability."[8] At the same time, some old stereotyped perceptions of gifted students as oddballs and nonconformists, or pathological or even supernaturally disturbed, were giving way to more favorable perceptions. Today, many see gifted students more often as well-adjusted persons who often excel physically, emotionally and socially as well as intellectually.

In fact, there may be danger of a new stereotype of gifted students according to which they excel at everything and have no serious problems or limitations at all. In her discussion of different intellectual, physical, emotional, intuitive and social characteristics of gifted and talented students, Barbara Clark identifies possible concomitant problems. For example, the unusually varied interests and curiosity a gifted student displays may be accompanied by difficulty conforming to group tasks, or taking on too many projects at one time. Persistent goal-directed behavior may be offset by a gifted student's stubbornness or uncooperativeness. Unusual sensitivity to the feelings of others may go hand in hand with unusual vulnerability to criticism from others; strong motivation can lead to early frustration and unrealized goals.

At least two considerations have been evident in all definitions of the gifted and talented. One is that these students possess educationally significant capacities. Behavioral characteristics indicative of the educational capacities of the gifted may include:

1. Extraordinary quantity of information, unusual retentiveness
2. Advanced comprehension
3. Unusually varied interests and curiosity

4. High level of language development
5. High level of verbal ability
6. Unusual capacity for processing information
7. Accelerated pace of thought processes
8. Flexible thought processes
9. Comprehensive synthesis
10. Early ability to delay closure
11. Heightened capacity for seeing unusual and diverse relationships
12. Ability to generate original ideas and solutions
13. Early development of differential thought processes
14. Early ability to use and form conceptual frameworks
15. An evaluative approach to themselves and others
16. Persistent, goal-directed behavior [9]

The second consideration in most definitions is an anticipated adult role involving "leadership and reconstruction at the frontiers of culture."[10] It is expected by some that self-actualization of the gifted will be as valuable for the rest of society as for gifted individuals themselves. Thus, one response to the perceived Soviet threat symbolized by Sputnik in 1957 was to look to this country's ablest mathematics and science students as our future leaders in the race to space.

In more recent years, emphasis on the social benefits of special programs has lessened. At the same time, emphasis on the task commitment and actual accomplishments of the gifted and talented has increased. Today, definitions of gifted incorporate three things: (1) high ability, (2) high creativity and (3) high task commitment. In addition, it has been recognized that, while some gifted or talented individuals demonstrate superior ability, creativity and commitment throughout their lives, others demonstrate superiority only during one period of growth and development or in one area of school activity.[11]

Changing definitions of gifted have been brought about by, or have led to, changing means for identifying gifted or talented students. The standardized intelligence test, once the sole instrument used for this purpose, is now more often one of several group and individual tests of intelligence and creativity which are utilized. In addition, testing has been coupled with nominations by teachers, parents, peers, and various experts to identify gifted and talented students. Identification also often includes affirmative action procedures to identify female, minority and handicapped gifted and talented.

The use of multiple criteria, multiple sources of data and multiple tests for identifying the gifted is, in part, a response to the critics of Lewis Terman's work who questioned his approach because of its apparent over-simplicity. Terman's population consisted of white middle-class children who were teacher selected, and then tested by means of a single instrument. However, who are gifted and talented and how they are selected continue to be important issues to consider when developing "gifted" programs.

What Curriculum Options?

Two specific questions about curriculum options exist: (1) what are the goals for programs for the talented and (2) what are the instructional organizations and methods for achieving stated goals?

Marsha Correll identifies the following goals for programs for the gifted and talented:

1. Achievement of fullest potential
2. Self-directedness
3. Acceptance of responsibility
4. Creative thinking and expression
5. Aesthetic awareness
6. Acceptance of divergent views
7. Pursuit of alternative solutions
8. Commitment to inquiry
9. Preparation for a satisfying lifestyle and career[12]

Like other statements for "gifted" programs this one includes a variety of goals. Like the definition of gifted and the means for identifying gifted and talented students, program goals have broadened somewhat as the movement has cycled through periods of growth and development in American schools.

Special programs for the gifted utilize one or more variations of three instructional methods in order to provide curriculum enrichment for achieving stated goals. The three methods traditionally used are grouping, acceleration, and guidance. Examples of grouping methods may include grouping within a regular class, special classes, seminars, after-school and Saturday classes, and special events. Acceleration methods include double grade promotion, advanced placement, tutoring, correspondence courses, and an extended school year. Examples of guidance methods are career and vocational counseling, community programs, conferences, and study groups.

Until very recently, however, these enrichment alternatives were limited pretty much to grouping. Such grouping included special assignments for gifted students included in traditional classroom groupings, special class groupings with alternative programs, and pullout groupings which provided special assignments or programs for gifted students in addition to those provided in the "regular" classroom. In the past, acceleration allowed a few gifted students opportunity for "grade skipping" (or double grade promotion). Guidance alternatives were rarely employed. Enrichment alternatives have been greatly expanded in the last decade.

A variety of other resources have been assembled as well. These include state policies and plans for implementing special programs, descriptions of exemplary programs, and a wide array of curriculum resources. On behalf of the Council for Exceptional Children (CEC), John Grossi has documented A Model State Policy, Legislation and State Plan for Education of Gifted and Talented Students. Corinne Clandening and Ruth Davies have collected summaries of existing state policies, model state by state guidelines, forty-two descriptions of school district programs and related materials. In an extensive collection of resources, Frances Karnes and Herschel Peddicord have identified twenty-four special programs for preschool children, elementary, secondary and performing arts students, eighty national and state leaders in this field, numerous local contacts, information services, alternative schools and programs, and teacher training options. Barbara Clark's work, previously cited, includes lists of characteristics and needs of gifted and talented students, organizations involved, curriculum strategies, materials and tests. Produced at the most recent peak of growth and development in this field, many valuable resources are available for expanding curriculum options programs for the gifted. The extent of use of these resources is in question.

The shifting of most federal support for education to the several states in the last three years has created concern about the current status of special programs. It is possible that, like the first federal initiative to support enrichment alternatives the latest ones have resulted in little change in schools. Virgil Ward presents perhaps the most negative assessment in stating that "what actually exists [today is]...a growing miscellany of practices in schools across the nation ... which fail yet to serve the gifted and talented."[13] More importantly, he asserts with respect to the traditionally employed curriculum options in special programs that "the unreflective reiteration of these insufficient programmatic resolutions [has] virtually blocked the advancement of theory"[14] in this regard.

The Common School

The arguments against special or separate programs for the gifted and talented are focused on the American public elementary and secondary schools. No argument is made at all with respect to nonpublic, early childhood, or post secondary schooling. The arguments which follow are related to a tension between equality and excellence in American public schooling, to the definition and identification of gifted and talented students, and to the curriculum options traditionally employed.

The relationship between equality and excellence in American public schooling is not accidental. Both themes reflect long-standing national beliefs and ideals. The nature of each results in a state of uneasiness, for many view "equality" as all-inclusive, but "excellence" as selective. Increasingly, however, we have come to depend upon the school to provide both. Schooling is but one of several institutions which can provide education, although in recent years in the United States schools have assumed and been given increasingly exclusive authority and responsibility for education. Historically, however, the American public school, the common school of Horace Mann and Thomas Jefferson, had neither exclusive responsibility nor exclusive authority for education in our democracy. As Lawrence Cremin put it:

> Mann's school would be common, not as a school
> for the common people ... but rather as a school
> common to all people. It would be open to all,
> provided by the state and local community as part
> of the birthright of every child. It would be
> for rich and poor alike, not only free but as good
> as any private institution, receiving children of
> all creeds, classes and backgrounds. In the warm
> associations of childhood Mann saw the opportunity
> to kindle a spirit of amity and respect which the
> conflicts of adult life could never destroy. In
> social harmony he located the primary goal of
> popular education.[15]

The primary goal of schooling requires equality of opportunity and common participation. But excellence is required too. As excellence and equality have been pursued by the schools in the twentieth century, particular attention to one often has been accompanied by temporary inattention to the other. Currently, critics view our schools as having lost sight of excellence. Such critics overlook the significant achievements in equality of school opportunity made in recent years by racial and ethnic minorities, women and the handicapped. They also fail to see an even more significant achievement in American public schooling in the 1980's, the mainstreaming of those same groups whose past participation in the common school has been on its fringes if at all.

To be sure, increased attention to excellence is required in our schools. But the attention to excellence surely should not be focused only on gifted and talented students, however they are defined and identified. Rather, the continuing tension between equality and excellence must be maintained. All students should achieve excellence!

Not Gifted, Different!

As noted, definitions of gifted and talented students make evident two considerations which are bases for support for traditional special programs. The first is that gifted students are thought by some to be generally advanced for their age, and that they possess educationally significant capacities. That consideration may have had specific meaning in the original focus on intellectual ability alone, in particular, on an intelligence quotient. However, the meaning of "generally advanced" has become increasingly blurred as the focus on the gifted has attempted to encompass other dimensions of intelligence and has moved from intellectual ability alone to considerations of creativity and task commitment. The broadening of definition by Commissioner Marland, the introduction of concomitant developmental problems among gifted, and the limitations of gifted and talented to particular phases of development and particular academic areas make "generally advanced" at best, arbitrary and, perhaps, meaningless.

However, the introduction of a number of refinements in how we have viewed the gifted during the past half-century does reveal that differences need to be considered as among individuals not among groups. Further, the identified differences among individual students may need to be considered with respect to specific purpose and task. There does not seem to exist a group of students which we can call gifted, or gifted and talented. Rather, there are individuals students who are gifted and talented with respect to purpose and task. In addition, there are perhaps as many important differences among gifted and talented students, identified as a group, as there are between gifted and talented students, on the one hand, and the remaining students, on the other hand. The more important thing about gifted and talented students is not that they are gifted and talented but that they are as different from one another as from other students.

Creating special groupings of gifted and talented students, or using traditional acceleration alternatives, are not defensible on the first definitional consideration above. Why schools have used such alternatives might be better understood as one more example of removing from the regular classroom, from the mainstream of the common school, students with whom many teachers and other school professionals have often had difficulty. Gifted and talented students are "independent, self-directed, persistent, keenly perceptive, nonconforming and highly motivated," in short, students whose learning styles have often been stumbling blocks for many traditional schools and teachers locked into the "one best way" thinking about teaching and learning of the past. Today, however, those stumbling blocks are seen by some as clues to teaching strategies which can accommodate a broad range of teaching and learning styles among gifted students as among others.[16]

Special programs also are not defensible on the second definitional consideration. Although emphasis on the social benefits of "gifted" programs has lessened in recent years, support based on probable social contributions lingers. However, a recent follow-up comparison of Terman's highest IQ (180 plus) subjects with a random sample of other subjects revealed no significant differences in educational achievement, career success, marriage and family, or lifestyle.[17] High IQ doesn't necessarily predict "transcendent achievement in some field," just an ability to do some academic work with relative ease.

The use of more than an IQ test in the identification of gifted and talented students today has addressed neither the consideration of possible social benefits nor the consideration given significant educational capacities. Indeed, the bias in Terman's screening and selection of gifted students is still evident despite the introduction of multiple criteria -- sources of data, tests and individuals -- for identifying gifted and talented students today. Clark, for example, identifies bias against underachievers, disadvantaged, culturally different students and females as continuing areas of concern in the identification process.[18]

The continuing growth of special programs is not, as advocates would argue, evidence of the school's increasing ability to respond effectively to diverse needs. Such programs are evidence of precisely the opposite condition, an inability to respond to diverse individual students which masks itself by separating groups identified as different in some way from the mainstream school population and providing special programs for those who, it turns out, have been rather arbitrarily included--or excluded.

Equality and Excellence

The stated goals of special programs, like the goals of public schooling generally, address dimensions of human growth and development, realms of knowledge, domains of learning, and arenas of life's activity. Those goals identified above are a typical statement of the goals for special programs generally. However, examination will show that such stated goals also are not unique to the schooling for gifted or talented students. Achievement of fullest potential, self-directedness, acceptance of responsibility, creative thinking and expression, aesthetic awareness, acceptance of divergent views, pursuit of alternative solutions, commitment to inquiry, and preparation for a satisfying lifestyle and career are goals for all students, not just for gifted or talented ones.

Curriculum options among special programs have increased in number in recent years. In some places, the options have changed in kind as well. Traditionally limited to "grade skipping" and limited special groupings, the curriculum options of the Ventura County, California, schools, for example, now include a variety of special groupings, acceleration possibilities and guidance alternatives which can begin to accommodate individual differences. In fact, the Ventura County curriculum options provide useful prescriptions for accommodating individual differences among students across the board, not just among the so-called gifted and talented. The curriculum options for PG/T, taken to a logical level of generality then, are not unique to the schooling of gifted and talented. They are options for all students, for each student considered individually.

Why, then, are special curriculum options required for gifted and talented students? Perhaps it is easier to create special groupings to which some students can be assigned than it is to address individual needs for all students. Perhaps it is easier to create acceleration mechanisms that allow some students to bypass some school opportunities than it is to address individual needs where we find them. Perhaps it is easier to provide special guidance for some students outside the mainstream curriculum than it is to provide meaningful experiences in the so-called "regular" school program. Perhaps the curriculum options in special programs are a kind of sleight of hand that allows reprieve from the fundamental challenge of the common school.

Like the mechanical solutions of today's school critics-- more school days, better paid teachers, mandatory homework-- programs have evolved from an obsolete way of thinking about individual differences and the relationship of equality and excellence in the common school. The obsolescence has per- sisted through more than sixty years of evolving programs for the gifted and talented. It is rooted in a way of thinking about individual student differences which has focused on de- fining and identifying special groups of gifted and talented students.

Equality of opportunity in the common school requires identifying the individual ways in which all students are gifted and talented. The obsolescence of special programs is rooted in a way of addressing differing student needs which focuses on providing curriculum options to groups of students rather than to individual students. Equality of opportunity requires making individual options available to individual students. The obsolescence is rooted in a way of thinking about excellence which reserves it for an elite. In the American public school, excellence must belong to all.

Notes

[1] Sidney P. Marland, Education of the Gifted and Talented, Re- port to the Congress of the United States by the U.S. Com- missioner of Education (Washington, D.C.: U. S. Government Printing Office, 1972).

[2] E. Paul Torrance, Gifted Children in the Classroom (New York: Macmillan, 1965).

[3] Joseph S. Renzulli and Elizabeth P. Stoddard, eds., Gifted and Talented Education in Perspective (Reston, Virginia: ERIC Clearinghouse on Handicapped and Gifted Children, Council for Exceptional Children, 1980).

[4] Barbara Clark, Growing Up Gifted (Columbus, Ohio: Charles E. Merrill, 1979).

[5] Lewis M. Terman, Genetic Studies of Genius, Volume I (Stan- ford, California: Stanford University Press, 1925), p. 14.

[6] Paul Witty, "Some Considerations in the Education of Gifted Children," Educational Administration and Supervision, XXVI (October, 1940), 516.

[7] National Education Association, The Identification and Education of Academically Talented Students (Washington, D.C.: The Association, 1950), p. 16.

[8] Marland, Education of the Gifted and Talented, p. 2.

[9] Clark, Growing Up Gifted, pp. 20-34.

[10] Virgil S. Ward, Differential Education for the Gifted (Ventura, California: Ventura County Superintendent of Schools Office, 1980), p. ix.

[11] Joseph S. Renzulli and L. H. Smith, "Revolving Door: A Truer Turn for the Gifted," Learning, IX (September, 1980), 91-93.

[12] Marsha M. Correll, Teaching the Gifted and Talented (Bloomington, Indiana: Phi Delta Kappa Educational Foundation, 1978), pp. 23-24.

[13] Ward, Differential Education for the Gifted, p. ix.

[14] Ibid, p. xiv.

[15] Lawrence A. Cremin, The Transformation of the School (New York: Vintage Books Edition, Random House, 1964).

[16] Shirley A. Griggs, "Counseling the Gifted and Talented Based on Learning Styles," Exceptional Children, L (February, 1984), 429-433.

[17] David H. Feldman, "A Follow-up of Subjects Scoring Above 180 IQ in Terman's Genetic Studies of Genius," Exceptional Children, L (April, 1984), 518-523.

[18] Clark, Growing Up Gifted, pp. 270-323.

PART THIRTEEN -- THE FUTURE FOR COLLEGES OF EDUCATION

What are the prospects for those institutions commonly charged with the preparation of the nation's elementary and secondary school teachers?

The American college of education is an outgrowth of the nineteenth century normal school whose humble beginnings consisted of an eleven week program for persons with the equivalent of an elementary school education. From such a start teacher training institutions have developed into colleges offering programs through the doctorate and engaging in research covering all aspects of education. Few people enter teaching today who have not completed state mandated course work at a college of education. On many campuses the preparation of teachers has become a major responsibility; at a good number it is the major responsibility.

Concern with the quality of teaching in some of our public schools has led in the 1980s to a number of reactions both within and outside the teaching profession, but none more provocative than the effort in several states to permit persons to teach who have had no specific training for the task. From one perspective this might be viewed as an at least temporary triumph of those who have long regarded colleges of education as inferior members of the campus community. Even at those universities which were founded to prepare teachers, or which languished as undergraduate schools until recognizing the profitability of teacher training, colleges of education often have been held in little regard. With the decline in the number of students preparing for teaching careers some institutions which over-expanded during the 1950s and 1960s have been reducing significantly the size of their education faculties. Is this a sign of changes to come? What are the prospects for teacher training institutions?

The first article examines the position of colleges of education beset by criticisms on one side from school teachers and administrators, and on the other side from university liberal arts colleagues. It asks whether school teaching really requires extensive university preparation, and suggests that teacher training may not belong at the university level. Education professors can and should give greater attention to matters of scholarship. As long as they continue to regard themselves as extensions of the lower schools, they will remain isolated from collegiate intellectual life.

311

The final article in this book contents that professional educators do have the capacity to shape the future course not only of educational preparation programs, but also of education itself. Current educational problems must be addressed in their entirety so that educators will not operate with a limited vision of their occupation, but rather with a recognition of the need for a blend of content information, methodology, and understanding of the environment within which learning takes place.

THOMAS R. LOPEZ is Professor of Education at the University of Toledo. His doctorate is from the University of New Mexico. DAVID M. BALZER is also Professor of Education at Toledo. He has taught at Pennsylvania State University and has been involved in teacher education programs in El Salvador, Saudi-Arabi, and Lesotho. His doctorate is from the University of Minnesota.

PHILIP J. RUSCHE is Dean of the College of Education and Allied Professions at the University of Toledo, and Professor in the college's Department of Educational Leadership. Formerly he held administrative and instructional posts at Marshall University and Northeastern University. His doctorate is from the University of Rochester.

POSSIBILITIES FOR THE SCHOLARLY LIFE IN COLLEGES OF EDUCATION

Thomas R. Lopez, Jr. and David M. Balzer

No one is neutral about colleges of education. Almost everyone with a bachelor's degree has opinions about such colleges, and delights in expressing them. Indeed, the mere mention of the college of education on any campus, or even at a cocktail party, is frequently enough to usher in a blast of unequivocated commentary. There is no doubt -- its detractors and critics are legion. Its defenders are few, their defenses muted. And its reputation, however deserved, is undeniable.

Our purpose in this essay is not to attack or defend colleges of education as such, but to offer an assessment of the possibilities on the question posed by the title. Colleges of education are, after all, only an administrative unit of the university that exists, presumably, to serve larger purposes. They have no inherent virtue or defect.

A substantial body of literature from the fields of educational history and the sociology of education details the institutional development of the contemporary college of education and the socio-dynamics of the so-called education professions. While we may draw upon some of that scholarship, here we want primarily to outline some general impressions on the basis of experiences as faculty members of an education department at a rather typical state university. We leave it to someone else to assess the possibilities from the vantage point of a graduate student. (Dare one hope for an undergraduate?)

Social scientists have developed an interesting body of knowledge on occupational "selection factors." Various kinds of people for varying reasons tend to be drawn into the ranks of different occupations (read "careers" or "professions"). Jobs influence the attitudes and behavior of the practitioners, and the practitioners' attitudes and behavior, in turn, influence the nature of the job in all kinds of interesting ways; that is no less true of school teaching than for any other endeavor. The paramount and most obvious characteristic of <u>the typical college of education is</u> that it is <u>populated</u>, with only a few exceptions, by students who are interested in careers in schools, by people who work in schools, and <u>by people who identify themselves with schools</u>. The outlooks of these people necessarily characterize the college of education in the same way that a particular university is marked by the people who attend it.

In discussing students who have indicated a desire for a school career or practitioners who are working on an advanced degree in whatever field, it is, however, simple-minded to think of them in terms of their college or departmental designations as such within the university. In the case of secondary school especially, programs leading to teaching certification are substantially the same irrespective of "college." What characterizes them for analytical purposes is not which administrative office houses their records or even their "majors" _per se_ but their career choices: school teacher, school administrator, school counselor, school nurse, or other school specialist. Most of them happen to be in colleges of education, but only incidentally. So while the discussion here is about "Education Majors," for convenience, it should be clear that the observations are about school people irrespective of the details of their college transcripts.

In most universities, the college of education, particularly the baccalaureate degree granting unit, is the "ghetto" of the institution. It doesn't require a sociological index of relative "prestige" to demonstrate that professional education (with exceptions) is close to the bottom among the disciplines and fields within the institution. Ghettos are created, of course, by external forces more often than not -- by prejudice, discrimination, denial of opportunity, political circumscriptions, for example. But ghettos are also partially created by factors that are located within the ghetto and within its inhabitants.

We should note that the reasons are historical in large measure for the "ghetto" status of colleges of education. The paidagogos of ancient Greece gave teaching the mark of slavery which has yet to disappear. In the Roman Empire Lucian satirically pointed out kings and viceroys in Hades who were punished for their misdeeds by being required to sell fish or to teach grammar. Colleges of education have inherited that legacy almost directly; and from securing a small corner on the campus to ultimately occupying a major position in the university represents a stormy history both for professional studies in education and for institutions of higher learning.

While part of the present marginal status of colleges of education is vestigial, part of the image of colleges of education on and off campus is based on myths and stereotypes. One need only to serve on a university-wide personnel commit-

tee, for instance, to find out that no single college has anything approaching a monopoly on manifest commitment to high
quality scholarship or to academic life; it seems, similarly,
that any philistines among us are randomly distributed, more
or less, throughout the campus(es), images to the contrary
notwithstanding. Nonetheless, one is easily struck by what
appears as the persuasive, crippling isolation of colleges of
education from general American scholarship and from much of
the intellectual life of the university.

Another impression of the campus observer about colleges
of education is that they are remarkable in their similarity
across the nation. This is no mean fact given the sheer number of them, the size of the country, and the organizational
independence of institutions and systems of higher education.
There are some, like the college of education at The University of New Mexico, which demonstrate pluralism to some extent in their students, faculty, and administration, and some
vitality in programs; that may be, however, as much a function of the university and its location as of any commitment
on the part of the college to create its own path. By and
large, one college of education seems, from a professor's
point of view, as dreary as the next. With the exception of
the few which are notorious, colleges of education not only
seem indistinguishable but they are institutionally undistin-
guished academically. Ten randomly selected professors of
education (from disparate fields) would be hard pressed to
agree on a list of colleges or graduate schools of education
that could be described as academically excellent. We suspect
that they would have trouble even agreeing to a list of "good"
ones (beyond their own alma maters, of course). There are, to
be sure, some academically strong graduate departments in colleges of education here and there. There are also some first
rate scholars, by any standard, who hold rank in colleges or
graduate schools of education. Their achievements, however,
seem personal and one can't be sure to what extent, if any,
the college of education is related, or even relevant, to
their work.

Individual excellence is, of course, uncommon by definition; colleges of education can hardly be singled out or criticized on that score. Further, institutional reputations may
have more to do with "images," sometimes manufactured, than
with actual achievements or even with seriousness of purpose.
Nonetheless, a third thing that strikes the observer of colleges of education is that, although they are frequently and
foolishly accused of creating them, colleges of education are
notoriously susceptible to "fadism" and patent medicine remedies to real or contrived educational ailments. Every con-

315

ceivable fad that erupts and spreads in the schools seems to find a place somewhere in the college of education. Some come and go with tedious regularity -- programs for the "gifted" (and the talented too) are a prime example. The list of new approaches in this or that subject to replace the "traditional" way (a term almost always used pejoratively) is too grim to recount here. The pattern, however, is significant: a few years go by and the schools and the colleges of education find that the "new" methods haven't worked any better than the old ones; but by then there is yet another new "movement" on the horizon, even if it is called "back to basics."

Some of the fads are manifestly silly. One need only peruse a topical schedule of summer workshops (always for liberal credit hours) for teachers, school administrators, and counselors or check the titles of "new courses" that are endlessly being developed; or scan the administrative or curriculum "specialties" that are available in college of education graduate programs. The "new" offerings are typically matched by newly developed "expertise" on the part of a portion of the faculty. Some are virulently anti-intellectual and vulgar -- the competency-based teacher education programs, for example, which budded in the early 1970's.

Undoubtedly most education professors to their credit were uninterested and uninvolved in the so-called competency movement. Possibly the majority opposed such approaches. In some fields and departments in education college, opposition was unified. Competency-based teacher education programs (C.B.T.E.) took their cue from the "management by objectives" movement which had been developed earlier in the Harvard Business School and which had been in vogue in some sectors of the American "Corporate Community." C.B.T.E. corresponded to increasing talk in the schools about "performance standards" for credits and diplomas, and competence testing for students. Under the stimulus of generous amounts of federal dollars (by university standards), some colleges of education developed C.B.T.E. programs at breakneck speed. Federal funds have, of course, since "dried up"; thus C.B.T.E. despite the hoopla, has received its just dessert. Like Viet Nam, many of us try to forget about it or even pretend that it never really happened.

A standard commercial formula had been applied in the case of C.B.T.E. to teacher training at those few institutions which in the language of the decade, "bought into it." The principle was: "If your product won't sell, and if you don't want to invest in research to build a better one, one that will sell, then put your money into marketing." The technique began with a name -- "Competency." Shades of President Harding! One can't help but wonder what an alternative "base" would be; and what was it before, incompetency? Teacher education at those institutions obviously was not improved. If anything, the quality of teacher education was diminished.

As a socio-political phenomenon, rather than as only a footnote in institutional history, the banality of the approach assumed more serious significance in Texas than elsewhere. A group of advocates of C.B.T.E. almost succeeded in having that approach, a prescribed and controversial teaching method, mandated not only in state colleges of education but in other parts of the universities as well. What zealots and a few allies in colleges of education could not win in the market place of ideas (or even in the commercial market), they attempted to win politically through ideologically capturing the machinery of government, in this case the Texas Department of Education, to impose their particular educational doctrine. Fortunately for Texas, there were enough people in and especially out of colleges of education who still respected academic freedom and who were tolerant of different points of view.

It is appropriate to make some other campus observations of things as they are. Colleges of education have been unable to establish admission standards beyond admission to the university. Public institutions in the midwest and south generally are required by law to admit virtually any high school graduate. That is as it should be. Public funding policies, however, have offered little inducement to those institutions and their component bureaucratic units to do anything but to maintain themselves and when possible to expand. Further, within the university one can hardly imagine, given intramural politics and program funding policies, real support of a serious effort on the part of the college of education to "upgrade" its programs. Present teacher training programs in large measure are lucrative sources of institutional revenue to support other university programs, including the coveted Graduate School. As it stands, and over the objection of many of the faculty of Education, little beyond a high school diploma and tuition money are tantamount to admission to teacher education.

There is incentive to retain all students on the part of every academic unit of the university, and there are serious legal problems, except in the most outrageous of cases, with efforts to exclude anyone for reasons other than grades and course credits. The problem is compounded by the fact, from

317

a scientific perspective, that successful teachers (much to the chagrin of academicians and those who identify themselves with them) may or may not be "high achievers" by university or scholarly standards. Moreover, such teachers, as identified by a variety of criteria and from varying vantage points, are not even necessarily academically disposed individuals! That phenomenon characterizes all clinical fields or occupations to some extent, but it is ironic that school teaching (or administering or counseling) is not different in that respect from any other so-called profession or applied field.

Aptitude test scores, for what the observation is worth, for undergraduates preparing themselves for education careers remain distressingly lower on nationally standardized tests than those of students in almost every other professional or academic field. The same generally holds true for the Graduate Records Examination. That includes those studying to be teachers, school administrators, and school counselors, although it should be noted there are some in almost any education field who score in the ninetieth percentile. Students in some education fields, for that matter, score consistently well-above university-wide norms on nationally standardized tests. Patterns of scores, as one might expect, are highly correlated with discipline and subject matter specialization in professional education. But what such scores mean in terms of personal ability, professional competence, or even scholarly achievement likewise remains a highly speculative matter.

Undergraduate education courses are widely called "Mickey Mouse" by many of the most serious students. Part of that reputation is primarily a reflected image of the wider culture, not necessarily of the academic quality of the college program. Courses in elementary education are frequently considered "easier" than courses in secondary education; clinical or applied courses and departments are typically considered less "substantive" than theoretic departments in college and graduate schools of education in a prestige hierarchy that corresponds almost exactly with the pecking order by age of students and subject matter found in the school system.

Part of the reputation is unadulterated prejudice. One suspects that the image for many of the courses in education could never be changed no matter what tailored modifications were made. Of course, evidence and rational discourse are of limited use in dealing with people whose minds are closed. Another possibility, suggested by a psychiatrist, is that many people, despite possible histories of school success, carry into adulthood a deep antipathy toward many of their former school teachers, which is subsequently directed toward colleges of education. To the extent that this is the case, one can only imagine the hatred some people who didn't succeed in school have for their former teachers, especially among members of minority groups.

Grade inflation is hardly the invention of colleges of education. Comparative university-wide tallies clearly reveal that A's and B's are not a localized phenomenon in the education building. As far as rigor is concerned, most people have a profoundly limited conception of what that is. Vocational education in high school, for example, to the extent that it requires application of theory and problem solving, or analytical skills, is in important ways intellectually more sophisticated and closer to a liberal education than a so-called "college-prep" course that might well consist of catechetical instruction and rote learning. Yet the images, and the ascribed characteristics are typically reversed. Variations of the same phenemonon appear on any university campus.

Nonetheless, many professors in education especially in the humanistic and behavioral studies, are distressed about the academic quality of much of the course work in colleges and graduate schools of education. Intellectual considerations, a concern for ideas, seem to occupy a lamentably small place in the professional literature, and above all, in the professional education enterprise of K-12 schooling. That reflects, of course, on the universities and the colleges of education. Regardless of what others may or may not be doing elsewhere in the university, education students are the focal concern. Typically what little reading is asked of education students all too often consists of professional or, even worse, institutional propaganda or intellectually unchallenging material. It is revealing to gather reading lists for education courses, or even better, to thumb through the books that undergraduate and graduate students are expected to read. Standards of scholarly performance established by professors for their graduate students and most especially the academic expectations students of education have for themselves compared to graduate students in other fields are generally modest.

Many education students, have become so accustomed to taking courses with lots of field work and "make-it-and-take-it" projects with so little reading that they are befuddled when handed a required reading list. As professors, we are not inculpable on this matter. What we do ask them to read sometimes says as much about us as it does them. In a graduate class of teachers, and especially school administrators and counselors, if one requires a term paper with a seemingly reasonable assumption that a graduate student should have some idea of what a term paper is, typically, we find mailboxes stuffed with five pages representing a quarter's work of "research" and study (ascriptively labeled higher education) for which someone expects an A signifying excellence. We should not be so surprised to run across our students in the library.

It can be left to colleagues in other departments to discuss the quality of work of education students in their courses, but for many, especially in the humanistic and behavioral studies, there is a mood of deep concern and even distress. One hesitates to embark on the discussion of academic quality in colleges of education out of respect for the serious scholars who sit among the others who have enrolled in our classes. The best students in education are by any objective measure as good as or better than any in the entire university. Indeed some departments have long standing traditions of high scholarship and performance. In fairness we should point out that among the very best students we have had in our classes have been elementary teachers. Here we are discussing a majority profile -- we admit our observations do violence to individuals.

Some Words About the Professoriate

A field researcher in the social sciences is usually well-advised, for the sake of his research if for no other reason, to make observations in "fields" and "neighborhoods" other than his own. However, it should be pointed out that "selection factors" operate for the education professoriate as they do for business, law, English, or any other discipline. Most members of education faculties have had extensive personal experience as teachers and administrators in the schools. A crucial difference between them, however, and their former colleagues is that they left those positions in the schools. Why did they leave? Were they more ambitious? Were they brighter, or more able? Is it because they were less willing to tolerate the working conditions and the climate of schools than those who remained? Or the quality of life? The money?

With a view toward the general subject under consideration, an observation that is commonly made is that for all their talent and advanced education and personal achievements, many people who hold faculty rank in colleges and schools of education professionally identify themselves with schools and something abstract called the "education profession" -- the world of K-12. Many, probably most, are not oriented to the university -- its values, traditions, and even its presumed work of research and scholarship. (That is likewise true, of course, of others at the university, but they do not concern us here.) They teach self-selected career aspirants to be teachers, counselors, administrators, etc. as they -- the professors, not the practitioners -- envision the profession. Because of their occupational experience and general professional self-identification (as well as their own college and graduate school experience), the education faculty tends to think of itself not primarily as a part of a university or as people who have chosen academic life, but as administrative extensions and campus agents of the "professional education establishment." A second possible implication is that traditions of academic freedom and governance may be marginally successful grafts on the education faculty: many faculty members became university professors as secondary careers, often after extensive school service.

Schools are very different with respect to governance. Public schools typically are governed bureaucratically as hierarchies. The values and procedures are at least nominally "professional" rather than "academic." It is not surprising that people would bring the practices and customs of high school and elementary school with them to the campus when they secure college positions. Attempts to transplant such modes and foster such attitudes on campus are not unknown. Indeed, there are abundant examples in colleges of education where such attempts have been successful.

One of the most curious aspects about school teaching is that classroom teaching is the entry-level slot in the profession. "Upward mobility" is through administration at the school and at the district level. Even at the university level, "teaching," especially undergraduates, is an activity that few professors are enthusiastic about. Working in the schools and particularly with children is viewed with distant sympathy, mild disdain, or even outright contempt on the part of a large portion of the university professoriate. Thus, the education professoriate is compromised in the eyes of their university colleagues to the extent that they attend to what is perceived as the mundane matters of the schoolhouse. Even within education colleges, working with undergraduates and especially working on-site in the schools (except for occasional forays as paid consultants to establish credibility with the practitioners), is widely viewed as a declasse assignment, best reserved for assistant professors.

The college of education is caught in a dilemma from which it has been unable to extricate itself. Professors of education (in the clinical fields especially) <u>qua</u> university professors tend to be seen by clinicians in the schools as utopians and "ivory-tower types." The anti-intellectualism that permeates American culture and plagues the ranks of school professionals finds an easy target in the visible, highly vulnerable education professoriate whose members are frequently seen in the corridors of schools. But that very involvement tends to invite criticism from colleagues, especially from the colleges of arts and sciences. The anti-intellectualism of the clinicians in the schools is thereby matched by the elitism of much of the university professoriate, who tend to view careers in schools as something people with talent avoid except under conditions of dire need. The extent to which education professors share that attitude is not known. In any case, both sets of attitudes converge on the college of education, as any professor of education will readily testify. The self-identification on the part of the education professoriate with school careerists further strains the collegial relationship with their fellow professors on campus.

Colleges of education are often frequently caught between management and labor. Labor unions tend to dismiss professors in colleges of education as allies of management and a mass producer of people competing for limited school jobs. Management tends to expect colleges of education to "produce" competent and cooperative (read "compliant") "team players" to do a job from the administrator's perspective. At the graduate level, the programs as in any professional school, are caught between the demands of both management and labor for attention to their immediate occupation concerns and problems. Both are impatient with <u>academic</u> concerns, generalized research, and "educational <u>studies</u>" as a liberal study to enhance the education of educators.

Universities and colleges of education have successfully solved the problem of the teacher shortage of the 1950's and early 60's. With the decline in the school-age population and the general over-supply of certificated teachers in most fields, the time is historically opportune from the academic viewpoint of the university, to seriously address the problem of teacher education and to upgrade the general quality of the clinical fields. Almost everyone recognizes that improvements are badly needed, but educational decisions are seldom made on educational criteria. Conflicting interest groups -- teachers unions, administrative associations -- do not have academic concerns and the perspectives and values of the university as their primary interest. And each group makes its demands on the university.

It has been suggested that anyone with a bachelor's degree should be eligible to teach if he can convince someone to hire him. That would profoundly expand the pool of prospective employees, so that if administrators didn't hire the right people it would not be that they didn't have enough choices. The teachers unions, of course, would fight such a plan with the same fervor that they oppose right-to-work laws. Their pleas for "academic quality" (i.e. restricted access to jobs) would be suddenly stilled. Their opposition to such a plan no doubt would be joined by many of the education professoriate. But their collective motives clearly could hardly be considered altruistic.

The fact of the matter may be that the jobs of school teaching, administering, and counseling, etc., are jobs that simply do not require extensive university-level work. Perhaps teacher training for purposes of certification could consist of two-year programs in the junior colleges. If a given teacher happens to have a bachelor's degree so much the better, but his college degree would accord him the same treatment as a police candidate with a bachelor's degree in criminal justice.

An observer has noted that one of the interesting unintended realizations that has occurred in colleges of education which adopted and implemented comprehensive so-called competency based teacher education programs is that the skills that are presumed to be desirable for entry-level teachers are startlingly few in number and rather low-level, that is, among skills that can be practically taught and learned in a four year college program. Such skills could easily be learned outside of a university environment, or perhaps learned on the job under contracted supervision.

Professionalism is a political process that has little to do with academic considerations or scholarship except insofar as schooling itself and certificates of competence are required. If school people want to become "professionalized" -- if they do not wish primarily to lead academic lives, as they clearly do not -- it will be up to them. University professors, including the education professoriate, cannot do it for them, nor should we. We have our own problems. We have our own institution, the university, to nourish; and we have our own fields to tend. Our work is not theirs. As long as we in education are in the teacher training and certificate recommending business, "educational studies" will continue to be hobbled, and graduate schools of education truncated as a possible vital place for ideas and scholarship. The dependent school teacher will perpetually suffer the fate of an artist whose work is governed by the tastes and moods of an insecure sponsor or patron.

Professors of education have been under a good deal of criticism recently as critics find fault with the public schools and try to force the blame on the universities. The critics don't know yet that professors of education don't own the public schools. If the truth be known, the professors of education have no more influence on the policies and conduct of school systems than the English Department has on the publishing houses or the political science department on the government. But scapegoats are nothing new.

Professor of English Richard Mitchell, for example, recently published a book on the "decline" of academic standards in the universities and especially on the "decline" of the English language. Despite his pontifications, languages do change, and whether those changes which he condemns represent devolution or simply change is a linguistic issue that deserves to be considered seriously, not closed by prejudice. What is particularly fascinating is that Mitchell singles out professors of education as responsible for what he views as debasement of the English language! One of the advantages of writing moralistic tracts under the label of "grammar" is that one need not feel compelled apparently to substantiate such charges with evidence. Not only does he not have much appreciation for the conservative, even puritanical language attitudes that permeate the entire education profession, including the schools of education, but Mitchell has no idea how much power we don't have! National language academies would covet such power. Most of the jargon and cant that Mitchell identifies are products of mass marketing bureaucracy, of business, or any number of powerful cultural sources -- not schools of education. Although the book is enjoying some attention in the popular press, it is not recognized in departments of linguistics as anything more than a layman's view of the subject, not unlike a host of others that have appeared recently on drug store book racks.

The Possibilities

Given the social status of school teaching and the related occupations in the schools, it is unlikely that colleges of education will soon be competing with professional schools such as engineering, law, and medicine for the same students. But we will continue to get our share of the most competent and most serious students found in the university -- as well as those who are a considerable distance behind them. In the graduate programs, students will continue to be people who are interested in "upgrading their credentials," moving up a notch or two on the wage scale, or enhancing their career prospects. Are colleges and graduate schools of education all that different from other schools in that regard? Who goes to the university for the "scholarly life"? Where would one go? Medical school? Law school? The sciences? What about the humanities?

A recent issue of The Chronicle of Higher Education carried a piece on the plight of the humanities. Professors of literature and especially history complained about the loss of their better students to fields that offer more promising careers, the quality of students who remain, and those humanities departments that tend to accept borderline candidates in order to continue to exist. The social sciences, as is well known, are in a similar state of depression. Further, liberal arts colleges increasingly offer professional vocational training to attract students or to keep the students they already have. The argument that liberal arts schools offer education for its own sake, that is to say, to those who pursue the scholarly life, while the professional schools offer "merely" "technical" or "vocational" preparation, is specious at best, although the issue of what should constitute a person's education is certainly an important one.

Some of the more prestigious universities no doubt will dismantle their undergraduate colleges of education and concentrate on developing prestigious and powerful graduate schools of education. That is probably what should be done in more places to promote serious educational research and to restore educational studies to their historic honorable place in western scholarship. It should not go unnoticed that they are doing so while familiar teacher education programs either through colleges of education or arts and science become less valuable as sources of institutional revenue. The large "service oriented" universities will continue presumably to provide university oversight of teacher training for urban schools.

The criticism that colleges of education get for the quality of teaching (and administration and counseling services) and the condition of public schools is not going to lessen. The word is not out that we don't own the schools and that we don't hire people to work in them. In labor-management disputes the college will remain in the middle. Management will demand that the colleges "produce" better employees who in turn are more "productive" and compliant, not necessarily who are more educated or effective as educators. Colleges of education will receive pot shots from labor as it attempts to wrest more control from management or the school board on matters that its leaders believe are in the best interest of its members or on occasion the interest of the union leadership itself and which may or may not be in the interest of the profession, to say nothing of children and the citizenry.

But such problematic conditions from a professor's point of view may enhance the possibilities for the scholarly life in schools and colleges and graduate schools of education as nothing else can. Policy issues and conflicting values, competing ideas and interest groups are grist for the analytical mill. Although it is clear that a great deal of money will not be given to education, there is potential for the scholarly life even under current conditions. The major institutions can be expected to go after the money in genetics research and lucrative contracts for applied research under the aegis of the Defense Department. The rest of us can follow other interests. The very openness of professional fields and ambiguity of educational studies give those who are interested a golden opportunity to provide definition and to pursue those studies. As far as the college itself is concerned, the place where we work, it is in important ways comparable to a typical multi-purpose state university -- the population represents the full range on almost any continuum. That will continue to be the case. The possibilities for the scholarly life whatever that might mean for an individual, are the possibilities one has for the life of his choosing -- and of his making -- in a city compared to life in a small town. As the flight attendants say, "Welcome to the metropolitan 'area.'"

COLLEGES OF EDUCATION: A QUESTION OF VIABILITY

Philip J. Rusche

Whether or not the training that takes place in colleges of education makes a difference in teaching effectiveness is a central issue currently being addressed by myriad groups throughout the United States. The question has been raised because of a perceived "crisis" in learning that many individuals view as threatening to the very fibre of our society. Although academic excellence is the primary focus of concern, colleges of education have come under much scrutiny leaving faculty worried not only about program viability but the very survival of colleges of education. To some extent, we in the profession have contributed to our own concern. We have been tardy in getting involved in this dialogue pertaining to academic excellence and, as might be expected, have been outright defensive. Such a posture has not been productive and has had the impact of removing us from a leadership role in shaping our future. If we do, in fact, believe that we make a difference, we must get involved and participate in identifying and correcting those things that have brought us to this state in professional education.

Are there problems associated with the quality of training found in professional education? Evidence supports that there is. Can these problems be alleviated? Obviously, the answer is in the affirmative. If we, as faculty in colleges of education can accept these facts, then perhaps we can ally with others to become partners in the problem solving process and demonstrate our viability. Up to this point in time, public denial by educators of difficulties has not been useful, especially when some faculty openly and many more privately admit serious concern regarding the competence of some students graduating from colleges of education. Open recognition and acceptance of dysfunctionalities in quality can focus attention on the causes of decline and promote appropriate remediation strategies. Educators themselves need to be central in examining, analyzing, and recommending changes in training lest positive dimensions of programs be lost in some type of educational purge already being seen in some states and in some institutions of higher education.

A multitude of factors affect academic excellence in professional education as they relate to training emphasis on the methodology, content, and context of teaching and learning. Students exiting from colleges of education seem to be quite

327

strong methodologically in both strategies of teaching and in technical skills. However, the content and context base apparently are marginal among far too many beginning educators. Content is, of course, the substantive knowledge the educator has of his specialized field of teaching such as English, history, mathematics or science. Equally critical, the context for teaching appears not to be understood by some prospective teachers. These are the understandings that assist an educator in interpolating learning into the complex social milieu of society today. Relating any content to the reality of another individual is frequently arduous even when one is well versed in both content and context. Methodology is rendered meaningless when the educator has little content knowledge or contextual perspective. Excellence is further impeded when marginality also is found in the preparation of basic skills necessary to teaching like reading, writing, computing, speaking and listening.

In positive terms, the majority of educators being prepared are competent, especially in terms of content and methodology. But, guilt by association with those of less quality hurts everyone in the profession. Context is a more pervasive problem for even a greater number of prospective teachers. They need to be stronger in their ability to define the purpose, nature and development of learning as well as the characteristics of learners and meaningful learning environments. We need not labor over the virtues or necessity of content, context or methodology. All are important; all need to be mastered for each contributes to both teaching and learning.

What educators must know is a matter of controversy; why some have limited training is more provocative. Yet education is a microcosm of society and it should not be surprising that the very same forces affecting other areas of society, also affect education. After World War I there was enormous expansion of teacher education programs throughout the nation. The supply of teachers, and other educators as well, never could keep up with the demand. The supply versus demand situation reached its turning point in the early 1970's. The National Council for Accreditation of Teacher Education had professionally accredited hundreds of institutions of higher education to train teachers by 1970. Many additional institutions also had programs but national professional accreditation was not an issue for them since certification is handled at the state level and this was the primary goal of these institutions.

The outcome was that for decades there was ample job availability, convenience for earning a degree and becoming certified, extensive upward and lateral mobility in teaching, all of which contributed to the general attractiveness of the profession. There was continuous growth, development and expansion of teacher training programs spurred on by money from national, state, local and private sources. There were many able students, especially women who were denied access to other professions, and both colleges and employers could be more selective in admissions, retention and graduation.

Suddenly, in the early 1970's the situation was reversed and perplexities developed. The last of the post-war baby boom children were in school or had graduated. This resulted in a dramatic decline in public and private school enrollments. The national economy started to decline and money was rapidly cut from educational budgets. Growth years had led to over regulation and stricter control which left schools and colleges with little flexibility or opportunity for creativity. Social restlessness, a desirable force for the larger society, placed many pressures on schools which they were not equipped to handle. Colleges had a difficult time responding to the variety of special interest groups, to court rulings, orders and mandates. National and state legislation placed additional burdens as did student and professional protests. In addition, there was simply over-specialization in the entire spectrum of the educational profession which resulted in resistance to ready adaptation. Each of the pressures was probably justified and good in its own right. But, taken as a group at a time of economic and student decline, they left schools and colleges crippled. Far too quickly, colleges of education found themselves with problems such as too many colleges and programs, not enough students in general and able students in particular, too many tenured faculty, too many highly specialized faculty, and rapidly decreasing funding. More could be identified, but the outcome of the stress would appear predictable.

Educational leaders should have anticipated the impending events and although some spoke out, they were not heeded. As in so many other areas of society, little planning was done and the obvious and inevitable was either ignored or resisted. In all fairness to educators, their programs were viewed as quite lucrative to colleges and universities. The large number of education students helped offset low enrollments in other areas and grant monies were very attractive. Hence, educational growth and expansion was not discouraged and limitations on scope and size were not entertained.

As might be expected, college faculty were not going to put themselves out of work nor were they going to admit their services were unnecessary or undesirable. It was business as usual on campus. Equal numbers of students were taken if available, and they were put through the same curriculum only with less quality control. The student still had to earn the same one hundred thirty to one hundred forty-five semester hours and continued to pursue the degree for at least eight to ten semesters. However, at the end he might or might not find employment and if he did it was often in a setting with less than adequate working conditions, earning a salary that was not comparable with other professionals, and job mobility was limited. Thus the profession lost much of its attractiveness. If business is continued as usual when demand and resources diminish something has to give, and in education it was quality that was negatively impacted. Maybe the case is exaggerated here, but the point needs to be made that the current problems in education are not just caused by students or teachers or professors or anyone else in particular. Everyone is partially at fault and energy utilized in attempting to affix blame is wasted. Effort should be directed at finding solutions to the issues involved.

An unacceptable trend is occurring in professional education which is a debilitating cycle that needs to be broken. As more experienced educators retire or exit the profession, they are sometimes replaced by less qualified individuals who have been graduated by colleges of education.

We need to make the profession more attractive; we need to rejuvenate college and school faculty and we need to increase expectations of those pursuing professional educational training. Simple solutions will not reverse the decline in educational skills, student achievement, or national test scores; nor will they arrest the growing functional illiteracy of young people and adults. There are still too many remedial courses necessary in schools and colleges and too much remediation needed to be undertaken by business and industry as well as public and private agencies. There is still a general skepticism on the part of the public about the effectiveness of public schooling. Additionally, it must be noted that also there is still a declining number of school age children, a sagging economy, court orders, legislative mandates, regulations, controls, social pressures, and the like. In other words, not only do we have the problems, but the causes are still with us.

The picture seems quite bleak and distressing. Indeed, education and educational preparation programs have had a few difficult years. Problems seem to have come so rapidly and in such great numbers that reaction by the profession became one of bewilderment and passivity instead of acceptance and activity. Suffice it to say that the entire profession has been in a state of shock and confusion.

The hysteria, however, appears to have run its course due to some forces that are bringing educators out of their lethargy. The marketplace, national attention, and educational leadership are starting to reverse the disconcerting trends. In the past, education relied on certification, accreditation, regulations and specialization to insure quality. In some respects these very controls that were instituted to promote excellence have contributed to inhibiting quality because college faculty found themselves with little recourse for initiating change. These are now being addressed because the marketplace dictated that business cannot go on as usual. There must be a new order of business that includes some type of quality guarantee. Educational programs at some institutions have closed down while many institutions are beginning to stabilize enrollments even though expected faculty-student ratios are not yet in balance. Employment difficulties appear to be easing and employers are taking a harder look at applicants. Nevertheless, the morality of graduating marginally prepared educators into a questionable job market versus fewer applicants and concern for job security by professors is still an issue that is unresolved on too many college campuses.

Like the marketplace, national attention on the output of education has had a major effect on education. Over twenty reports and studies have been conducted regarding educational excellence. The National Commission on Excellence in Education, the Southern Regional Education Board and The Carnegie Foundation for the Advancement of Teaching are just several of the prestigious groups articulating concerns and solutions. Such studies have focused on basic skills proficiency, a broad-based liberal education, specialized knowledge fields, methodological skills, higher college entrance and exit requirements and competency testing throughout. However, less attention has been paid regarding the quality of life for the educator, including salary and working conditions.

Nevertheless, this is the first time in the history of the nation that education has been the beneficiary of national focus. Issues have been raised and preferences expressed. Many recommendations have been forthcoming. For example, it has been suggested that schools could be improved if there were more use of technology, more computer learning, more homework, a longer school day and year, teacher evaluation, merit pay, more science and mathematics, more humanities, more individualized learning, more educational competition between public and private schools, greater curriculum offerings, more achievement testing, more extensive graduation requirements, and many, many more. Conversely, educational preparation programs could be improved if there were fewer schools of education, more content required, stricter admissions standards, less rigid curriculum patterns, graduation examinations, emphasis on research, more extensive specialization requirements, better pedagogical courses, more relevant curriculum delivery systems, more teachers trained, better teachers trained, and many, many, more.

Which of these suggestions hold promise is at present unclear. Study and dialogue are needed among constituent groups. There is no indication that the federal government will, at this point in time, provide direction or assistance. State and local officials seem to be more prone to action but such action appears headed in the direction of more rules, regulations and controls which have not proven effective in the past. The marketplace will continue to be a catalyst.

Therefore, an appeal to educators is appropriate. These are not hopeless times, but rather a setting for excitement and challenge in education. Fresh insights are needed as are renewed enthusiasm, professional rejuvenation, reflection and risk taking. In short, there is a need for leadership that can best come from the profession itself.

Right now it would appear as if most faculty in colleges of education have little interest in assuming leadership in resolving educational issues. Ironically, such passive behavior reinforces the allegations of critics and lends credence to what they are saying in opposition to colleges of education. It may well be that the extent to which educational faculty do become involved and do participate in issue resolution will be the final determiner of the future viability of colleges of education. If we refuse to show we make a difference, it is naive to believe that anyone else will do it for us. Educational faculty reticence is difficult to understand. Each professional group certainly has some personality traits of its own but professional educators are by far the most timid and professionally conservative enclave in higher education. Only speculation can suggest reasons for such behavior and research well could be warranted concerning the attitudes and behaviors of education faculty. No doubt, concepts of our own self image have partially been shaped by past training and experience, by the nature of educational training programs and by the characteristics of institutions of higher education.

A common criticism of educational programs is that curricula are not challenging and that course work lacks rigor. Allegations abound that education faculty do not demand enough of themselves or others and that their professional contributions are devoid of academic substance and intellectual integrity. The perceptions may or may not be fair but they are perceptions that need to be assessed and affirmed or proven inaccurate. Curriculum and course outcomes have not been proven ineffective. However, as a group, educational faculty are notoriously lacking in scholarly productivity of the type generally promulgated in higher education, so criticism of quality is a bit premature. Lack of contribution should be the concern, not the research itself. Therefore, we do leave ourselves open to continuing criticism when we refute research emotionally or embrace unsubstantiated criticism. Frequently we seem to be our own worst adversaries who do not have faith in what we are about.

Most faculty in colleges of education have been elementary, middle childhood or secondary teachers earlier in their professional careers. A few individuals have not made the transition from school to college very well. Outstanding school teachers are not necessarily effective faculty in institutions of higher education since role expectations differ dramatically at various academic levels. This is not a negative commentary, but instead a statement of fact: schools and colleges are not the same. Neither is impugned, they are just different. Notable teaching is a prized commodity throughout all education, but in higher education, along with synthesizing and transmitting knowledge one must work to create information. Besides teaching, higher education faculty are given time to reflect, research, write, develop and refine knowledge as well as engage in public service. School faculty are not often charged with these tasks nor are they given supporting time or recognition for undertaking these activities. Education faculty, once on the college campus, do not always understand, appreciate, or accept this difference.

While many college programs, most obvious in the arts and sciences, promote the non-teaching aspects of academic professional life, teacher training programs stress the pedagogical instructional functions that are required of faculty in schools. Through initial and advanced training studies, one set of students, usually found in the humanities and sciences, is nurtured on research and development of a chosen specific academic discipline. Another group, usually found in professional colleges like education, view themselves more in accord with the applied aspects of their profession. One must be cautious in making comparisons since orientations are not the same and dissimilar approaches are used in achieving intended goals. This is as it should be, but institutions of higher education cannot resist making comparisons and when comparison is made, education faculties on occasion do not compare well because they are judged using criteria for which past training and experience provide little preparation. The thrust of a professor of English is not the same as that of a professor of English education; mathematics is not the same as mathematics education. Generally, the focus of professors in content fields in the humanities, sciences and arts all differ from those in education and other professional colleges. The interpretation of scholarly productivity by professional colleges is broader than that in liberal arts but all are measured in similar terms in the higher education setting. Even at the graduate level in professional education, stress is not always on research in the typical sense because advanced programs are frequently used for additional certification or movement from one personnel area to another in the schools. Without extensive training in the classical tradition of scholarship, many educational faculty are forced to use an heuristic approach in securing the skills, attitudes and techniques essential to emulate research found in other colleges. Educators themselves are self-conscious about their scholarly reputation and tend to apologize for their perceived shortcomings, avoid colleagues in other disciplines, and sometimes exhibit an outright contempt for research and theory. It is ridiculous to assert that educators are incapable of research when actually they have not been trained or nurtured like colleagues in other disciplines.

Nevertheless, education faculty can neither dismiss nor ignore the research mission of higher education, and indeed some excellent research has been contributed by education faculty. Quantity of research may be more of a problem than quality of research. Perhaps the concern is that we do not research, instead of being unable to research, and that we do not publish instead of not being able to publish. Each of these omissions can and should be rectified. We do not do ourselves or the profession justice by avoiding scholarly activities which are normal expectations in higher education; we just make criticism more believable. Lack of scholarly productivity affects the image of everyone associated with professional education. Perhaps worse is that in the absence of research data, we are less willing to experiment on our training programs and turn to fads that come and go regularly in education. Professional educators react differently to this particular type of criticism than do faculty in other professional colleges. It may be that other professional college faculty care less because they can always return to their

334

former employment and receive at least equal remuneration and prestige. Whatever the reason, we educators are quite sensitive about our image. Training programs, especially advanced graduate programs, should address this dimension of professional education and ensure that all graduates have the full range of skills required to function at any level in education.

If past training and experience have posed problems for educators, these difficulties are being perpetuated by current program delivery systems. Educational programs really are not much different than they were thirty or more years ago. General education, enhanced with a specialization and appropriate pedagogy is the framework for training, with the same number and distribution of credit hours that have been in effect for years. In professional education courses, emphasis is placed on the methods of instruction and content is viewed more as the prerogative of other colleges. We have students in our college courses for only about thirty or forty percent of their programs. We continue to try to build more learning into these courses which limits time for study, reflection and development. Increased societal demands, more elaborate certification requirements, and extensive field experience all place added burdens on both education students and professors. Examining theory and integrating theory into practice demands personal attention and exhaustive discussion. The discussion format of classes makes course work suspect and is often viewed by the immature student as nonessential and just plain meaningless. Therefore, the nature of current training programs can adversely condition the attitudes of professional educators. So, once again, explanations can be found relative to the image of professional education which should not be used as excuses but as challenges to be faced and resolved.

Finally, the very nature of institutions of higher education has inhibited a more positive image for professional education. Teaching is an important priority of higher education and few faculty in colleges other than education have had formal instructional preparation yet are perceived as successful teachers. As a result, they look at teaching as a natural outgrowth of scholarship and see little need or value in what is done in colleges of education. Once again concepts are being confused. College age students cannot be compared directly to younger students and the dynamics of college are not the same as earlier schooling. But, it is interesting to note that as the competition for college students has increased over the past few years, quality of teaching throughout higher education has been an issue.

Complex forces have come together to create the debilitating cycle mentioned earlier. Colleges of education have reached a low point brought on by both external forces in the larger society, and by the internal mechanisms of institutions of higher education and our low self-esteem. Currently we feel we are perceived as being non-essential, unappreciated, and without respect or proper reward. In times of plenty we were left alone but now with hardship we feel assailed and somewhat insecure. We almost appear willing to buy into the myth of professional education inferiority which could lead us to a self-fulfilling prophecy of demise.

What has been written here might be overstated and sound like an effort to make excuses for the neglect that we have been guilty of in professional education. Such is not the intention. Instead, an attempt has been made to punctuate the broad-based causes of problems confronting education in general and educational preparation specifically. The message is intended to support the contention that we should not be held accountable for what we cannot control. We should be judged on the merit of our performance in areas that we can control. Our courses can be more meaningful; our curricula can be more demanding; we can study, research and write; we can provide community service; we can prepare educators for higher education roles; we can be equals in higher education. Indeed, in most respects we have already demonstrated our ability, but we are still questioned. If we have the will to guide our own future and work toward excellence, the opportunity to move forward is present. With confidence, we must prove that we do now and will continue to make a difference in teaching and learning. By our own actions, we will remain quite viable.